THE
ATTACK LAMBS

MARK GEPPERT

Copyright © Mark Geppert
Second edition published by South East Asia Prayer Center
P.O. Box 127, Oakmont, PA 15139
info@seapc.org

Originally published as "Every Place Your Foot Shall Tread — The Attack Lambs"
by SOAR Publishers
P. O. Box 215 Vail, AZ 85641, USA

Cover design by Uncomn Creative.
Bible Verse references and edits by Genre Baker.

ISBN-978-1-7344882-1-0 (paperback)
ISBN-978-1-7344882-0-3 (eBook)

DEDICATION

It has been said that behind every successful man there is a wonderful woman.

This is certainly true in my case.

I dedicate this book to my wife, Ellie.

Thank you for your trust, encouragement, and sacrifice.

GET ACCESS TO THE FREE COMPANION E-COURSE AND VIDEO SERIES!

VISIT: THEATTACKLAMBS.COM

Thank you for taking the time to read this book. This Updated and Revised version of *The Attack Lambs* includes stories of how we have seen God work as we have joined in His mission through prayer. These principles were tested 30 years ago on the streets of Singapore, and have been repeated again and again throughout the nations as people have stepped out in faith to pray and establish an atmosphere over their neighborhoods, cities, and nations.

It is my prayer that as you go through this material, that you would be encouraged and equipped as you do your part in God's Kingdom work.

CONTENTS

FOREWORD

When I first met Mark Geppert in 1985 in Hong Kong I had no idea this historic meeting would lead to a global partnership between Mark's ministry and mine to help evangelize some of the world's most difficult regions and people groups. Mark's unique calling to pray open closed doors has been a powerful asset to ministries like Every Home for Christ, the ministry I lead. That calling and anointing has helped us go through those once closed doors to reach multitudes with the Good News.

Since writing the foreword for the first edition of Attack Lambs some years ago, the partnership between Every Home for Christ and Mark and Matt Geppert has resulted in greater things than we ever could have imagined. In one nation alone (that for security reasons cannot be named) I can report that some 25 least-reached people groups (previously on a list of some of the most difficult-to-reach peoples on earth) now have thriving church planting movements among them. In one region of that specific nation we've heard that some 40,000 people have now come to know Jesus as Savior, where not long ago, there were few if any believers among them and no churches of any kind to our knowledge. Now there are literally hundreds of thriving congregations.

This growth is no accident. The Geppert family has spent all those years faithfully walking by the simple and profound truths shared in this book. Their passion to see salvation come to the lost in all the earth has led them to carry out these strategies in all corners of the world. They have seen untold lives and entire communities transformed by the gospel as a result. One of the greatest encouragements to me in this regard is how Mark's son Matt has followed in his father's footsteps. I'm not sure I've ever seen a son of a great leader carry such a pronounced anointing from his father in such a way that there is little if any difference in the transfer of a mantle of a ministry. What a glorious heritage and legacy passed on to a whole new generation of warring lambs who will help finish the Great Commission, hopefully in this very generation. I would not be at all surprised if that very thing happens!

The insights offered in the anointed pages of this timely book have been tried and tested by countless believers who have embraced the call to world-changing prayer and walked the way of precious Attack Lambs who have gone before them. But make no mistake about it—this book, revised for such a time as this—is like a whole new message to a whole new generation. It is alive with faith and saturated with passion. I trust that as you embrace the training in these pages you will see wonders unfold in kingdom impact before your very eyes. Become an Attack Lamb—an Agent of Spirit-anointed transformation for this generation! And don't be surprised if you hear some lambs roar!

—*Dick Eastman*
International President, Every Home for Christ
And President of America's National Prayer Committee

PREFACE

It has been 20 wonderful years since some friends made it possible to publish The Attack Lambs. The book has been well received and is currently printed in English, Chinese, Hindi, Spanish, Khmer, and Thai. We have taught the Attack Lambs Seminars in all of Asia with a team of teachers taking people to the pressure points in their cities and call-ing upon an unchanging God who hears and answers prayer to pour out His Holy Spirit on those places.

Our relationship with Dr. Dick Eastman and Every Home for Christ has resulted in millions of people in the most remote parts of the earth having the opportunity to know Jesus. The numbers are recorded in heaven's accounting; but we know that by bringing prayer and mission together, the will of God is manifested in righteousness, peace, and joy in the Holy Spirit.

The South East Asia Prayer Center, which I serve, is now active in 122 nations in mobile prayer strategies. My son, Matthew, has taken up the mantle which is why you are reading an e-book. Matt and his global team have accepted the challenge of getting this teaching into more languages and nations. He believes in the message and its application because he has seen it work all his adult life.

We are making some changes in the original text as, with the translations, we have found that some locations and events are not as clear as they could be. But we have in no way altered the teaching. This stuff works. In China, Latin America, India, and especially Southeast Asia we are seeing tangible results to the simple truth that if you get dust on your boots from your city streets, you have authority to invoke the presence and power of the Resurrected King of Kings and bring change.

The Second Edition Updates appear at the end of each chapter of the original text. With over 300,000 copies of the original in distribution around the world, you can imagine the amount of feedback we receive and to date none of it is negative. Please join with the thousands of Attack Lambs who are putting a Holy Spirit bootprint on their communities and proclaiming that Jesus is Lord. Please learn from and use this book and let us know your testimony as an Attack Lamb.

We will be glad to walk with you and stand before the throne. We will even let you stand in front because we love you and that is really why this book has been written.

Just one more word before you walk through these pages. If you are going to repeat any of the stories in this book, please keep them small. They have a tendency to grow with the telling and when they come back to me, I am embarrassed. Give the glory to Jesus.

He is the only One worthy of the glory, and honor, and power, and might, and dominion. Please join me in walking before Him in every village and among every tribe. He'll be back soon.

—*Mark Geppert*
South East Asia Prayer Center
SEAPC@hotmail.com

CHAPTER 1

THE SERPENT IS BOUND

My traveling companion, an evangelical pastor, and I approached the guard station situated about a kilometer from the Chinese border. We were inside Laos on a weather-beaten road, and had no papers to allow us entry into China. Wanting to pray as close to the Chinese border as possible, perhaps being able to see into the land as we did, we felt this station might be as far as we dared go.

During the last several minutes Pastor had been telling me about how he didn't care for any of the "weird stuff" we charismatics do, like praying in tongues. It made him very nervous. "Don't do any of that stuff, ok? No praying in tongues," he said. For the sake of harmony I agreed, feeling like a boxer who'd been told he can't throw his best punch. When we found a place to pray we stopped.

First, we worshiped but, in the back of my mind, I'm thinking, "OK, Lord, how am I going to pray?" As I worshiped I was released from the cares and doubts and worries of how I would pray, and surrendered myself to the sweetness of His presence. It was like my heavenly Father and I were sitting together, indulging in our totally trusting and honest relationship. In those moments His Spirit touches ours in a way that wipes away fears and tears and gives us clarity.

A SIMPLE PRAYER

I opened my mouth to pray and out came a very simple prayer. "Lord, we pray that the Serpent would be bound in Laos." That was it. It was so simple, I repeated it again. For a moment I was tempted to be embarrassed, but I've learned that the most powerful prayer is the one the Holy Spirit prays through you. It was also accurate. Just how accurate, I was to learn only a couple of hours later.

We didn't expect to be able to go into China, so when the guard asked us if we wanted to go in we said, "No."

"You can go in if you like," he offered, not knowing about our lack of papers.

"We do not have the necessary papers," we explained, "but we would like to just go across the border and pray."

"You can go ahead," he replied, "I won't check your papers. Just make sure you come back."

As we walked the remaining "klick" to the border we were praising God. Once we were on China's soil we worshiped God and prayed for that nation. No praying in tongues here either, of course. After a short while we returned to the border station, much to the relief of the guard, though he gave no indication he was worried.

When we got back to the spot where we had prayed earlier we found a 12-foot python tied firmly to a tree. Wow! The Serpent really had been bound!

We asked around among the men at that place if they knew who had tied the snake to the tree. "We haven't seen anyone," they said. We asked them if they had ever known anyone to tie a snake to a tree like that. "No," they said. "When we catch a snake we kill him right there and cut him up for food." They had never seen such a thing, either.

Now I grant you it wasn't a burning bush; but, for us it might as well have been. God had demonstrated His commitment to answering our prayer.

Just recently I received a report that in the village just down the road from that spot, 200 people of a remote tribe had received Christ from hearing only one cassette in their own language. Praise God!

We had attacked as lambs, quietly, without arrogance and in love, and God had given us the victory. If we had prayed in tongues or done some type of prophetic demonstration or made a declaration over the land, we would have missed God. Instead, we were acting in obedience to the Holy Spirit. We prayed the prayer He had instructed us to pray, as simple as it was. More importantly, our intercession sprang from the fountainhead of a worshipful attitude. Somewhere along the way the lesson that all successful spiritual endeavor comes as a result of an attitude of worship had seeped into our prayer bones and the 12-foot proof of its truth was right in front of us — tied to that tree.

GOING ON THE OFFENSIVE

This idea of a lamb being aggressive seems a bit strange, I know. After all, the very image of a lamb suggests it would be the least likely candidate for the role of attacker.

First of all, they are young. Then, they are small. They have no natural defense systems to speak of. They are not the brightest of critters, nor are they the fastest. All in all, they lack nearly everything necessary to take on successfully their natural enemies, the wolf or the bear. However, that is the point. Who would suspect such an unlikely animal to have the capability, let alone the desire, to go on the offensive against its enemies? Even if a lamb could somehow muster the desire, it still has no weapons with which to defend itself, let alone attack.

Oh, but if they could, wouldn't the wolf and the bear be in for a shock. Appearing harmless, but full of power and might. I know, not in this lifetime, right? No matter how hard we think about it nothing comes to mind as to how a lamb might transform itself into such an aggressive creature. And so, the question...

HOW?

How do you suppose a lamb might be victorious over, say, a wolf? If you guessed run to the shepherd and let him fight your battle for you, you're right. It is the shepherd who has the rod and staff and slingshot, or maybe today a .357 magnum. The power resides with him. The lamb can make use of the shepherd's weapons, but not in its own strength. The lamb must rely on the strength of the shepherd.

So it is for us and our Good Shepherd Jesus. Yes, we have weapons of warfare to overcome our enemy, the Devil: the blood of Jesus, the word of our testimony, the name of Jesus, and the various gifts of the Holy Spirit. But these weapons all operate by the Holy Spirit who lives in us.

In us. There's a key! Unlike a lamb, we don't have to run far to find the Source of our power. He is in us. The Holy Spirit, God Himself, our Helper dwelling **in us** and working through us. Through us. There's another key! We don't secure the victory ourselves. It is the Holy Spirit within us who works **through us**.

What, then, is our part? That's simple…not necessarily easy, but it is simple. We have to train ourselves to be aligned with and sensitive to the prompting of the Holy Spirit. Then we must become obedient to His direction. It is simply a matter of teamwork.

ATTACKED BY A GATE?

Tradition says that as sheep we are to be meek and mild, give no offense, endure all things and return only love. Sounds pretty good, huh? But when these things are spoken of, it is in reference to our attitude toward others in the Body of Christ or the world which desperately needs Jesus.

Then what should our attitude be toward the realm of darkness, Satan's domain? In a word…ATTACK. Not in our own strength, but in the Lord's. Not at our own direction, but at His. And not with our own plan, with His. Remember He is the Lion of the Tribe of Judah, not us. But, some will protest, we are His Body. Doesn't that mean we do the fighting? Oh yes, indeed, but while the victory is ours, the battle is the Lord's. That means we fight the battle designed by the Lord, with His strategies, executing His plan, utilizing His resources and weapons. It's all up to our Commander-in-Chief Jesus, but we claim the victory!

Jesus gave us the definitive stance to take when He spoke to Simon Peter after his disciple's declaration of the revelation God gave him: **"You (Jesus) are the Christ, the Son of the living God"** (Matthew 16:16). After praising Simon and changing his name Jesus said, **"…upon this rock [of revelation], I will build my church, and the gates of hell shall not prevail against it"** (Matthew 16:18).

It is quite clear that Jesus' church and the gates of hell were going to come into a great conflict. I have just one question: when was the last time you were attacked by a gate?

Gates do not attack, they defend. They are solidly immobile. Their posts are dug down deep and set firmly. Gates are reinforced, locked and guarded to prevent successful entry. They are built to withstand attack; they do not initiate it. That's our job! We are to be taking the fight to the Enemy's territory in the power of the Holy Spirit. We do that by becoming "Attack Lambs."

And how do we do **that?** Good question, thank you for asking because that is what this book is all about. It is painfully clear that the Body of Christ does not have within itself the power to defeat Satan. But the good news is we don't have to. Jesus has already done that for us.

What is happening in these last days is that we are learning how to enforce that defeat by stepping out of the way and letting God effect the victory through us, rather than trying to achieve it on our own. We are learning how to work with the Lord, to be attuned to His Holy Spirit and to walk in obedience to His direction. The result is…

WE WIN!

Say it to yourself. Say it out loud, "We win!" Let that fact that it's a done deal penetrate your thinking down to the floor of your soul. Let it take root there and continue on into the depths of your spirit man. We win.

The world system wants to convince us we can't win. We're only sheep. But, they're too late. We've already won. Jesus did that for us. It's like a friend of mine who had broken his ankle (twice actually), and the Lord healed it both times, in two different ways. It's too late to tell that man, "God doesn't heal anymore." He knows better; he has already experienced it.

So don't you believe it when the world tells you that you can't win. You already have! Jesus won the victory for you and, if you are a believer, it's yours!

Our job then is to walk in that victory. Again, simple, but not necessarily easy. Let's use the letters from the acrostic **W-I-N** to help us understand what the foundation of our success is.

WORSHIP

The first letter of **WIN** is **W**, which stands for worship. Worship is not only something we do; more importantly, it is an ongoing attitude we should have toward God. All successful spiritual endeavor comes forth from an attitude of worship. Why? Because as worship focuses us on the Lord, it brings clarity. This clarity causes us to see the affairs of this life for what they are. It releases us to see that we are seated in heavenly places in Christ, with Him at the right hand of the Father (Ephesians 2:6[1]). We can see that the blood of Jesus has set us free from the presence and power of the Enemy (Hebrews 9:12[2]).

Like so many endeavors in life, spiritual warfare has a mental side. In nearly every sport the mental game is far more important to ultimate victory than the skill level. So too, in spiritual warfare the mental attitude of worship is what sets us apart for victory and provides that non-skid foundation for our attack.

---

1. [6]and raised us up together, and made us sit together in the heavenly places in Christ Jesus
2. [12]Not with the blood of goats and calves, but with His own blood He entered the Most Holy Place once for all, having obtained eternal redemption

In worship, all fear is driven from us. We fellowship in our acceptance by the Father (Ephesians 1:6[3]). We are righteous before the Almighty because of our Redeemer and the thought of it changes our being. In fact, as we join with Him through the worship experience, we begin to adopt His confidence, calling, and character.

His will becomes ours, His timing our timing, His power our power, His purity our purity, His vision our vision. Through worship we experience the effectual exchange of our nature for His nature. We are no longer lost in sin. We are no longer lost at all. We are no longer losers.

The fact that we can have intimate communion with the God of the universe through worship is a power connection we cannot do without. It is an uplink and a downlink at the same time. And it is vital to our success.

Unlike false gods, God wants us to know Him and His will. Every other religion on earth has a god that is hidden from the people. He dwells on a mountain top or in a shrouded holy place. He is inaccessible to mankind. He is said to tower over the people and demand sacrifice that they may come up to him. Only Jesus has come down from heaven to meet us.

As we are incapable of attaining heaven through our own works, (which is the basis of all false religion), Jesus left heaven to reach us. This is the message of the Gospel. It is this fact which separates us as Christians from all other religions. This is good news for all mankind. There is a true God whose love has brought Him to earth to make the way of ascension for those who believe in Him.

THE SONG OF SURRENDER

As we mentioned earlier, one of our primary tasks is to align ourselves with the will of God. The will of God is not difficult to discern. In fact, here it is:

---

3. [6]to the praise of the glory of His grace, by which He made us accepted in the Beloved

It is the will of God that every man, woman, and child on the face of the earth has the opportunity to receive Jesus Christ as his or her personal Lord and Savior in this generation.

Obviously, the entire revealed will of the Father encompasses more than just this one statement, but nearly every aspect of His will and purpose marches under this banner. If the Father were to have a mission statement this would be it, the most quoted verse in the Bible, **"For God so loved the world that He gave His only begotten Son, that whoever believes in Him should not perish but have everlasting life"** (John 3:16). This is the divine mandate for all of history.

But now we must come face to face with another question. How do **we** fit into this exalted purpose? It is so natural a question our minds assume it must be the right question. It's not. What we are really asking with this question is, how can I, with what talents and abilities I have, be used of God for His purposes? Wrong question.

THE RIGHT QUESTION

The right question is, (are you ready), am I available to God to be used by Him? Yes, of course, you answer. Not so fast, my good friend.

We are all kingdom builders, of one kind or another. Either His or ours. Most people try to build their own kingdom while paying homage to His. This will not work. Others try to develop a kingdom of their own within the kingdom of God. This will not work either.

The greatest prayer of Scripture, the Lord's Prayer, is the foundation of all spiritual warfare. Contained in it is one phrase which is the heart of worship, the song of surrender. It was the supreme prayer of Christ as He set His steps to the cross for you: **"Your kingdom come. Your will be done, on earth as it is in heaven."** (Matthew 6:10).

For those who wish to chart their own course in the kingdom, this is the end of the line. For those who would claim Christ's riches for their own extravagance, this is the bill of reckoning. And for those who try to heal the sick or raise the dead and count the percentages of success, this is the great humbler.

But, for those who will pray for others, live in humility and reach out to the lost, this is the anchor of their souls. You see, it is the surrendered life that the Lord can and will use. To whatever extent you lose your life for the sake of the gospel of Jesus, to that same extent you will find it anew in Him, in His glory, His power, and His passion. Your **availability** is far more important to the Father than your **ability**.

CALLED UP INTO HEAVEN

The reason John was called up into heaven to see the heavenly vision he describes in the book of Revelation was so he could see from the heavenly perspective. It was so he could see the heavenly purpose, and the heavenly worship which undergirds every declaration of the kingdom of God on the earth.

All the other religions of the earth have their hidden, inaccessible, mystical realms. Only Christ has opened the door to the heavenlies and calls us, not only to see but to enter in. Like John, we too have been called to see from a heavenly perspective.

Worship is key because it gives us the correct perspective. God's ways are higher than ours. His ways are perfect and our natural understanding is imperfect. But Paul tells us we have received **"the Spirit who is from God, that we might know the things that have been freely given to us by God"** (1 Corinthians 2:12b). In verse ten he declares that God has revealed these things to us by His Spirit.

God wants us to know His ways, His strategies, His methods, but He can only show them to us within the context of our relationship with Him, and worship is the material of that bloodbought relationship. Heaven is open to a worshiping heart.

As John was immediately **"in the Spirit,"** so we too, as we enter into worship according to His will, are caught up in the Holy Spirit. Sure, our body stays on the earth and we are certainly aware of our surroundings. In fact, we become more acutely aware as the power of the Holy Spirit to reveal the calamity of man begins to be activated. We are made aware, by the Holy Spirit, of the heavenly plan and purpose.

The things of earth grow strangely dim. In fact we no longer consider our previous preoccupations. Philippians 2 begins to live as we let the mind of Christ be in us. We think from a heavenly perspective and the heartbeat of God begins to set a pace for our lives. The rhythm of His heavenly presence communicates that pace to our limbs, directing us in His plan.

IN THE SPIRIT

In the Spirit we are free from the desires of the flesh. "Me," "My," and "Mine" give way to "You, Lord." We worship "You" and the "I Am" begins to dwell in our praise. Just as in John's vision, all eyes turn to the One upon the throne.

Our purpose, our plan, and our presence fade away and His purpose, His plan, and His presence take their place.

Sweet surrender to the worship of God is the release necessary for you and me to truly become His ambassadors. Old things must pass away and all things must become new. We are the instruments of His will in the earth. That will becomes clear as we look upon His throne. We are no longer preoccupied with self; we can clearly hear what the Holy Spirit is saying, "Go ye into all the earth..."

When we are in the Spirit, we are limitless. There is no thought of purse or person. The cost of serving Him is nothing compared to His cost in serving us. He gave all for you and you know it in the Spirit. He is the only One worthy to receive blessing, honor, power and might. He is the only One who has defeated the Enemy and has taken His rightful place on the throne. When you are in the Spirit and you are worshiping Him, only His Person is accepted. You will bow down...gladly.

FOR THIS REASON

It is for this reason the trumpet call to worship has drawn you into His glorious presence so that you might be delivered from yourself, and be set free to participate in His majestic purpose. You bow down like everything else in John's vision. You are on your face before God.

In this position, you would never think of telling Him what to do. You only cry, "Holy, holy, holy" to the One who is on that throne! There is no way you are going to think about a single care of this life when you are before the One. His grandeur answers all your questions for life. Will He provide? He is the Provider. Will He heal the sick? He is the Healer. No man will glory in His presence. No flesh will stand before Him. He is the only One talking in this picture.

Paul's letter to the Philippians declares,

That at the name of Jesus every knee should bow, of those in heaven, and of those on earth, and of those under the earth, and that every tongue should confess that Jesus Christ is Lord, to the glory of God the Father.
Philippians 2:10–11

When you are worshiping it doesn't matter where your problem comes from. It doesn't matter where it tries to hide. It doesn't even matter that the power which binds someone you care about might be from the Devil himself? When you are in the Spirit, you know that power is going to bow down at the mention of that glorious name, JESUS!

When our focus is on the One who is on the throne our message is based upon His victory. Lenin is in his tomb. Mao is in his tomb.

I have visited the bones of Buddha in his tomb. Mohammed is in his tomb. But Jesus rose from His tomb to prove He is the Son of God. His victory over death validates His claim of Messiahship. As the Scripture says, **it is by grace we are saved, through faith, _and that not of ourselves,_ but it is a gift of God** (Ephesians 2:9[4], emphasis

---

4. [8]For by grace you have been saved through faith, and that not of yourselves; it is the gift of God, 9 not of works, lest anyone should boast

added). When a man tells me that he can get to heaven by his works, I realize either he has a very dim view of heaven or an overly bright view of himself.

THE DEVIL'S LIE

The movie *Star Wars* popularized the concept that the spiritual realm has two equal sides to it, one good and one evil. A light side and a dark side, if you will. The assumption made was that they were both more or less equal, with right on the side of light, and cunning on the dark side. Luke Skywalker was constantly being tempted to join the dark side because its power seemed stronger. In the end, however, Hollywood gave the victory to the good side of the force, (it's a better story that way), and we were left with the feeling that the light side had somehow pulled out a win over a much superior force.

In the real world of the spirit nothing could be farther from the truth. While the Devil would love to have you believe he is the negative, and therefore equal opposite, of Jesus Christ, it just isn't true.

Jesus has always existed with the Father.

Satan is merely a created being.

Jesus has authentic spiritual power.

Satan can only counterfeit, lie and deceive.

Jesus has a home in heaven.

Satan was cast down from heaven.

All power and authority was given to Jesus in heaven and earth.

Satan has no authority except what we give him.

Jesus is the equal of God and is God.

Satan is merely a defeated and fallen angel.

And we are the ones who will judge the angels.

THE ABSURD ASSERTION

To assert, therefore, that Jesus and Satan are opposite equals is totally absurd. In fact, the Devil isn't even present in the vision John has of heaven. But guess what? We are. That's right. People were there doing what Satan would not: worshiping the Lord. When we worship the Lord we are giving to Him the very thing Satan covets for himself. No wonder worship upsets him so. The truth is, as a pastor friend of mine puts it, "Greaaaat BIG God. Little bitty devil."

You belong in heaven. The Devil doesn't. You were made to operate effectively in the kingdom of heaven here on earth. He can't. You can operate in Jesus' full authority, using the Name of the King of the universe to overcome the tide of evil in this world. And, your Enemy has already been defeated by the very One in whose name you operate, Jesus.

We are a part of a heavenly celebration. Jesus has given us great victory. We are in the earth to celebrate that victory before God and a defeated Enemy. When we go out to pray as Attack Lambs, we are not going to gain a victory. We are going to celebrate a victory that has already been won. Hallelujah!

....

In Revelation 4, John is called up to the heavenlies by a voice that sounded like a trumpet.

"After these things I looked, and behold, a door standing open in heaven (worship opens the doorway to the throne room). And the first voice which I heard was like a trumpet speaking with me saying, "Come up here, and I will show you things which must take place after this."[5]

It is God's will that we know His plans and purposes. He wants you to be informed.

─────────────

5. Revelation 4:1 NKJV

"Immediately I was in the Spirit; and behold, a throne set in heaven, and One sat on the throne."[6]

From this, we see that spiritual understanding comes when we are in the Spirit. As we worship, giving attention to the person and presence of the One, the eyes of our understanding are enlightened and we begin to realize more deeply what God is saying to us. **As we practice this presence, we will also become more adept at knowing what He wants to say through us to those for whom we are praying.**

All focus in the heavenly vision is on the One on the throne. This intensity of focus must become the Attack Lamb's discipline for there are many voices in the earth and so many distractions. As we go out, there is the noise of the nonbelievers, the noise of the culture, and so very many discussions and thoughts that try to enter in. Maintaining focus on the One on the throne is key to releasing the anointing to set people free.

MANAGEMENT IS BOOKED

"Around the throne were twenty-four thrones and; on the thrones, I saw twenty-four elders."[7]

The management positions in heaven are fully booked. You are not there to tell God what to do, but rather to worship. To ascribe glory, honor, power, might, and dominion to the One who is on the throne.

We are not in management but in sales. So often people try to tell God what to do. If you can do that, then we should worship you because you have power over an Absolute which would make you God.

John is being told that he will receive information in this setting. It is a time to listen, not to speak. The invitation into the throne room of God is an awesome opportunity to hear from Him. It is amazing to

6. Revelation 4:2 NKJV
7. Revelation 4:4 NKJV

me that the Creator of the entire universe, who holds all the galaxies in the span of His hand, takes time to speak to us individually. What is more astonishing is the number of people who will just be still and listen. They are few when compared to those who feel they have to say something.

WE HAVE BEASTS TOO

"And in the midst of the throne and around the throne were four living creatures full of eyes in front and in back."[8]

In many of the temples among Chinese and Indian people, there are depictions of dragons and serpents. There are gargoyles and all sorts of underworld creatures. Often local people express a fear of going into the temple to stand in the gap for the families of the temple. I quickly point them to this verse. We have beasts as well, and our beasts are bigger than their beasts because our beasts are in the presence of God. **Remember, we are not there for the beasts, we are there to free the people.**

"And they do not rest day and night, saying: 'Holy, holy, holy, Lord God Almighty, Who was and is and is to come!' Whenever the living creatures give glory and honor and thanks to Him who sits on the throne, who lives forever and ever the twenty-four elders fall down before Him who sits on the throne and worship Him who lives forever and ever, and cast their crowns before the throne, saying: "You are worthy, O Lord, to receive glory and honor and power; for You created all things, and by your will they exist and were created."[9]

FOCUS ON THE THRONE

All focus is on the One who is on the throne. When you hear people glorify the devil, or call him by some familiar name, remember that the One on the throne is the **only** one worthy of such praise. He

8. Revelation 4:6 NKJV
9. Revelation 4:8-11 NKJV

is the creator of all things, is supreme over all things, and controls all things by the counsel of His will. Therefore, He alone is to be worshipped.

When I hear people expound about the power of the enemy, I wonder whose side they are on. Why would you glorify the enemy of your soul by ascribing power, might, or dominion to the one Jesus defeated? This does not make sense to me. I try to correct such a mistake, and if they persist to exalt the enemy, then I just walk away because nothing good is going to come of such conversation.

SPIRITUAL SUCCESS

Revelation 5 continues the throne room vision:

"No one in heaven or on earth or under the earth was able to open the scroll, or to look at it. So I wept much, because no one was found worthy to open and read the scroll, or to look upon it. But one of the elders said to me, 'Do not weep. Behold, the Lion of the Tribe of Judah, the Root of David, has prevailed to open the scroll and to loose its seven seals.'

"And I looked, and behold, in the midst of the throne and of the four living creatures, and in the midst of the elders, stood a Lamb as though it had been slain, having seven horns and seven eyes, which are the seven Spirits of God sent out into all the earth. Then He came and took the scroll out of the right hand of Him who sat on the throne.

"Now when He had taken the scroll, the four living creatures and twenty-four elders fell down before the Lamb, each having a harp, and golden bowls full of incense, which are the prayers of the saints. And they sang a new song, saying: 'You are worthy to take the scroll, and to open its seals; for You were slain, and have redeemed us to God by Your blood out of every tribe and tongue and people and nation, and have made us kings and priests to our God; and we shall reign on the earth.'

"Then I looked, and I heard the voice of many angels around the throne, and the living creatures, and the elders; and the numbers of them was ten thousand times ten thousand, and thousands of thousands, saying with a loud voice: 'Worthy is the Lamb who was slain to receive power and riches and wisdom, and strength and honor and glory and blessing!'

"And every creature which is in heaven and on the earth and under the earth and such as are in the sea, and all that are in them, saying: 'Blessing and honor and glory and power, be to Him who sits on the throne and to the Lamb, forever and ever!'

"Then the four living creatures said 'Amen!' And the twenty-four elders fell down and worshipped Him who lives forever and ever."[10]

All success in the spirit realm flows forth from an atmosphere of praise and worship. When we turn our focus to the throne and begin to praise the Lord, we are invited, as John was, to come to a higher plane, to see the majesty and power of the Lamb. We realize that He is the only One worthy of glory, honor, power, might, and dominion. We join with the authority of the throne and the elders to participate in the plan and purpose of God to bring even tongue, tribe, and nation to the knowledge of Jesus. By knowing who is with us in this vision, and with this purpose, we gain confidence that in the end, we win. You have been made a powerful king and a passionate priest and are commissioned to walk and pray among the nations. It is your role to agree with the vision, focus on the Lamb, avoid distraction, walk in the presence, and bring heaven to earth through your obedience.

TWO IMPORTANT POINTS

In the 20 years of walking in worship since publishing the First Edition, I have taken two of these points deeply to heart. **First, I will ascribe with my mouth glory, honor, power, might, and dominion**

---

10. Revelation 5:3-14 NKJV

only to the Lamb. That is to say, I will not ascribe any of those things to the enemy. When people start telling me about how mighty the enemy is, I ask why he is not seen or mentioned in this vision. All glory and honor belong to Jesus.

The second is: **Wherever I am, when I turn my focus to Jesus, He releases the powerful dynamic of this throne room in my life, enabling me to fulfill my calling as an Attack Lamb, a mighty warrior clothed in the gentleness of the Lamb. Life laid down to bring others to the throne.**

Oh, and by the way, after the serpent was bound, we traveled the length and breadth of Laos proclaiming the Kingdom of God is at hand. First came a few believers, then the Lao Christian Movement, then the Lao International Foundation for Poverty Alleviation. On the day the serpent was bound, a certain people group had just three people who knew Jesus and today there are over 2,000 worshipping in their villages. Many members of the government have given their lives to Christ. There is now a network of replicating churches throughout Laos.

Video clip from televised LIFPA Concert 2010

CHAPTER 2

THE 90-PERCENT SOLUTION

We stood behind a wide yellow line. It was painted on the floor and up the walls of the two-story cell block in the Armstrong County jail in Kittanning, Pennsylvania. Rows of cells lined the walls of the big room on either side of us and stacked above them was another row of cells. I didn't know what the temperature was, but it felt cold; cold in my soul. Concrete and steel were the only sights to see. The guards straddled the line as the cell doors clanged open and they called to the men to come out. But the inmates just called back insults from behind the barred cells.

"What do we do now," I wondered? We had come with hearts filled with hope and compassion for these men, but their hardness was a slap in our faces. No one moved from their cells. The ministry team was looking to me, their pastor, for leadership. *"Tell us what to do,"* their eyes said. I didn't know.

In my heart I could feel the love of Jesus for these men, and His compassion to see them freed. I could see Him, the King of kings, proclaiming their release and out of my spirit, at the prompting of the Holy Spirit within, I began to sing. The team joined in and we sang the anthem of heaven in praise to Jesus. "Holy, holy, holy Lord, God of power and might, heaven and earth are filled with your glory…"

After a few moments the jeers and insults stopped. A soft shuffling sound began as men slowly emerged from their cells. Warm tears started flowing from closed eyelids and cascading down uplifted faces as the loving presence of God entered this man-made hell. His glory filled the place and saturated the very walls. The shuffling sound of feet on concrete became entwined with the sound of angel's wings as we sang. I had obeyed the simplest of promptings and God had poured Himself out to them.

Opening my eyes, I was aware of the faces of those who had been touched by God, but my attention was drawn above them to an area at the top of the flight of metal steps which connected the upper and lower cell blocks. There I saw a white Figure, brilliant in sparkling silver and pure white light. He was taller than eight feet and His face was light energy without describable feature. As we sang, there emanated from the folds of His flowing robe a cloudlike presence which flowed down the stairs and throughout the main floor of the cell block and into each and every cell. Every man there was touched.

The effect of this presence was deliverance. Hardened men wept as we continued to sing praises to the Lord. They confessed sin. They found forgiveness. They opened their hearts to the Lord. They declared His glory. They entered into the presence and will of God. This heavenly vision was a reality on earth as that night Jesus visited that jail.

Someone smarter than I has said, "90 percent of almost anything is just showing up." It was surely true that night. We did nothing more than show up and do our 10 percent. And that consisted of singing the song He prompted us to sing. God did the rest. So it is with our next foundation block for success.

GAP STANDERS

As we drove home, I realized in an even greater way the call of God on my life. I realized that He needs people to go into the prisons of the earth and proclaim His glory among the heathen. I realized that Jesus was moving in a mighty way and that the most hardened of men would melt in His presence. He just needed someone to go and sing that song, pray that prayer, reach out to that man, take that territory for Him.

I became aware in that instant that the One at the head of the stairs was able to reach to the farthest corner of that cell block, or to the ends of the earth to save, or heal and deliver as long as one of His witnesses would go out and sing His praises before the heathen. That night it was actual singing, but showing forth His glory could have taken many forms.

After an experience like that it would have been tempting to start a "singing ministry," but I did not form a band, hire backup singers or get an agent. I took that heavenly song and vision and through His direction and provision began to travel around the world praising Him. We've done it both in sanctuaries and streets. I have seen Him do the impossible for rich and poor, simple and wise. Jesus continues to use those who will go forth, and He backs up His Word with signs and wonders.

What happened that day in the Armstrong County jail is really simple. A large gap existed between those men and God. God needed someone to come and fill that gap, to pray on behalf of those men for their reconciliation to God. We were available, and with no special talent or abilities, (if you've ever heard my singing you would know how true this is), we were able to stand in the gap for those men. Then God Himself bridged the gap of sin and brought salvation and true freedom to the captives.

A "gap" is a space between two places. For most people that gap is between where they are spiritually and where they ought to be. I'm glad that you are thinking about others. That is really good. As long as you are aware there are gaps in your life, you will have the humility to pray for the gaps in others. The hard question is, are you willing to stand in those gaps for them? Those gaps create the doorways through which the enemy's lies enter in.

HOW GAPS DEVELOP

The soul of man longs for the fulfilling presence of God. Man, however, entertains other desires that lead to fulfillment apart from

Christ and, therefore, to sin. Sin is fundamentally the fulfillment of lust. When any other person, place, or thing is substituted for the fulfilling presence of God, disappointment will follow as surely as wet follows rain.

A person without Christ is not able to access the heavens and receive from God. It's like trying to tune in a TV when you don't have an antenna; there is no established uplink. God only responds to one prayer of the sinner: one special prayer that confesses and repents of a sinful state and asks forgiveness; the prayer that asks Jesus to be Lord and Savior. With that prayer, all of heaven's benefits become available and the gap is closed.

When people look for the perfect church, they begin by attending services. Eventually they affirm that God is indeed in their midst. They decide to stay a while and begin to build relationship. They begin to put their trust in the pastor or another leader of the fellowship. Along with the joy of new Christian relationship there begins a gentle warning of the Holy Spirit, "Do not put your trust in man. Stay close to Me."

This believer continues to look to the pastor as a wonderful person given to them by God to fulfill all his spiritual needs (so far, so good). Then one day the usual fulfilling ministry does not flow. Oops. Not that they are offended, it is just that their expectations have not been met. A gap has appeared. Satan looks for these gaps. He sows seeds of discord and tells the believer, "You deserve more; I mean after all, look at all you've done for this church." Sound familiar? We have all heard it at one time or another.

But what does such disappointment with our church life really indicate? Disappointment indicates misdirected desire. Our focus has shifted from a desire for a relationship with the Lord to a desire for relationship with the pastor. Besides, pastor seems to meet our spiritual needs almost better than God does. Such a desire indicates a gap has formed in the relationship the believer has been developing with the Lord. Usually by this point corporate worship has replaced individual worship in his life.

ENTER THE ENEMY

Now the Enemy enters the picture with thoughts of rejection and dislike. Thoughts are the arrows he shoots through the gaps. Attacking the mind of the Christian, he will sow one of two lies. He will either give the believer a short list of reasons why he should no longer appreciate the pastor, or convince the believer the pastor no longer appreciates him. Either way, the results are the same; discord, strife, envy, etc.

The same set of circumstances gives rise to the alarming number of divorces among Christians. Rather than having Jesus as the source of fulfillment, couples look to each other. They develop certain expectations of each other and impose demands. When these are not fulfilled, the same Divider is there to sow the same kinds of thoughts. A couple with over twenty years in a wonderful marriage will tell you they have fallen "out of love" with each other. A gap has widened until it is a gaping hole through which the life of the marriage is being sucked out. The resulting devastation will effect generations.

If you can see the gaps in your life, the lives of others, the church, or your nation, it is because you are seeing from the vantage point of God's great love for His people and the world. Because you have that vision, God is calling you to get into that gap and to pray. God is allowing you to see things as He does so that through your prayers there can be agreement on the earth with His perfect plan for mankind.

What intercession really means is to intervene between parties with a view to reconciling differences. This is no great revelation; it is the definition of the word from Webster's Dictionary. But, part of the problem for the modern church is so many other things have been substituted for standing in the gap to effect that reconciliation. So often it is very instructive to see what something is not, in order to see what it is. After all, in wanting to be "gap standers" or intercessors we would certainly not want to be led...

DOWN THE GARDEN PATH

Have you ever seen this scenario? A sincere group of people decide they have been called to "Intercessory Ministry." They begin to meet as a small group, usually at a time which is not convenient for anyone else in the church. A general call is given to the church for prayer requests to be given to this "special group of intercessors" whom the Lord has "raised up."

After several months, the first directive suggestions begin to trickle out from the group. They feel that they have seen the will of God for the church and for individuals in it, particularly members of the leadership team. Soon they are talking to the younger singles about their life direction.

Given respect by the leadership and common courtesy by church members, they grow in intensity. Now they are aware of the "ruler spirits and strongholds" which are set against the church. These are rumored to have appeared to them in their prayer meetings. Often they claim to be aware of the spiritual forces which are operating in the lives of leadership. They become very spiritual in demeanor. They will not open their intensity or spirituality to question by those who are younger in the Lord or less experienced.

Now spiritual visitation becomes a part of their "prayer time." They do warfare against demonic forces which somehow never seem to totally lift from the church. They develop an image to accompany the word "intercession." It conveys an air of knowing more than anyone else in their church body...even the pastor.

Soon, they begin to "discern" spiritual activity in each other. They spend their prayer time "ministering" to each other. They focus on the enemy's attack on them because they are "prime intercessors." The inference is that if they who are so strong in the Lord are having these difficulties, how can mere believers survive. Those who hear about these things decide they will never be able to sustain a prayer ministry. They determine that they are far too weak for such warfare.

STAYING ON COURSE

I am not mocking the process of spiritual discernment, but this group, however well-intentioned at their beginning, have moved far away from true intercession. Their self-focus and self-orientation has culminated in spiritual pride, and taken them far off course. Paul warns us to **"Let no one cheat you of your reward, taking delight in false humility,..."** (Colossians 2:18[11]a). It is this false humility through which the Enemy has begun to defeat this otherwise sincere group.

There is a phrase you will begin to hear from group members like these, which will tell you they are close to this point. They will say they are being called to a time of personal cleansing before they can handle any more prayer requests. They will begin to stress the importance of preparation of the intercessor over the Lord's ability to provide grace to cover their weaknesses.

Gosh, doesn't that sound spiritual? The problem is, it isn't correct.

It is understood in our walk with Jesus that we are not worthy to be included in His plans. That will never change. In fact, the celebration of our weakness opens our hearts for the worship of His excellence. Paul says, **"Therefore most gladly I will rather boast in my infirmities, that the power of Christ may rest upon me"** (2 Corinthians 12:9b). He knew he could rejoice that the kingdom of God was not altered by the strength of his performance on any given day. This is no small concept; it is spiritual reality. We must have our heads on straight about this matter. It is vital to the flow of the power of the Holy Spirit in our lives.

FALLING INTO THE TRAP

Our group of would-be intercessors has fallen into the trap of "self perfection" to attain a throne room position with Christ. The

---

11. [18]Let no one cheat you of your reward, taking delight in false humility and worship of angels, intruding into those things which he has not seen, vainly puffed up by his fleshly mind

problem is that the access to the throne of God is given through the blood of the Lamb, not by works of righteousness. The very best prayer and the very best works do not gain us access to grace. Grace is gained by one thing only, and that is the precious, all-powerful blood of Christ.

If you are part of a group like this, please ask yourself if this expression is becoming frequent among you. If it is, remind yourselves of the grace of God in calling you to ministry. Remind each other of your simple first love experience with Christ in prayer. Read Andrew Murray and Charles Finney on prayer. Work your way back to true humility which cries out to the Lord in utter amazement that I should even have a place in the plan of the Savior to be saved by His blood.

You and your group can be used in a mighty way when you hurdle the high place of humility. Get it settled in your spirit that the only worthy One is Christ. You are not going to arrive at any higher a pinnacle of perfection for you already have access to the throne room. Do not allow the Devil to tempt you with what you already have.

TEARING DOWN OUR OWN STRONGHOLDS

We receive clear caution in the Word that the strongholds we must tear down are those of our own minds.

> **Casting down arguments and every high thing that exalts itself against the knowledge of God, bringing every thought into captivity to the obedience of Christ;...**   **2 Corinthians 10:5**

It is the imaginations, the inflated thoughts of self worth, which lift themselves against the knowledge of Christ. They must be brought under subjection to the truth. Your personal knowledge of Jesus Christ has lifted you to be a coworker with Him. You do not attain any higher position than the one you presently have. You are seated with Christ at the right hand of the Father. To attempt to pull yourself higher is to do exactly what Lucifer did.

> **For you have said in your heart: 'I will ascend into heaven, I will exalt my throne above the stars of God;...I will ascend above the heights of the clouds, I will be like the Most High.**   **Isaiah 14:13,14**

We must be happy in the realization of what we have in Christ. This is why Paul prays for the Ephesians that the eyes of their understanding might be enlightened (Ephesians 1:18[12]). When we realize all that Christ has given us, we cease from our own labors and enter into the rest which He has provided. His power through us causes even the demons to bow down.

Those who do not remind themselves daily of their weakness will finally come to their leadership with "direction from God" for the body. At this point they are no longer teachable; correction is out of the question. The pastoral team does not follow their input and division occurs. More than one church split has happened just this way. We had the same temptation in our ministry several years ago.

WORN THE SHOES – WALKED THE PATH

Many years ago, as a young pastor, I was amazed to see this process in operation. One day one of the group of "intercessors" burst into my office declaring she knew what direction the church should take with one of our families. Now, as a pastor, I was wondering how she had obtained such detailed information about one of our church families. I listened quite closely to her energetic call for me to discipline them.

I was more inclined to mercy. Somehow the thought of telling someone they could no longer be a part of the church was a little much for me. I felt that was far beyond my job description. As I appealed

---

12. [18]the eyes of your understanding being enlightened; that you may know what is the hope of His calling, what are the riches of the glory of His inheritance in the saints

for mercy and longsuffering in the situation, I was rebuked as being typical of all pastoral leadership, that is, unable to take a stand for Christ. I refrained from pointing out that for years I had risked my life on the mission fields of the world.

As the lady left in the same haste with which she had entered,

I reflected on a few things. God's mercy exceeds His wrath. He is longsuffering with us all, and thank God for it. He adds to the church daily as He sees fit. Jesus said He would build the church and cautioned strongly against offending any one of His sheep.

I chose mercy.

That same prayer group happened to be holding a retreat for women over the next weekend, and I made a point to see her again. The following Monday she appeared at my door in quite a state of excitement. She told me about the glorious time they had at the retreat, and I was impressed with what I saw as a certain change about her. Then she gave me the news.

"You should have seen God move," she said. "He led us to cast the lying spirits out of each other." She was thrilled.

I couldn't help it. I had to ask the obvious question. "If a lying spirit had been cast out of you, then it's a good thing we didn't do as you had suggested last week, isn't it?" Her enthusiasm dampened a little bit.

When she left my office I was deeply troubled. How had this happened in our church? These were very nice people. They had formed the group with all good intentions to intercede. I feel to this day they were very sincere and had only good motives in what they were doing, but what had happened?

TRUE INTERCESSION

The second letter in our **W-I-N** acrostic is **I** and it stands for intercession…true intercession.

The problem was this group had never known or completely understood the true definition of intercession. They had their own idea of the call to intercessory prayer, but had not gained a biblical understanding of what intercession really is. Rather than being instruments for reconciling differences, they had become instruments for division, questioning leaders and stumbling babes. They had gotten out of the gap and had begun to lord a false spirituality over the flock.

I thank God He did intervene in our lives. Today they continue to meet and to seek His face. I have no doubt that as the Holy Spirit leads them, they pray for me and I thank God for that. But in those years, we all had many lessons to learn. Our zeal was beyond question, but we had very little experience.

A healthy ministry of intercession reaches out to and includes people. Exclusivity is the enemy of God's purpose. If every man, woman, and child on this planet is going to have the opportunity to receive Jesus Christ as Lord and Savior, we must include people in prayer rather than exclude them.

While intercession can include a lot of things, e.g. worship, prayer, prophetic acts, etc., one thing it must include is intervention. To "intervene" in this case is like playing the role of referee in a boxing match. He is irrelevant until he is needed; then he steps between the combatants and sets things in motion correctly again.

How do you like irrelevance? Very few people do. That is why so many folks doing the work of God declare themselves to be a "ministry." They are not content to just disappear from the mainstream and seek the Lord. It is in the heart of man to have a title. We are conditioned by the world's system to look out for number one. To take care of ourselves. To promote ourselves. To make sure we save face in every circumstance.

We want our labor to be for something significant. Does it bother you when people say, "All we can do now is pray." Or, "I guess we'll just have to trust the Lord on this one." Who else **would** you trust?

And why wait till the bitter end to pray? Men ought always to pray (1 Thessalonians 5:17[13]). Ephesians 6:18[14] goes a step further encouraging us to pray always in the Spirit.

Indeed our work in the Lord is in vain if we fail to pray. Jesus spent night and day in prayer. He said, **"...the Son can do nothing of Himself, but what He sees the Father do; for whatever He does, the Son also does in like manner"** (John 5:19b). How do you suppose He gained such insight? He walked among man in continual communication with the Father. That is prayer walking.

Have you ever wondered how Jesus managed to spend so much time among people and they still didn't know who He was? He made himself of no reputation. He did not have an advance team; at least not one you could see. He was a study in avoiding the ways of man for He had a heavenly vision: to effect the perfect will of God in His life and the lives of those with whom He came in contact. What is the perfect will of God? That every man, woman and child have the opportunity to hear the Gospel in a way they can understand it. The result: He attained the highest reputation ever afforded anyone in all of recorded history.

JESUS IN THE GAP

In 1983 I was trekking in Nepal. At that time it was illegal to change religion in that beautiful land. The jail terms were one year for converting, three years for leading someone to the Lord, and six years per person for water baptism.

We were trekking from village to village, distributing Christian literature and praying for the sick. The previous day we had handed out about two hundred tracts and the response had been very great. Now we walked into the town of Gaighat, Sagamatha Province. This very busy village was Panchat, a sort of county seat.

---

13. [17]pray without ceasing
14. [18]praying always with all prayer and supplication in the Spirit, being watchful to this end with all perseverance and supplication for all the saints

We entered the place in the heat of the day and stopped to rest on a low stone wall adjacent to the local school. The children were attracted to the two very different-looking Westerners. They ran over to see us and were very curious about what might be in our rattan baskets. Our porters, also weary from the journey, were looking forward to spending the night in this town and had left us there on the wall to fend for ourselves, while they went to make arrangements. The crowd of children grew and two of the braver boys, perhaps ten years of age, began to open the baskets. We let them.

BUSTED

Across the way from us was a man in legal garb. Attorneys in Nepal have a very distinctive haircut and robe. This was obviously a man of some legal influence. As the children began to open the baskets and shout with joy at the books they found, this man turned and hastily headed toward the police station.

Calling to the porters, I expressed my concern, but they were not inclined to move quickly. So we Westerners took off as fast as we could go and left them behind. We were certain there was going to be a problem. We were right.

As the oldest and heaviest of our team, I was the one the police caught up with first. The arrest was very professional, but the arresting officer did tell me I was in a lot of trouble. The Chief District Officer (CDO) had ordered my arrest for preaching Christianity through the books we carried. The officer was under orders to stop my flight and to bring me at once before the CDO.

As I walked back down the trail to face certain difficulty, the Lord spoke to me, "If you deny Me before man, I will deny you before the Father."

The voice was as clear as day. The certainty of its tenor gripped my heart so that minutes later when the CDO asked, "Are you a Christian?" it was very easy to say, "Yes." When he further asked, "Are you a baptized Christian?" It was even easier to say, "Yes, sir,

I have been baptized three times," (once as a child, once as an adult believer, and once in the Holy Spirit).

"I LIVE TO MAKE INTERCESSION FOR YOU"

As I said that, the same voice spoke to me saying, "I live to make intercession for you." It was so real. No one else in the room heard it. The CDO never heard it. But there was Jesus telling me He had the situation under control. He was standing in a major gap in my life that day. He was drawing together these events and the perfect plan of the Father.

After lengthy dialogue in which I shared the message of the Gospel with the CDO, he decided to let me go, along with our team. His exact words were, "I have decided to show you grace." Where did a Hindu official come up with the word "grace?" God was speaking through him. Instead of six hundred years in jail, I was going on with the rest of our scheduled trek.

Six months later, that same man walked out of his office and from a clear blue sky was struck dead by lightning. It was reported in the Kathmandu paper and the Christian brothers in Nepal saved the clipping for me. For years I thought about that lightning strike as retribution; you know, "**Touch not mine anointed, and do my prophets no harm**" (1 Chronicles 16:22). But one morning the Lord corrected me. "Rather," He suggested, "see how much it took for Me to get a pampered, self-centered, Christian preacher (that would be me, in case you hadn't guessed) over to Nepal to share the faith with that man, knowing he had just six months to live."

You see, Jesus was in the gap for **him**, too. The CDO neither knew Him nor knew where to find Him, but had a need to know Him. God orchestrated the arrest, used the Nepali attorney and even my size to bring us to the gap. Jesus was busy interceding and, indeed, I have never been better cared for. The plan of man was made to conform to the plan of God, and the intercessor was unseen throughout.

FIRST BLOOD

Philippians 2 teaches us that Jesus made Himself of no reputation and served us in the great gap of Gethsemane. The blood of the covenant was first shed there. Not Pilate, nor the high priest, nor the Devil extracted the first drops of that cleansing flow. They dropped as sweat from His body in the agony of intercession. The blood began to flow in a place where no one else could see it. Intercession is a private matter.

Yet, intercession is so powerful that all the sin of man can be washed away by it. God was in Christ reconciling man to himself. He was in Gethsemane as the Intercessor for you. Yes, the plan of man was made to conform to the plan of God that every man, woman, and child on the earth would have the opportunity to know Jesus as their Lord and Savior. Jesus prayed that for you in that garden. He lifted you before the Father before you were born.

He paid the price and now He has the greatest reputation. He has defeated the Devil above the earth, on the earth, and under the earth. He has risen far above every power and principality. He has opened the gates of heaven and now lives in the gap for you (Hebrews 7:25[15]). You have an Advocate with the Father. Go ahead and thank Him!

IT WORKS FOR YOU TOO

You do not have to be preoccupied with how you are doing. The One who can open the seals has taken up His position as intercessor for you. Receive that gift with thanksgiving and be happy for He lives to intercede for you. You are the object of His love. He looks upon you with delight as He sees His own prayers answered daily in your life. You are a joy to Him. You are accepted in the Beloved. Jesus loves you. Jesus accepts you. As a born-again believer, you are just as if you had never sinned in His sight.

---

15. [25]Therefore He is also able to save to the uttermost those who come to God through Him, since He always lives to make intercession for them

When you have that locked into your spirit and your relationship with Him is secure, you are ready to step into the gap for others. You will be able to appear as an irrelevant or extraneous feature without it bothering you. You will have exchanged the desire for prominence for the desire to be significant. You'll know the event is not about you. You'll know you were called there to pray, not posture, not parade, not even to preach.

Step into that gap. Intervene. Take up that position of humility that declares your weakness and the Lord's strength. Appeal to God's ultimate purpose on someone else's behalf. You are in the gap as a result of your relationship with Jesus, just as He is in the gap for you as a result of His relationship with His Father.

....

Times were difficult for the rebuilding of Jerusalem. God looked for a man who would stand in the gap and build the wall. There were very strong forces aligned against the team that went out to reclaim this promised land. Initially, the city and its temple were built as a dwelling place for the Lord, but as the people turned to the idols of the land, His presence abode no more. The restoration is a great story told in the books of Nehemiah and Ezra with prophetic insight from Jeremiah and Ezekiel and an inspiration for us to stand in the gaps and build walls in places where the Lord once moved; but, has moved along.

Radical concept, I know, but in our city of Pittsburgh we have places where David Brainerd walked and prayed, Billy Graham held revival meetings with thousands responding, Kathryn Kuhlman was used by God in miraculous healing ministry, and the Catholic Charismatic Movement was birthed when the Lord poured out His Spirit on four Roman Catholic priests.

Today we battle the same forces that hit every major city in America. Each morning we are awakened to the toll of young people who have died as the result of drugs or drug-related murders. Abortions are performed on-demand in the shade of one of the nation's greatest Children's Hospitals and the birthplace of Mr. Rogers Neighborhood.

"Intercession" has taken many forms as each stream of the Church has tried to address the needs. As part of the community, we have been teaching Attack Lambs to go out into the community and worship the Lord, releasing the power of heaven on earth. In a word, stand in the gap. There are racial, political, communication, and economic gaps; in fact, there are so many disagreements that agreement is hard to find. Unity in the community is a fleeting commodity.

INTERCEDE

Searching for a definition of "intercede," I came across my copy of Webster's Dictionary of the English Language. The first definition of intercede is simply *to pray*. And I certainly agree that lives are changed through prayer.

It was the second definition that caught my eye. To Intercede is *to intervene between two with a view of reconciling their differences.*

Wow, that is exactly what we are talking about. Find that space between where someone is and where they could be, enter the space, and talk to God about them until you receive something from Him to say to them. The Apostle says we have this ministry of reconciliation and we see Jesus on the cross, reconciling God to man and man to God. He was in the gap and so can you be.

The active word or verb in the definition is to intervene. Webster defines intervene as *to enter in or appear as an extraneous or irrelevant circumstance.* In other words, we enter in, drawing no attention to ourselves. We are very Lamb like, gentle, kind, courteous, nonconfrontational until the wolf that holds the people turns to attack us. When we discern evil, out comes the Lion who dwells within us.

As we maintain focus on the throne and Lordship of Jesus, we release the anointing that breaks the yokes of bondage and we fill the gap with God's presence dispelling the evil that lurked there.

24/7 PRAYER

Praying over Hong Kong from top of ICC building in 2012

But what about the wall. Our friend and mentor, Dick Eastman partnered with another dear friend Dr. Agatha Chan and set out to raise up 24/7 prayer centers in each of the 19 sections of Hong Kong. For ten years the prayer warriors have walked from their section to the prayer location to pray for that great city. Their cry has been for righteousness, peace, and joy in the Holy Spirit. As I write, we are seeing changes in Hong Kong that will eventually guarantee the three.

Agatha's walls and the concept have been beautifully built at the Jericho Center for Global Evangelism, the international headquarters of Every Home for Christ in Colorado Springs, Colorado. You can go there and see the walls, book a prayer closet, and join in "wall building" around the world.

God is looking for those who will enter the gap, release the anointing, and change their city. It is great to know it, it is greater to do it.

Rainbow and eagle during prayer time in Hong Kong 2012

CHAPTER 3

ABRAHAM, OUR EXAMPLE

Prayer Walking

Abraham was a family man. When God instructed him to leave his family and separate himself to God's purpose, he took along his nephew Lot. We have no idea what agreements were made amongst the members of the family, but we do know the patriarch was, or felt he was, responsible for Lot.

Abraham was obedient, coming to rest in a place of peace called the plains of Mamre, when the Lord came by (Genesis 18). Remember the Spirit of the Lord is moving in all the earth looking for those through whom He can be glorified. Abraham had put himself in the gap, albeit unknowingly, and God found him. How did he place himself in the gap, you ask?

Abraham worshiped. That is, he got up from his rest and beckoned to the Lord to come and fellowship with him. Abraham made himself available to God. He called to Him. What an example! All successful Christian endeavor comes from an attitude of worship. He got up from the place of peace where he was content and called upon the Lord for a time of fellowship. When worship moves into fellowship you have stepped into the gap.

God and Abraham had a meal together. The blood of the calf of sacrifice speaks of acceptance in the Beloved because of their existing covenant. The bread and wine speak of the new covenant which is to come in Jesus. Abraham had relationship with God. The "Father of Faith" and the "Father of the Spirit" ate together. The purpose of man is about to conform to the purpose of God.

THE AFTER DINNER WALK

After dinner, the Lord excused Himself and headed on down the road. Abraham followed the Eastern custom and saw his Guest off in proper fashion. They walked together for a while and the Lord was mindful of Scripture He would be inspiring a couple thousand years later, **"He will do nothing without first telling His servants the prophets"** (Amos 3:7[16] author's paraphrase). He thought for awhile about the man with whom He was walking and the reason for His journey. *"Abraham is a just man and is going to serve me all his days,"* the Lord thought. *"Is it right for me to do something without telling him?"*

Have you ever wondered what God is thinking about as you linger in His presence? So often we sing a few songs and then rush

16. [7]Surely the Lord God does nothing, Unless He reveals His secret to His servants the prophets

on to the announcements or the day's schedule or program. This text tells us God is thinking about us in covenant terms. He is making a decision. In this case He is determining the present from His knowledge of the future. He relates to you not according to what you have been, but according to what you shall be.

He shares His mission with Abraham. God is going to purge the people of Sodom of sin and its consequences, perhaps even AIDS. That's right. Sodom and Gomorrah are homosexual communities. How do we know that? From Genesis 19:5[17]. The men of the city wanted to have sexual relations with the angels for they were fair to look upon. Where did you think the term sodomy came from?

When God tells Abraham His plan to destroy Sodom, Abraham appeals for the life of Lot, his nephew who is living there. Abraham and God dialogue as they walk. This is prayer walking. Abraham finally steps in front of God. Talk about standing in the gap for someone! He beseeches God to spare the city for the sake of its righteous people. First, he asks that the city be spared if there are fifty righteous people. God agrees. Abraham reduces the number and asks again. Again, God agrees. Abraham continues reducing the number and asking until finally he stops at ten righteous people. But there aren't even ten. Still, God's mercy exceeds His wrath, so He spares those who call upon Him and destroys the rest. What a message for today. He spares those who call upon Him and destroys the rest.

Of course, Lot has to leave all that is associated with living in Sodom. But his wife cannot separate from her love for those things or the city and turns as if to return. She is turned to a pillar of salt. The entire region is barren to this day. Whatever virus was there was terminated.

Abraham stood in the gap for Lot and his family, and did so boldly. We can do the same for our families, and do it just as boldly because we operate under a better covenant with better promises.

---

17. [5]And they called to Lot and said to him, "Where are the men who came to you tonight? Bring them out to us that we may know them carnally."

INTERCESSORS TODAY

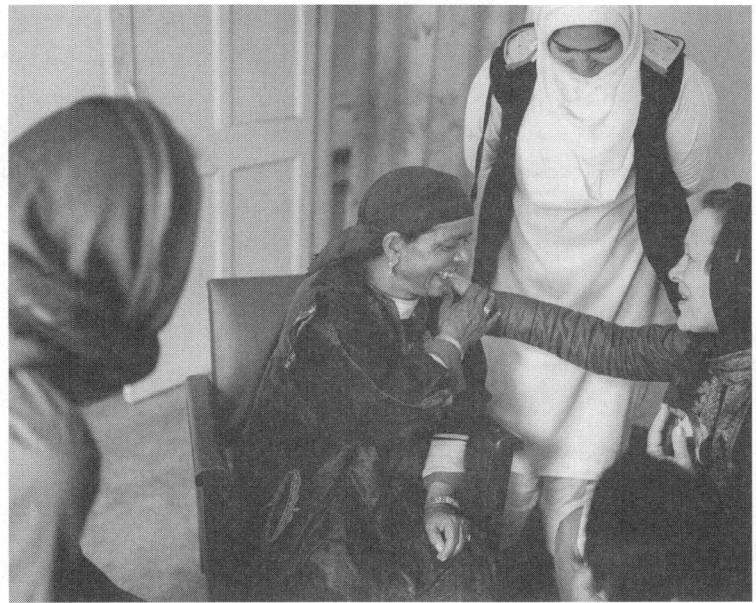

Praying for people during medical outreach in Kashmir June 2018

I hear politicians and "do gooders," and the media is filled with issues and non-answers. But where are the intercessors? They are walking with God. They appear as irrelevant or extraneous. They are not on TV; they are not included at the summits on AIDs, and they are scorned if they say anything. Eventually, when the way of man has run its course, the problem will be brought to the feet of Christ. At that time, one of those whom the world thought was homophobic will have divine wisdom and God's mercy will be made manifest.

Exodus 32 and 33 are a study on developing an intercessory relationship. As we join the action in verse 30, the people have sinned a great sin. Moses, as their leader, has to take a course of action. He steps into the gap. He returns to the Lord.

Can you imagine saying to a teenager caught cheating in school, "I am going to go and see if I can make atonement for you?" To make atonement means to make up for some error or deficiency; in the extreme it means to give your life as payment.

In other words, Moses is saying he is going to go before God in the place of the guilty to plead for them. The innocent sacrificing himself for the guilty! Will you give yourself to a life of prayer? Will you be a Moses standing before God? Will you be an Abraham standing in God's way bargaining for the life of another?

In Exodus 32:32[18] Moses makes an extraordinary request. He has so identified with the people he is willing to bear the consequence of their sin. He gives God a choice: forgive their sin or blot his own name out of the book of life.

The Lord's response is that sin and its consequence are a personal matter. Each person must bear the consequence of his own sin. Further, the context tells us that, while they were subsequently led through the wilderness by the Angel of the Lord, Israel was still plagued because of the golden calf they had made to worship (Exodus 32:35[19]).

GOD'S SOLUTION — PRAYER WALKING

In spite of Israel's failings, God makes a great commitment to Moses in the next few sentences. He says He will come along on the trip. He is going to walk in the midst of the people to prevent the spoken plague from destroying them before they arrive at His promise. He describes them as a stiff-necked people. As such, they will always have a gap between them and God, but since He loves them, in response to Moses' plea, He will close the gap.

When told this news, the people are sad. Not that they are going to get the promise, but that God is in their midst because they are stiff-necked. Is this a great gap? You are in one about the same size. You tell your loved ones Jesus wants to walk with them and, instead of being happy, they are sad. You tell your young folks if they will

---

18. [32]Yet now, if You will forgive their sin—but if not, I pray, blot me out of Your book which You have written."
19. [35]So the Lord plagued the people because of what they did with the calf which Aaron made

walk with the Lord they will be blessed and, instead of going for the promise, they are sad about the condition.

It was the same for Isaiah and for Jesus. You remember that Isaiah was going to be rejected, by 90 percent of the people (Isaiah 6:9[20]). Jesus was despised and rejected, a man of sorrows and acquainted with grief (Isaiah 53:3[21]). He was eventually abandoned to the cross by even His best friends on earth. But there in Gethsemane, when even the closest could not fellowship with Him in prayer, He was met by the Father and the angels ministered to Him. He was sustained by that heavenly vision.

THE KEY TO SUCCESS AS AN INTERCESSOR

God establishes relationship with the intercessor. The people go out of the camp to find God in the tabernacle and nothing happens. Moses goes to the same place and the glory of God manifests as the two friends discuss the pressures of leading six million stubborn people in a way they have never gone.

God meets Moses in the gap. This causes all of the people to turn their attention toward that tent. They had not seen the presence of God before now. They had seen His power against Egypt. They had covered their door posts against His wrath, but they had not seen His glory. As Moses and God fellowship in the tabernacle, the cloudy pillar appears to the people and they do what the Lord has placed in their hearts. They worship. **All successful Christian endeavor comes from an attitude of worship.** The people only wanted to see God's ways; Moses wanted His presence!

Moses leaves the tabernacle of intercession to return to his role of leadership. The people now honor him because he met with God face to face. One young man remains in the tabernacle. He is learning the lessons of the presence of God which will enable him to lead the

---

20. [9]And He said, "Go, and tell this people: 'Keep on hearing, but do not understand; Keep on seeing, but do not perceive.'
21. [3]A Man of sorrows and acquainted with grief. And we hid, as it were, our faces from Him; He was despised, and we did not esteem Him

next generation of these people. He is communing with the Person of God who will one day meet him before the closed gate of Jericho and instruct him in how to take the land. He is Joshua.

The hours of worship in the tabernacle gave Joshua great faith. He was ready to receive the promise God had given for he had spent time in fellowship with the One whose word is true. In Numbers 14[22] this confidence causes him to proclaim to the people the Lord will give them the land as He has promised. Indeed, it is Joshua who contends with the people for the promise.

AN UNHAPPY PEOPLE

Yet the people are not happy with Moses. In fact, they take up stones to kill him. Why is it that the one who seeks God and appeals to faith is always the target for the stones of those who rebel? Could it be that the offended ones are also trying to fill the gap? Do they sense the distance? Has the peaceful presence and powerful purpose of God become distant to them as well?

God's response is He will disinherit them, He will destroy them, He will make a new and mightier nation who will enter in (Numbers 14:12[23]). For the moment, Moses is the only one who can stand in the gap. He does not appeal to the Lord's nature of longsuffering. He does not call out for protection for himself or his young leaders. Instead, he appeals to God's ultimate purpose.

THE APPEAL TO ULTIMATE PURPOSE

He reminds the Lord that should God destroy this people, the nations will have no reason to believe His promises either (v. 15[24]).

22. [8]If the Lord delights in us, then He will bring us into this land and give it to us, 'a land which flows with milk and honey.'
23. [12]"... I will strike them with the pestilence and disinherit them, and I will make of you a nation greater and mightier than they."
24. [15]Now if You kill these people as one man, then the nations which have heard of Your fame will speak, saying, 16 'Because the Lord was not able to bring this people to the land which He swore to give them, therefore He killed them in the wilderness.'

It is the will of God that every man, woman, and child on the earth hear the Gospel in a way he or she can understand. So to destroy the people called by His name would defeat His own purpose. How many years of solitary intercession and relationship building do you think it took for Moses to understand the impact his counsel would have on the heart of God?

Do you intercede according to the ultimate plan of God? Are you asking Him to fulfill His plan or yours? We know if we ask anything according to His will He hears us and grants the petition we desire of Him (1 John 5:14–15[25]). If you are living your life to fulfill His purpose, that every man, woman, and child would have the opportunity to receive Jesus in your generation, then ask Him to remember the promise of all things that pertain to life and godliness, ask on in confidence.

Moses' appeal to ultimate purpose released pardon and the declaration that the glory of the Lord will fill all the earth (Numbers 14:20–21[26]). Because there was an intercessor in the gap, the plan of God did not stop with a rebellious and stiff-necked people, but continued on to the next generation.

Caleb is selected as the "seed bearer" to the promised land. Caleb was selected for two reasons. First, he was not of the same spirit as the others, he was the elder of the tribe of Judah, hence bearing the title, "The Lion of the tribe of Judah." Not only did he have the title and the anointing, he was also obedient. He followed the Lord fully.

THE PURPOSE OF THE WILDERNESS EXPERIENCE

Those who did not obey the Lord were led into a wilderness designed for death. The function of the Old Testament wilderness was to see the death of the previous generation and the training of

---

25. [14]Now this is the confidence that we have in Him, that if we ask anything according to His will, He hears us. 15 And if we know that He hears us, whatever we ask, we know that we have the petitions that we have asked of Him
26. [20]Then the Lord said: "I have pardoned, according to your word; 21 but truly, as I live, all the earth shall be filled with the glory of the Lord

the subsequent. It is the same in our wilderness experience. Death of the old, preparation of the new. Moses stood in the gap for those who would die. Even though they had caused so many problems for him, we see in Deuteronomy 9:25–29[27] his heart of prayer for them.

He first mentions he has fasted and prayed for them for forty days. Wow, what a gap! Imagine having to fast for forty days before receiving the assurance God was going to hear your prayer. Can you imagine how many times in those six weeks without food he wanted to say, "OK, God, blast them!"

Moses' motive had been God's declaration of destruction of the nation. Can you grasp the fear of God this man had to believe Him so strongly that food was set aside and faith took its place? He is not praying to an extension of his father image. He is not gazing through crystals or burning incense to a rock that cannot speak. Moses is talking to the true and living God who has dramatically demonstrated His awesome power.

They had met at a bush, walked the deserts together, faced Pharaoh, and parted the Red Sea. Moses had seen the hand of God in deliverance and destruction. There was no doubt the Power with whom he spoke could do whatever He desired.

ULTIMATE PURPOSE AGAIN

Moses reminds God of His love for the people, the fact that He had chosen them. He makes a strong point of all the Lord has done for these people in bringing them out of Egypt. He asks God not to

27. [25]"Thus I prostrated myself before the Lord; forty days and forty nights I kept prostrating myself, because the Lord had said He would destroy you. [26]Therefore I prayed to the Lord, and said: 'O Lord God, do not destroy Your people and Your inheritance whom You have redeemed through Your greatness, whom You have brought out of Egypt with a mighty hand. [27]Remember Your servants, Abraham, Isaac, and Jacob; do not look on the stubbornness of this people, or on their wickedness or their sin, [28]lest the land from which You brought us should say, "Because the Lord was not able to bring them to the land which He promised them, and because He hated them, He has brought them out to kill them in the wilderness." [29]Yet they are Your people and Your inheritance, whom You brought out by Your mighty power and by Your outstretched arm.'

consider the nature of these who had groaned in Egypt but, as the Lord of Abraham, Isaac, and Jacob, to remember those whose lives God had chosen to bear His own name among men. For, he concludes, God is the God of the living, not the dead.

Then he appeals to God's ultimate purpose, **"You do not want the nations to reject You by saying You could not do what You said You would do"** (Deuteronomy 9:28[28]). This is powerful prayer. It is the character of God which is shown forth in His actions. Moses realizes the Devil is waiting to see the outcome of the rebellion of Israel.

Satan has his heralds, the kings of the nations, ready to shout the news throughout the earth that the mighty God who threw him out of heaven has been defeated by the fear in His own people; that God made a mistake in choosing man. The kings of the nations are under his deceiving power to attack those chosen vessels of the Seed of Abraham.

Would God abandon His promise to His friend? Will He abandon you when you are stubborn and rebellious? The Enemy would love to tell you that God is ashamed of you. That your salvation is not valid for the day-to-day failures in your life. He will try to get you to believe, instead of standing in the gap for others, you are such a mess yourself you should have an army of intercessors standing in the gap for you.

How did Moses quiet all of these thoughts? The same way Jesus did, he fasted. He took away the enemy's device of lust and appetite. His appetite was for the Lord.

In the power of position in God's gap, Moses prayed according to the Word of God. "You have said you will bring them out," he reminds the Lord. It is the character of God to fulfill His promises to man. Therefore He will have to change His nature to destroy the

---

28. [28]lest the land from which You brought us should say, "Because the Lord was not able to bring them to the land which He promised them, and because He hated them, He has brought them out to kill them in the wilderness."

people at this point. Moses has used a powerful tool of intercession: prayer according to the Word of the Lord.

IT'S YOUR TURN NOW

With local nursing students who assisted in the
outreaches in Kashmir June 2018

Now, have you seen some new gaps? How about those family members? Can you think of a teen who needs your prayers? How about the life of your church? Is the worship in the heavenlies? Is the preacher in the Word? How about those people on your TV who are so obviously unreached?

Take a few moments right now and intercede for one of the gaps you are aware of. We'll still be here when you come back. Pray. Step into that gap. Intervene. Take up the position of humility which declares your weakness and the Lord's strength. Pray according to the plan of God. Appeal to His ultimate purpose that every man, woman, and child know His Son. Agree with God for a while, we will wait here for you.

Let the Lord form a prayer list for you. Get paper and a pen and let Him lead you from name to name. Write them down with today's date and get ready to hear the answer. God is not slack concerning His promises (2 Peter 3:9[29]). Go ahead, give yourself to it and you will find yourself in the place of success for an intercessor: the presence of God Himself.

....

In the 43 years of practicing these teachings, two points in chapter three have become the very fiber of our relationship with God. Abraham is the example of the first and Moses of the second.

FATHER OF FAITH

All success in the spirit realm flows out of an atmosphere of praise and worship. Abraham got up from his repose and went to greet God. It was not a time of difficulty; it was a hunger for the person and presence of God. Abraham sought a dialogue, a discussion, a conversation with God. He recognized the presence and immediately wanted to know what the Lord was doing and to spend time lingering in His presence. This is the true heart desire of all who know the Lord.

Abraham prepares a place and a meal for God. This is the highest form of praise, to dedicate time and place to entertain the presence of the Lord.

God responds by joining Abraham in the meal. He is never too busy to fellowship with the one who will prepare a place for His presence. Of course, the covenant is celebrated in the bread and wine, and the redemptive nature of God in the sacrificial calf. Abraham's offering is well received. And the two fellowship at the table.

---

29. [9]The Lord is not slack concerning His promise, as some count slackness, but is longsuffering toward us, not willing that any should perish but that all should come to repentance

In Genesis 14, we find another covenant time when these two met. Abraham instituted the tithe when the king of Salem came out to meet him in the valley. Melchizedek brought bread and wine to that event. The "Father in Spirit" covenanted with the "Father of Faith" through the exchange of the tithe and the elements of communion. The Spirit of one would come upon the daughter of the other and the Redeemer of Mankind would be born. All God and all Man, He would be the Lamb who would open the scroll.

God withdraws to go on about His purpose. He waits to see if the man will alter his daily plan to walk along with him. Will Abraham get up and go? Huge point here, don't miss it. So often the Lord meets us, settles down with us, and then waits to see if we will follow Him.

Abraham continues the dialogue getting up from the place of repose and beginning to walk with God in His purpose. Big point here. Those schools are out there, those government centers are out there. Are we going to repose in our comfort zones, or get up and go with God?

Abraham's walking with God releases a further dialogue which we might call a "word of knowledge." One of the gifts of the Holy Spirit found in 1 Corinthians 12, this gift gives understanding to the "what" in God's action. When Abraham takes those first prayer walking steps, he joins in God's purpose and plan. They begin to discuss what is happening.

Lot has been crying out day and night, vexed in his spirit, righteous by the relationship of his uncle, his prayers have been heard (2 Peter 2:7-8[30]). Lot has been living surrounded by the sin of Sodom and Gomorrah and crying out to God. God has heard the cry and will visit to see if it is so before pouring out His judgment on the city. Continued walking reveals the "why."

---

30. [7]and delivered righteous Lot, who was oppressed by the filthy conduct of the wicked [8](for that righteous man, dwelling among them, tormented his righteous soul from day to day by seeing and hearing their lawless deeds)

Abraham steps into the gap. He stands before the Lord, impeding His progress to try to reconcile the people and God. That is the definition of intercession. Sure, Lot had abandoned him. Certainly, he could have taken offense; no, he did not condone the sinful practice of the people, but he entered in to appeal for reconciliation.

It is this history from Genesis 18 that has molded much of my dialogue with God, and I trust it will do the same for yours. The judgment was an outpouring of salt on the region of Sodom, which remains to this day. God in His mercy destroyed the virus that had the potential to destroy the promised land.

Lot and his daughters were spared. He chose a cave over humbling himself and returning to his uncle and got very drunk, so he did not realize he was committing incest with his daughters. Two nations were formed, Ammon and Moab, who would plague the seed of Abraham.

But Abraham remained in covenant with God and was given all the land he could see. His worshipping heart gave God all the glory for the land and all that was in it. He was great in all the earth and the fullness of his worship relationship was seen in the fact that through His seed salvation and knowledge of God are seen in all the earth.

Once I saw these outcomes, I realized that all success in the spirit realm flows forth from the dialogue of Praise and Worship. I encourage you to take time in the presence of God. Offer a sacrifice of praise and follow Him into dialogue. Hear what He has to say and surrender your time and material to Him. Set aside a time and a place to meet with Him. It does not have to be fancy, perhaps a parking spot at work or a quiet place in your home. Wherever you put it, He will meet you there. Getting up from the routine of repose of life is the key.

He rewards those who diligently seek Him.

THE MEEKEST MAN

The second principle from this chapter that has really shaped my approach to being an Attack Lamb comes from the conversation between the Almighty God and the Meekest man on the earth.

Starting from the burning bush, and continuing to the Transfiguration, Moses and God talk over the establishment of the children of Israel (God's Ultimate Purpose); but, especially, Moses's personal battle with anger.

I am a man of passion. When I see the killing fields, concentration camps, gulags, and lynchings, my blood begins to boil. I can't stand bullies and arrogance in any form. I believe that every child is sacred and is sent from God for His purpose. When I see what man does to man, I cannot accept the humanist philosophy.

But, the wrath of man does not accomplish the righteousness of God. So, I cannot stand in the gap for injustice until I can do so in the peaceful presence of the One who was worthy to open the scroll. This has been a challenge as I have been permitted to walk in some of the most corrupt cities in this world. I have seen atrocities face-to-face, rescued young people from brothels, faced down corruption in governments and schools, communications and businesses, until I have come to realize, as Moses did, that the cost of losing my temper even in a "justifiable" outburst of "righteous indignation" is too great.

Moses said to God, I am going to kill them all, and God said, you can't.

God said to Moses, I am going to kill them all, and Moses said, you can't.

Moses got so frustrated at their unbelief that he not only threw the book at them; but also hit the Rock who was Christ. As a result, he never entered the Promised Land only seeing it from afar. When he died, his body was given to Satan from whom it had to be retrieved for the Mount of Transfiguration where he counseled Christ on His mission (Jude 1:9[31]; Matthew 17:1-13[32]).

Jesus was encouraged by Moses and Elijah that day. One said the resurrection is true and you can trust it; the other said, when they hit you, do not hit back, remember your ultimate purpose, to redeem the children of Abraham.

When we are the Lamb, Jesus will be the Lion. We must stand in the gap, maintain focus on Him, and crying, "Lord do you see this? How long are you going to allow this? Let God arise and His enemies be scattered."

A SOFTENED HEART

In March of 1999, about the time the first edition was being released, USA Today published a half-page story they picked up from Reuters about four missionaries who had to seek cover in a police station in Indonesia as a mob tried to kill them. Reuters reported very accurately that the team was only praying in that province. Their lives

---

31. [9]Yet Michael the archangel, in contending with the devil, when he disputed about the body of Moses, dared not bring against him a reviling accusation, but said, "The Lord rebuke you!"

32. [1]Now after six days Jesus took Peter, James, and John his brother, led them up on a high mountain by themselves; [2]and He was transfigured before them. His face shone like the sun, and His clothes became as white as the light. [3]And behold, Moses and Elijah appeared to them, talking with Him. [4]Then Peter answered and said to Jesus, "Lord, it is good for us to be here; if You wish, let us make here three tabernacles: one for You, one for Moses, and one for Elijah." [5]While he was still speaking, behold, a bright cloud overshadowed them; and suddenly a voice came out of the cloud, saying, "This is My beloved Son, in whom I am well pleased. Hear Him!" [6]And when the disciples heard it, they fell on their faces and were greatly afraid. [7]But Jesus came and touched them and said, "Arise, and do not be afraid." [8]When they had lifted up their eyes, they saw no one but Jesus only.

[9]Now as they came down from the mountain, Jesus commanded them, saying, "Tell the vision to no one until the Son of Man is risen from the dead." [10]And His disciples asked Him, saying, "Why then do the scribes say that Elijah must come first?" [11]Jesus answered and said to them, "Indeed, Elijah is coming first and will restore all things. [12]But I say to you that Elijah has come already, and they did not know him but did to him whatever they wished. Likewise the Son of Man is also about to suffer at their hands." [13]Then the disciples understood that He spoke to them of John the Baptist.

threatened, jailed because of the ensuing riot, they were expelled to Singapore. Reuters posited that this was another example of Islamic resistance to other faiths.

It was a pretty accurate report and when I saw it, I was glad they had not published our names. The details of the event and lessons learned from it can be found in our book *A Faith to Die For*. It took four sessions with a Christian psychologist before I could be in crowds, but my anger against Muslim people became very intense. I justified my feelings by repeating the Islamic teaching that Mohammed is actually the embodiment of the Comforter that Jesus promised in John 14 and 16. This is blasphemy of the Holy Spirit and cannot be pardoned.

You can imagine my amazement when God gave me instructions to go to Srinagar, Kashmir and pray for the 99% Muslim population. Thirteen years had passed and at some point, God had softened my heart so that I could pray for people who had been moments from taking my life. Now we are embraced by the community in Kashmir and have seen many, young and old, be reconciled to Jesus as the Son of God and their Savior.

The Lamb was the One who opened the scrolls and the Lamb is the One who will deliver the nations. He was an Attack Lamb who identified with humanity. He endured verbal and physical abuse from those He came to save. Can we be any different?

Praying for people during medical outreach in Kashmir June 2018

CHAPTER 4

NEUTRALIZE THE ENEMY

2018 Prayer walk team in Guatemala

My early days as a missionary were spent in the wonderful country of Guatemala. In those days Guatemala was recovering from the earthquake of 1976. God had used the quake to open the doors for evangelical and charismatic ministries to flood the land with the good news of Jesus. Following on the heels of a century of missions work, this army of soul gatherers found great success, a tribute to the seed which had been sown there.

For my part, the Lord had given me a burden for small villages in what we called the "marginal" areas. These were settlements which had sprung up around the capital as people came in search of a better life. In the course of working among these people I became intrigued with the villages from which they had come and, after a couple of years, found myself walking among those villages with a small day bag stuffed with Spanish Bibles.

I would drive each day to the road's end and then walk the footpaths looking for someone who could read Spanish. When I found a reader I would give him or her a Bible and a reading assignment with the agreement that he or she would read the assignment to those in the family who could not read. Each week I would return, answer questions, and give the next assignment.

Often the oldest child in a family was the only one who could read, and the proud father would assure me he would gather the rest of the family each day to hear from the Book.

In this simple way we found success in reaching many villages with the Word of God. Good news spreads fast and soon there were house groups, and churches were beginning to organize. People were waiting for me on the appointed days to claim a Bible for their family. In natural progression, there were healings and salvations and baptisms and churches formed.

It seemed too good to last and, of course, it did not go unchallenged by the Devil.

THE MASTER'S STRATEGY

One morning as I went out to the villages, I was blessed to have the company of a precious brother, Gilbert Dilley. Gilbert and his family had moved from Indiana to work in the reconstruction and he was pastoring those of us who had formed a Sunday night fellowship in English. He was interested to see how our ministry was coming along.

We arrived in the town of San Jose del Golfo and were joined by the elder there, Lazuro Ochoa Catalan, and two policemen. One of the policemen was a new brother in the church. He delivered the news to me that I was not going out to the villages as there was a very important meeting awaiting our arrival. I mildly suggested I had to go because the people would be waiting, and it wasn't right to disappoint them. He firmly assured me I was not going but would attend this meeting.

San Jose is the municipal center of government for about thirty small villages extending from the Atlantic Coast Highway to the Motagua River just fifteen miles east of Guatemala City. The Lord had given us small groups in each of the villages and a church in San Jose. Our influence was building in the area and had caught the attention of the government.

As we entered the large meeting room of the town hall, I recognized most of the men. The mayor of San Jose was there as well as the sub-mayors who presided over each community where I had been distributing Bibles. They were easily distinguished by their hats and official sticks.

The mayor greeted me and thanked me for being there. He wanted to know who Gilbert was and said Lazuro did not have to stay but could if he wanted to. Two of the closest friends I will ever know, both men said they would be glad to stay.

The mayor explained that this was a special and very important meeting because these men wanted me to declare my intention in their communities. When I asked him exactly how important, he said it would be the most important meeting I would probably ever attend.

CALLED TO ORDER

Mark teaching in Guatemala - May 1983

Calling the meeting to order, the mayor had each man stand in front of a chair all of which formed a circle. He explained to the men who I was, although most of them knew me. He took great pains to formally introduce Gilbert and Lazuro and expressed their desire to remain. He explained my Spanish was fine so there was no need for translation. I would understand their questions and could answer quite well.

While all this was going on I was in the Spirit quietly asking God to neutralize the power of the Enemy arrayed against us so His work could go on to bear fruit.

When the mayor suggested we start with questions, I immediately jumped in with what the Lord had given me, not knowing where it would lead or even what the next step would be.

"I realize this is a very important meeting and I want to express my appreciation for your coming all the way to be here. May I suggest, since this is such an important meeting, we follow a custom which we have in my country for such occasions."

They thought that was a good idea and so I explained to them, "In meetings of this importance in my country, we always start with prayer."

They looked at each other and again at me. They were not men of prayer.

"Since this is such an important meeting," I continued to cover their hesitation, "it is important the prayer be done properly. Just custom you understand."

They were getting a little upset with the length of time this was taking, but they were going along with it, just to be customarily correct.

"Now in prayers like this it is customary for us as men to pray with our hats off."

They looked to the mayor who, with a condescending shrug, removed his hat. They too removed their hats and looked around at each other. I cannot recall another meeting in Latin America in which all men had their hats off.

NERVOUS OBEDIENCE

Now I was nervous, but I continued as the Lord gave me instructions.

"Since this is such an important meeting, and we surely want it to go well, perhaps we should follow custom another step."

The mayor was not smiling when his eye caught mine. I had pushed this about as far as I was going to be able.

"Perhaps," I suggested, "we should join hands to pray."

Latin men do not stand around with their hats off holding hands. They looked to the mayor and then to me; you could see the fire in their eyes. I took the hands of Gilbert and Lazuro and they in turn reached out for the others. The men placed their hats and sticks on the chairs behind them and took hands. A nervous laughter went through the place.

Now, feeling very hung out there by the Lord, I said, "I know that many of you are not used to praying and since this has to be right, may I suggest I lead you in prayer and you all repeat the prayer after me."

Somewhat relieved, they were quick to agree.

"Lord Jesus," I began, and they followed. "Forgive me of my sins. Come into my life as my personal Savior and Lord. Give me the power to be a good man and a good leader for my people, in Jesus name."

EARTH SHAKING EXPERIENCE

Nueva Esperanza in the Limonada February 1983

When they said "in Jesus name," the earth literally shook! There was an earthquake. The place shook violently from side to side as well as up and down. I was scared to death. Holding Gilbert and Lazuro's hands tightly, I did not open my eyes.

The quake measured 6.5 we found out later. The mayors ran from the building as they were afraid the terra cotta tiles would come crashing down through the wooden rafters and crush our skulls. Taking no thought for important hats or sticks, they dashed from the building.

Now, when a tremor stops, there is complete silence. Dogs do not bark, birds do not chirp, all creation stands still waiting to see if it is going to happen again. As the dust cleared around us, we three stood petrified by the impact of what had happened!

One by one the men re-entered the room, found their hats and sticks, nodded to us and went off to find out the condition of their village. Finally, the head mayor came back in. He put on his hat and, drawing himself to full stature, he said, "I do not know how you did that; but I am authorized to tell you that whatever you need in any of these villages, you have only to ask the man who was in this room and he will get it for you. You are to come tomorrow with your passport and those of your family and friends and you will receive courtesy visas. From this day forward you are the invited guests of the government of Guatemala, you have no need to stop for immigration or customs and, should the national police stop you for any reason, just show them this seal and you will be conducted safely and speedily to your destination."

Satan had not only been neutralized, his attack had been turned against him.

WE WIN!

The third letter in our acrostic **W-I-N** is **N** for **neutralize**.

I want to tell you, God will literally move heaven and earth to achieve His ultimate purpose. He wants every man, woman, and child on this planet to hear the message of His Son in a way they can understand. He wants you to stand in the gap, to enter into key locations in your city, country, and around this globe to call upon His name and see His power manifest.

He is the God of Acts chapter four, He is the God of Abraham, Isaac, and Jacob who changes not. He is the One to whom you are talking when you pray. It is He who has saved you and it is He who is calling you to pray.

Just as He will dwell above the blood on the mercy seat, between the angels, He will dwell above your life and His glory will be seen through you. The irresistible power of the love of Jesus will flow through you and thirty villages full of souls will be released by the power of God. All you have to do is enter in. Get into the gaps in your town and wait upon the Lord. Let the Enemy work his plan because it is going to be to your and the Lord's advantage. Let them capture the ark if need be so the glory can be carried to the nations.

WE HAVE THE SOLUTION

Through the fall of man, Satan gained an advantage in the earth. This is universally accepted. From the temples of Buddhism to the halls of great governments, this fact of the fall of man is testified to. We have the only solution to neutralize the power of the Devil. The disciples reported the demons were subject to them in the name of Jesus (Luke 10:17[33]). These first followers of Christ testified His name was above all names.

As we enter the gap, as we stand between the place of the Enemy and the lives of the people, we are used of God to neutralize the power of the Devil. I suggest you make a weekly trip to the campus of your son or daughter. If you don't have family, think about those young people whom you observe in the community. Go to that school and walk around it. Quietly declare the name of Jesus. Go with the intent of intercession. Don't make a big show, but do pray. Stand in that gap once a week and pray. Watch the news, watch the neighbors, watch your kids, you will hear the good report as you continue to pray.

---

33. [17]Then the seventy returned with joy, saying, "Lord, even the demons are subject to us in Your name."

Get four friends and cover the school week. Each one take a day. Just go the one hour and walk around or stand quietly somewhere and observe and pray. The Lord will give you the place as the power of the Devil is neutralized!!

There is no better place to be! **W-I-N**...We win. Shout it!

Worship...

Intercede...

Neutralize the Enemy...in your family, in your town, in your state, in your nation, around the world!

W...I...N. WE WIN!

••••••••••••••

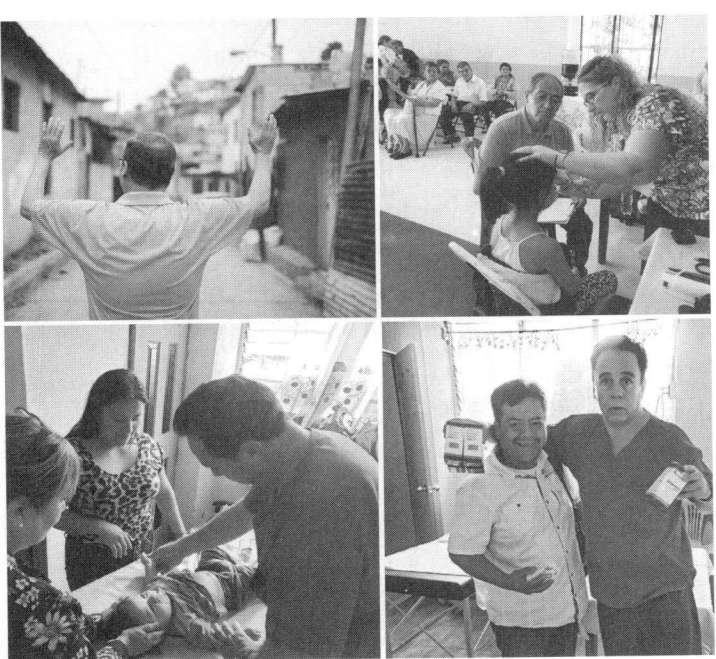

Guatemala

If you would like to come on down to Guatemala and go out to the San José del Golfo area, we would love to show you what the neutralization of the enemy can do. Guatemala went through one of history's most amazing revivals. At one point, after the neutralization, it was estimated that 65% of the population had come to Christ. There were reports from Amalonga of huge harvests of crops, several times larger and more abundant than ever.

Churches grew to the thousands. Women's Aglow Fellowship (now known as Aglow International) was birthed and within two months had over a thousand members. Jesus was doing amazing things in signs and wonders with healings becoming commonplace in every stream of the church.

Five young men who we were blessed to help with tuition for ministry education became pastors of churches totaling 60,000 people.

The village GDP increased ten-fold as the Lord blessed the farmer, the buyer, the seller, and the consumer. The government saw tremendous change as solid Christian leadership began to bless rather than extort the people. It was a time of amazing change and rapid growth.

The power of the enemy to rob, kill, and destroy was negated by Attack Lambs who stepped into every gap they could find.

GROWTH IN GUATEMALA

Today the church has matured and is sending Guatemalans into major gaps in the earth. From Palestine to Lhasa, those who were looked down upon by all other American people have been raised up by the Lord to take the freedom they have found and multiply it to the oppressed. In Syria and Africa, they are calling people to pray and share their testimony of deliverance. God has chosen the least to reach the rest.

Hector Zetino is typical of the fruit of that revival as are Amilcar Cabrera and Jorge H. Lopez. Very different in their approach to the ministry, these three have the common thread of prayer and the testimony that Jesus has raised them up. In each life, there was a "gap," and somebody stepped into that "gap," took action in prayer, and looked forward to their potential in the Lord, not stopped by their present state.

Now, they go out and identify a gap. They take worship teams into that gap. The anointing released in worship dispels the forces that hold the populations and they come to know the Lord. Jorge does this in meetings of thousands in Asia, Amilcar does this in Palestine with Jew and Muslims alike and Hector is back in the Barrio where he was once a gangster. His team of ten former gangsters is negating the forces ensnaring this new generation. Each of these men is a lamb on the outside but never let their meek humility fool you, the Lion lives within.

The invitation is real. Contact SEAPC and we will be glad to put you in touch with these and many others who realize the key: stand in the gap and neutralize the power of the enemy.

Pastor Hector Zetino

CHAPTER 5

THE FOURFOLD FOUNDATION

2005 NHO Kids Camp

THIS will be the shortest chapter in the book, but one of the most important. I've set it apart so it will be a clear path for you to follow in your own prayer life as you intercede for those you love and those God has called you to intercede for.

How is that prayer list of yours doing? Mine lists the names of family members and heads of state, Christian workers and their families. One of the things I like to do is put up pictures of people in my prayer room and just look around and pray for each one. Yes, you can send me one and I'll put you up there with the rest. I'm not promising you letters, and please do not send money for the prayers, but I will pray for you.

On the subject of prayer habits, let me share with you something Dick Eastman of "Every Home for Christ" taught me a long time ago. It is a habit of prayer which is according to the Word of God and has proven to be wonderful for me. It is found in detail in Appendix A of his great book, *The Hour That Changes the World*.

There are four areas of prayer which Dick suggests. I have made them the foundation of my prayer time. They make a great structure on which to build an hour of prayer. It was these four which sustained me during years of prayer for changes in the Soviet Union.

First, we pray for **Workers**. Jesus said we were to pray the Lord of the harvest that He would send laborers into the harvest (Luke 10:2[34]). As I walk the nations of the earth and pray for the souls of the people, my constant cry is for workers. The harvest is ready. We need workers. Not just from our country, but nationals as well. Not just eager beavers, but trained harvesters.

2012 NHO Kids Camp

---

34. [2]Then He said to them, "The harvest truly is great, but the laborers are few; therefore pray the Lord of the harvest to send out laborers into His harvest

Second, we pray for **Open Doors**. Paul said it this way, "**[Pray]...
that God would open unto us a door of utterance,**" (Colossians 4:3[35]
KJV). There is no such thing as a closed door to a praying person.
Because we are in touch with a heavenly vision and a spiritual kingdom, we can see beyond the limitations of negativism and the present
situation. The Russians used to tell us "Nyet" when we tried to witness, bring Bibles, hand out tracts, sing Christian songs, or fellowship
with Soviet Christians. We heard it as, "Not yet."

Each time we were rebuffed we would reassure ourselves by saying
that we were one day closer to the opening. We would ride the Trans-
Siberian Railway and speak revival to the countryside. We would get
down for a couple days in major cities and walk about in them calling
upon the Lord to drive out the darkness to open the door.

During those years I often said that communism would fall and
the Gospel would be preached throughout Europe. I was rebuked
many times by people who had to have communism to fulfill their
end-time plan. We just kept praying, "Open the door." How we rejoice
today as so many souls have entered in to praise the Lord, and volumes
of testimony have been written about the churches in those cities.

Third, we pray for **Fruit**. Jesus told the disciples in the upper
room that He would pray the Father would give them fruit for their
labors. We call forth the fruit of righteousness when we pray. We
speak fruitfulness to your ministry. Fruitfulness means souls are
saved and prayers are answered. Jesus will give us the fruit of our
labors because it comes from the vine and not the branches. He is the
vine, we are the branches. Your fruit is His fruit.

Fourth, we pray for **Finances**. Actually, we pray for the entire
material realm. I do not want to own a Boeing 747. I have no place to
put it. But, I do need a seat on one fairly often. As we pray the hour
of prayer, we loose full provision for the Church so our workers can
go through open doors and bring forth much fruit. The Lord does
answer prayers.

---

35. [3]meanwhile praying also for us, that God would open to us a door for the word,
to speak the mystery of Christ, for which I am also in chains

Often I am asked about our funding strategy. My answer is the condition of my knees and one fourth of my prayer life. Jesus had no gimmicks in His earthly ministry, and we don't need to use any in conducting His ministry now. He not only provides, He is both the Provider and the Provision. His command contains His provision. He said, "Ask," and so we do.

That's all. May I suggest you memorize this fourfold foundation for prayer? When you don't know what to pray for, this will get you started.

············

2018 NHO Kids Camp

From the time I read Dick Eastman's book, *The Hour That Changes the World*, I have made every effort to daily set aside an hour for prayer. Being the independent sort that I am, and not having the discipline to follow the clock set forth in the main teaching of the book, I have grasped with both hands the suggestion found in the appendix A: take an hour, divide it into quarters, use the first quarter to pray for workers, the second for doors to open, the third for fruit that multiplies, and the fourth quarter to pray for finances.

This hour of prayer has become a core fiber of the South East Asia Prayer Center and is strongly suggested to every person we employ. Without the hour of prayer, we are going nowhere in growth. That means that we will not be able to fulfill the Lord's calling upon the ministry to create new, and network existing, prayer cells. People who pray multiply into more people who pray.

While we are involved in evangelism, church planting, discipleship, leadership development, medical, educational, parenting, and micro-economic development, we are not deceived. All of these platforms have come to pass at the hand of the Lord through prayer.

In the 20 years since the publication of the first edition of Attack Lambs, for which Dr. Eastman was very gracious to write the foreword, we have faithfully followed this hour of prayer and have seen the Lord multiply our efforts from Singapore into 122 nations. Doors have opened in amazing ways first in the Tibet Autonomous Region of China, and then in the Mainland. We are seeing Kashmir open. The USSR burst into pieces and the eastern European republics were delivered from the clutches of atheistic communism. Jesus has responded to the cry of His people.

Workers, doors, fruit, and finances have been multiplied unto us. In each of our ministry areas, we have seen tremendous growth allowing us to equip many Asians, Latinos, and Indians for the work of multiplying the power of prayer. More than 3,000 groups are meeting regularly for prayer. Our budget has reached over 3 million per year while maintaining 7% or below administration cost. The company performing our outside audit is amazed each year as we have seen the Lord grow us at 15% per year and maintain a 65% donor retention average.

We are not deceived. We have not done this. Jesus responds to faithful prayer. If we are working ten hours a day then the first hour is a tithe to Him in prayer. It is an act of humility, to enjoy fellowship and the refreshing of His presence. If tithing our finances insures them from the consumption of the devourer, how much more the tithing of our time?

If there is a single message to this second edition, it would have to be, "Do it."

As our friend and board member, Dr. Chris Marshall says, "Information without application is just information." This hour of prayer works.

CHAPTER 6

SING YOUR SONG

My second son, Matthew, changed schools in the sixth grade. We had just returned from Asia and Matt had never been in a public school. He was quite used to the Christian custom of singing praise songs to start the school day. At first he thought he was the "odd ball," but one day he came bouncing home with the declaration that he had figured it out.

"The reason they don't sing," he reported, "is they don't have anything to sing about. They don't know about Jesus."

Matthew saw his purpose as sharing with his classmates the joy of Jesus. But he didn't do it in the flesh. Spiritual work must be done in a spiritual way. I began to walk our dog around the school each day. The dog needed the exercise and it gave us the chance to "spy out the land," and claim the school and the kids for the Lord. You know the end, of course, the Lord is faithful and many of the faculty and children have a song today.

Spiritual warfare is just that simple. In the sincere attempt to convey the tremendous importance of intercession and spiritual warfare, many have complicated this valuable ministry to an unattainable level. In this section we are going to experience the joy of a very simple acrostic, **S.I.N.G.** It is the key to becoming an Attack Lamb.

It stands for:

Spy out the land

Intercede

Use the Name

Cut the Grass

SPY OUT THE LAND

In Matthew 10 Jesus commissions His twelve disciples. Come with me to that point and let's together observe the way in which He accomplishes this very important task. To find the flow of action, let's back up to the last two verses of chapter nine, verses 37 and 38:

Then He said to His disciples, "The harvest truly is plentiful, but the laborers are few. Therefore pray the Lord of the harvest to send out laborers into His harvest."

What a strategy! When I saw it, I was astounded at its subtle simplicity.

Jesus is asking His disciples, and us, to pray according to His ultimate purpose; that every man, woman, and child on the face of the earth will have the opportunity to receive Him as their personal Lord and Savior. He is asking each of us to pray for workers. Yet, He is the Lord of the harvest, He is the One who owns the harvest, He is the One who will send the harvesters, and yet He commands our participation in prayer.

We have an important position! He has commanded you to pray that He will send forth the laborers. Why is He doing that? Because He wants to include you in the powerful stream of His ultimate purpose.

See what happens next. The Lord calls to Himself those very ones whom He had commanded to pray. By virtue of their praying for laborers they have placed themselves in the gap of intercession and in a position to be called into His purpose. Now, with His call, they become the answers to their own prayers!

Since I saw this powerful truth, I no longer ask people to come to the mission field. I just ask them to pray that someone will hear the call and join us in the flood of God's purpose. As their trickle of faith receives a deluge of power through the Holy Spirit, they join the flow which is flooding the globe with the good news of Jesus Christ.

Do you need workers for children's ministry? Do you need men with a heart to labor to add that education wing? Do you need volunteers to deliver meals or to sidewalk counsel? Don't put people on the spot, instead, ask them to pray that someone will come forward to do it. They will respond to God's call for they are being, through prayer, included in His ultimate purpose.

ATTACK LAMBS

Jesus said, **"Behold, I send you out as sheep in the midst of wolves. Therefore be wise as serpents and harmless as doves"** (Matthew 10:16). Did He call you a sheep? No! You are no more a sheep than the Holy Spirit is a bird! He said you are "as a sheep." You are after the fashion of a sheep. Big difference!

Just think about this. You are out there as a sheep. The wolf sees you. *"How 'bout a lamb chop for dinner?"* he says to himself.

You can feel him sneaking up on you. Do you know what that feels like? I get a little queeze in the stomach. Or else I get what my sons call the "willies." At any rate, there are wolves around.

Maybe there are places you pass by on your way home from work or school where you feel this discerning chill. The radar goes off and your wolf alarm sounds. How about a particular boss or teacher? Have there been any that make you want to cry out, "I rebuke you in Jesus' name!"?

There are wolves in the area. They sneak up on the sheep and pounce. They sink their claws in from behind. They grab that wool and tear it back. Dinner is served! Or so they think.

But wait! The wool comes off too easily. The wolf has been fooled. Something else is inside this sheepskin. It is a LION! It is the Lion of the tribe of Judah. **"…greater is he that is in you than he that is in the world"** (1 John 4:4[36]). You are not a sheep at all! You are the temple of the Holy Ghost. Jesus Christ lives in you!

You are a Wolf Shocker! That wolf has just put the grab on an **Attack Lamb!**

JESUS, OUR EXAMPLE

When the Devil came against Jesus in the wilderness, who was in trouble? Was Jesus in trouble? Never. He is the King of kings and the Lord of lords. He is the same yesterday, today, and forever! He is not now, nor has He ever been, less than the Devil. It was the Devil who was in trouble. He was being set up for defeat on the earth. And the good news is when he tries to sink those claws into you, he is being set up again!

Why would Jesus want you to walk around and entrap the Devil? Why would He lead you into places where the Enemy operates? Why would He call you and send you into places of demonic strength? Because it is His ultimate purpose that every man, woman, and child will have the opportunity to receive Him. He knows where the obstacles dwell and He has included you in His purpose as an Attack Lamb to set to flight those enemies of the Gospel which have hindered people from hearing His name.

Why doesn't He just blast them Himself and have it done? This is my question every day. Because He has chosen to include the Church in His plan to reach the nations. I have debated with Him just as Moses did over Israel. I have expressed my frustration over people who will not pray, or give, or go. He always has the same response, "Pray ye the Lord of the harvest…"

---

36. [4]You are of God, little children, and have overcome them, because He who is in you is greater than he who is in the world

You're an Attack Lamb in the army of Jesus Christ. But as you go forth in the guise of a sheep, you are directed by His voice, word, and sovereign providence. Like a spy with a constant communication uplink to headquarters, you have the perfect cover. You're a sheep. Who would suspect anything from a sheep?

FINDING THE GAPS

There are gaps all around you. They have become the caverns of daily living from which the wolves prey upon those who have not yet met Christ. As an Attack Lamb it is your job to walk about and see where the wolves are. You are a spy for the Lord walking about the promised land of your school, your community, your place of work. You are there to discern and neutralize the powers that hold back your friends from receiving Jesus as their Lord.

Tomorrow morning as you prepare for work, ask the Lord to use you as an Attack Lamb. You will have a different sort of day. You will be walking as the housing for the Lion of the tribe of Judah. Might as well wear a "Wolves Beware" shirt. You will go to that place of work or study and it will look totally different to you. You will see it in the perspective of a heavenly vision. As you enter, many angels will be there with you. The elders will be catching the prayers you offer and pouring them out before the throne. The beasts will be bowing down and crying, "Holy, holy, holy is the Lord."

Imagine the look on your colleague's face as the radiant power of Jesus flows forth from your eyes. You are going to perceive how the Enemy has worked in that place, and how you are going to neutralize him in the lives of those for whom Christ died. I am so glad you are there. In that gap. Waiting for the Lord to move through you. Pray, pray, pray.

YOUR PLACE IN THE SPACE

You have a place in the space between man and God. It's called **Intercession**, and it is the second letter in our **S-I-N-G** acrostic.

You are His ambassador to men, and their advocate with Him (2 Corinthians 5:20[37]). What an important place to be. That is why you are who you are, live where you do, shop where you do, were hired where you work, and went to school where you did. The Lord has had His hand on you all the time. He has ordered your steps to accomplish His ultimate purpose. Now you are in that gap between Him and them. What should you do?

Matthew 10 is an instruction manual for Attack Lambs. It addresses specific ministry, the power we have, the way to travel, the amount of money we need, how to know where we should stay, how to react when ill-treated. All of life is defined for us in those verses.

Verse 27 is our labor management agreement. **"Whatever I tell you in the dark, speak in the light; and what you hear in the ear, preach on the housetops."** We are going to see into the heavenly realm and then act in the earthly one. We are going to hear the direction of God and have the boldness to do it. This prayer stuff is all right! Have you ever heard a deal like that?

You go into the gaps in your town and wait on the Lord. He will show you the heavenly vision and the way to reach the people there. When you have that word, you can do as He has shown you and you will be a winner of souls!

A DAY IN PITTSBURGH, IN THE GAP

One day I was standing in a doorway in downtown Pittsburgh. There is a large bus stop and a welfare office on the corner. People deal drugs there and make contacts for different things. The police are there, but they are outnumbered. As long as everything flows along in a peaceful way, they remain calm.

That day I was standing there with the motor running; that is to say, I was praying softly in tongues. I was there and a young man separated himself from the crowd and walked over to me. I had no

---

37. [20]Now then, we are ambassadors for Christ, as though God were pleading through us: we implore you on Christ's behalf, be reconciled to God.

sign. I was not passing out tracts, although I love to do that. I was just standing there with the motor running and this young man walked right up to me as though he had been told to go see me. Then, without either of us saying "hello," he began to speak.

"I'm sorry," he said in a mournful drone. "I'm so sorry."

"Excuse me?" I responded gently.

"I'm sorry for my life," he continued. "My life is a mess."

"Tell Jesus you're sorry," I said softly. "He can forgive you."

"Jesus, I'm sorry," his drone continued. "Forgive me, my life is a mess."

We stood there quietly for a few minutes. I heard nothing by the Spirit to say, so I said nothing. I saw nothing to do, so I did nothing. After a few moments he turned to me and held out his hand.

"Thank you so much," he said with joy. "Thank you so much." His face shone and he squared up his shoulders, and with a smile on his face walked happily up the street.

The peace and presence of God touched his lost soul. I saw the transformation in his eyes and heard it in his voice. It was one of the most beautiful miracles I've ever witnessed. That young man had found forgiveness.

No sign, no PA system, no tracts, just being in that gap with the motor running. **The end result of successful spiritual warfare is souls saved.** This is the reason Jesus has invested His great power in us. This is the reason you are reading this book. Think about all that had to happen for you to read this sentence. Jesus had to put together a wonderful plan to equip you as an Attack Lamb and He did it. Wow, you are a part of a great plan. You are a worker in His harvest. You are so special.

THE NO-NAME WARRIORS

In the tenth chapter of the gospel of Luke, we see seventy others going forth. I love these guys. They were the No-Names of the New

Testament. Attack Lambs, every one. They came to the Lord in response to the prayer for workers and they were ready to be sent. Jesus gives them the same power He gave the apostles. They can cast out devils, heal the sick, raise the dead, give eyesight to the blind. Man, these are some kind of sheep among wolves.

They have a great time of ministry and return to give Him their report. They tell Jesus what, to them, is the most exciting thing, "… **even the demons are subject to us in Your name**" (Luke 10:17b[38]). Jesus understood their excitement, I'm sure. But He called them back to a greater cause for rejoicing, namely that their names were written down in heaven.

He was requiring proper perspective from them. Why? Because all power flows from relationship with the source of that power. In this case, from the Lord Himself. Maintain that relationship and we won't have to worry about power.

There is truly no greater cause for celebration than our salvation. Having said that, the disciple's report is still true. Demons **are** subject to the name of Jesus.

These seventy disciples used a wonderful word in their report. They said the devils are subject unto us. This word *subject* is the Greek word which we transliterate, *hupotasso*. It means to "voluntarily order yourself under the affairs of another." We most often translate this word as "submit."

When you join a church, you "*hupotasso*." You submit. You see what time the services begin and you arrange your schedule to be on time. You do this through several acts of your will. You determine to be there. You set other schedule entries around that fixed time.

When you marry, you "*hupotasso*." You submit. You spend years listening to your intended's plans and you order your steps to accommodate that plan. You submit to each other in the fear of God. You prefer one another and live to see the other's dreams fulfilled. You do

---

38. [17]Then the seventy returned with joy, saying, "Lord, even the demons are subject to us in Your name."

this voluntarily. It is an act of your will. You determine to leave all other plans and people and to cleave to your spouse and to be one in Christ.

Successful marriages reflect this principle of *hupotasso*. A marriage breaks apart as soon as one party determines to have his or her will, his or her way, upon his or her demands. Love does not demand, it seeks to serve.

You also apply the principle of *hupotasso* where you work. You have a set time to be there to keep the business running well for the benefit of all. You set the events of your life voluntarily so that the best production possible is accomplished. You have seen that the Lord honors those who submit. *Hupotasso* is a big word with Him.

The seventy others reported to the Lord that as they went about in the gaps of their world, the devils voluntarily submitted to them. This was not a dialogue with demons. This was not shouting at a lying spirit to give his name. (I have always wondered how a lying spirit was going to do that.) This was not pouring oil down a person's throat to have them vomit up a spirit of this or that. This is power through prayer. This is authority on the scene. The devils **voluntarily** ordered themselves under this authority.

THE ODD ANSWER

Jesus gave his 70 disciples what I have always considered an odd answer when they returned rejoicing over the demons being subject to them. He declared, **"I saw Satan fall like lightning from heaven"** (Luke 10:17 NKJV). What He was saying was, the battle has already been won. Satan and his demonic band have already lost and forfeited their place in heaven. His power, and therefore his authority, has been broken. Naturally the demons who operate under Satan's broken authority would be subject to the name of Jesus in the lives of the people to whom they went. Through this same fact of our authority in the name of Jesus the devils are subject to us today. The Enemy is cast down still today by the name of Jesus.

So now, the question of our century. Why has the world not been reached with the good news of Jesus?

Answer: because we do not go to them. Why do we not go to them and declare this glorious Gospel of good news that Jesus has set them free?

Two reasons. First, we are too busy with our own stuff, too self-involved, self-oriented and selfish. Second, we think we **are** sheep.

But we are not!

BE WHAT YOU ARE

Jesus has made you an Attack Lamb. The devils will order themselves under you; the power of the Devil is broken in your life. Get out there and bash some wolves! Use what God has given you. Jesus said to these no-name warriors, **"I give you the authority…over all the power of the enemy, *and nothing shall by any means hurt you*"** (Luke 10:19³⁹ emphasis added).

Attack Lambs do not sit back and let the pusher take their kids! They get out there in the gap and pray! Attack Lambs do not allow the Devil to kill an entire generation of babies! They get out there and pray. You will find Attack Lambs in doorways, standing quietly on street corners, walking around government buildings, in the audience of the Senate and Parliament. You will find them in tour groups of the White House and in the Forbidden City of China. You will find them in business in Riyadh and booking flights to Mecca. You will find Attack Lambs in every sector of society.

They are spying out the land. They are driving out the devils. They are neutralizing the effect of Satan on the world's population, and all the while they look like gentle little lambs at play. I tell you the truth, in all the places I have walked, I have not raised my voice above a conversational tone. I have caused no demonstration but, in the power of the Holy Spirit through prayer, I have seen walls come

39. ¹⁹Behold, I give you the authority to trample on serpents and scorpions, and over all the power of the enemy, and nothing shall by any means hurt you

down, gremlins leave Kremlins, abortion clinics close and young men walk up to repent.

You are an Attack Lamb. You have power over all the devices of the Devil. Get out there. Set apart one lunch per week and fast and walk around the place where you work and pray for the people. Pray for workers, pray for open doors, pray for fruit for every Christian ministry and business, pray for a financial/material flow to prosper the Gospel in that place.

You are an Attack Lamb. Take one morning a week and get out to that local school. Walk around that place or get to a convenient place to pray and wait upon the Lord. Pray for workers, doors, fruit, and finances. Look and listen to the heavenly vision for that place. Cry out to God for the people. Walk around and make those devils voluntarily bow down. They will for it is the Word of God and it is true. It is not by might or power that these children shall be loosed, it is by the Spirit of the Lord as you get into that gap between God and man and cry out for those souls. Get on out there. It is for His purpose that you were born. Fulfill your destiny, get in that gap.

THE SECRET

We were starting a Christian School in a small Pennsylvania community. There was resistance from the school board to allow us the rented use of an existing school building. They just would not even put the topic on their agenda.

Meeting after meeting, we went and just sat there. We looked very foolish to them. Our prayers were constant and we waited on the Lord to see how He was going to accomplish His desire to train up young men and women in His ways. The members of the board did not recognize us or give us any opportunity to speak. They were trying to pretend we were not even there.

In actual fact, it was not these men and women with whom we were doing battle. It was a combined spiritual force which we shall detail when we get to the "N" in our acrostic. We were sitting there as Attack Lambs.

For several months we sent letters asking to be heard, then we would sit and pray and have no response. We were encouraged to cause a demonstration, but thought it not Lamb-like. We claimed hupotasso power and rejoiced in our salvation. I must say the school board meetings in that town were quite boring.

Finally one night as the board was leaving, one of the members passing me stopped. He turned and said, "Aren't you Mark Geppert?"

I assured him I was.

"Didn't I used to fix your father's car?" he asked.

I assured him he had.

"Are you part of this group?" He looked at the three of us.

I said I was, and asked if he had seen our letters.

"Come next month," he said.

That was it for direction.

VICTORY IN JESUS

We used that building for years and finally bought it. The Lord delivered it into our hands through a mechanic who sat with doctors, deciding issues in a school from which he had never graduated. Attack Lambs learn to rejoice in Jesus and wait for Him to move for them.

Attack Lambs are spies for Jesus. We are His eyes in the earth. As we maintain a heavenly vision, He leads us to the caverns of wolves. He causes us to stand at the mouth of their dens and pray. As we do, sometimes the wolves attempt to attack us. You are irresistible to them. However, when the name of Jesus is invoked, they voluntarily order themselves under you. Since you are voluntarily ordered under Jesus, the power of the Enemy in that place is neutralized and the

Gospel can go forth. As you walk in His presence, you will manifest His power and accomplish His purpose.

Jesus cautioned the seventy no-name disciples to keep the source of their joy rooted in the reality of their relationship with Him. He said not to rejoice over earthly success, but rather that we have relationship with the Father. This simple statement is the SECRET to victory in spiritual warfare. Remember, all power flows out of relationship to the source of that power.

As we go into the gap, looking for all the world like little sheep, the power of God goes with us. We are the temple of the Holy Ghost. We are a home for the Lion of the tribe of Judah. He will manifest His great power when the wool is pulled from us.

············

Wow, do I love this chapter. My son, Matthew, is now the president of the ministry that was birthed out of prayer walking. He is mobilizing prayer teams in 122 nations led by wonderful local people and resulting in nation-changing visitation of the Holy Spirit.

One of our closest friends, who has walked with me from the publication of the first edition and whose picture was on the cover of the first printing, has commented that this teaching is simple, but it is not easy. He has faced strong resistance from the flesh to go out and pray. We say we will take a day and walk around our city, but when that morning comes, it seems the smartphone and Facebook, business and unexpected calamity take all the time and attention.

There is a discipline involved in going around a city for a week. Joshua needed reassurance from the Lord before even he could take those first steps to praise the Lord around Jericho. I often think about the time and resources we expend in asking people to pray for just one hour. To ask them to set aside every sin and weight that restrains them, and to walk in a place for a day, is unthinkable.

My good friend Charles was the first to walk in Singapore with me. A mutual friend and great church leader, Prof. Koo En Teck, instructed Charles to walk with me when he heard the teaching. Charles agreed and it was so wonderful as we had many divine appointments just like the young man at the doorway had been in Pittsburgh. Charles called his wife and friends from the walk and very excitedly relayed to them the faithfulness of the Lord. Little did I know that, because of the condition of his body, walking was not a thing he would normally do. He overcame and did the four-hour walk touching five pressure points (which we will talk about in chapter 18) in that great city.

THE STORY IS NOT ABOUT YOU.

Charles and I felt like two of the seventy sent out in Luke 10. Like us, they were not famous. They did not have to take a bag of clothes, two pairs of shoes, or a supply of money. All they had to do was walk their city and be available for the Holy Spirit to set up situations for them. By walking out the Attack Lambs teaching we became very familiar with the verses of Luke 10.

Two points of the chapter became vital to us with the Spanish translation of Attack Lambs. We realized that the verb in Luke 10:17[40] is translated a little differently in Spanish. For English readers and believers, there is the sense of the Attack Lamb having to "pull-down" Powers and Principalities from the heavenlies. This thought gives rise to questions of personal spiritual strength and combat with different levels of demonic forces. And results in qualifying statements about who is strong enough to "do battle" at which level. But in Spanish and Greek, there is no "pull-down." Instead, they bow by their own volition.

Your obedience (bowing down to the direction of Jesus to stand in the gap) releases the spiritual truth that the lesser must bow to the greater. So, in Greek and Spanish, the demons subject themselves to you as you are subject to Christ.

So, Jesus said in essence, "Maintain your focus on the One to whom you are submitted."

---

40. [17]Then the seventy returned with joy, saying, "Lord, even the demons are subject to us in Your name."

If our focus is on the demons, we will become fearful and be distracted from the throne.

If our focus is on our own strength or weakness, we will conclude weakness or become prideful at the number of demons and of what level we have cast out, and be distracted from the throne.

But, when we keep our focus on the One who is Worthy, His great power flows through us and breaks the bondage that has plagued the people. Thy Kingdom Come, Thy Will be Done.

With this understanding came one of our favorite phrases, "This story is not about you."

THE OTHERS

The second point that became very clear is a wordplay that does not translate well, but we will give it a try. Matthew 10 is the commissioning of the Apostles or "sent ones." Indeed, they are the cornerstones of the church and were set apart by their time with Jesus. Matthew 10 marks their growth point from Disciples to Apostles as we teach in our book, *A Faith to Die For*. They are the famous people. Cathedrals and cities will be named for them. They will write epistles and their words will carry the church into its destiny. We call them in Spanish, "Los Famosos."

In Luke 10 we find seventy or seventy-two others. They are not famous. Their names are not recorded. Cities are not named for them and they wrote no words that were carried on through the centuries. They are "the others." In Spanish, "los otros."

Attack Lambs are not a specially called and anointed few. The definition of intercession is that we intervene between two with a view of reconciling their differences. Intervene means to enter in or appear as an irrelevant or extraneous circumstance. Our North American culture requires relevance. *I have to be somebody. I am important. The situation could not be improved if it weren't for me.* Saul has slain his thousands, but, David his tens of thousands.

Attack Lambs are the "others." The no-names who have pulled down the lofty titles and simply go where the Lord tells them to go, to do what He has told them to do: see the harvest, pray for workers, build relationships with people at the table, heal the sick, and get dust from the city. But, above all, maintain the focus on the throne and avoid thoughts about yourself. In Spanish, we are "Nosotros."

Ellos no son famosos, sino los otros como nosotros. They are not famous, but others, like us.

The desire to be famous as a prayer warrior is the precipice to which Satan took Jesus in the wilderness.

"Ascribe honor to me," the devil said. "And I will give you the nations." In today's jargon, "Just say I am the Ruling Spirit or the Controlling Spirit, give me title, power, and glory, when you address me. Do it with respect, and I will give you the people who are under my control." The devil is a liar, claiming what he has never had. Psalm 24 clearly declares, "The earth is the Lord's and the fullness thereof, the nations and those who dwell therein."

Jesus said to the devil, "Get out." He did not dialogue with demons. Knowing who He was and His authority for the purpose, He said just two words. This has been a great lesson for us over these years. Once we understood that our obedience was the greatest act of worship and that the game was to maintain focus on the throne and to give glory only to the Lamb, we began to see the anointing break the yokes of bondage. So, these two phrases became ours by experience:

"Don't set your focus on the hocus pocus."

"Obedience releases anointing and anointing breaks the yoke."

CHAPTER 7

PARK THE ARK

Mark with local leaders - unknown location - October 1982

God told Moses, "Build a box.

"Use simple acacia wood.

"Cover it with gold on the outside.

"Cover it with gold on the inside.

"Put three things in the box.

"The tablets of the Law,

"A pot of manna,

"And Aaron's rod that budded.

"Put a gold covered lid on the box.

"Put a crown of gold around the lid.

"Stand an angel with wings extended over the box on one side.

"Stand an angel with wings extended over the box on the other side.

"Within the crown and under their wings is the mercy seat.

"Sprinkle the blood of the lamb of sacrifice on the mercy seat.

"My Presence will dwell in power above the mercy seat.

And flow out to the people from there" (Exodus 25, author's paraphrase)

The "box" would be called the ark of the testimony. It was made of simple wood and covered with gold. Three things were placed in it: the tablets of the Law, carved by God Himself, a pot of the perfect food which sustained the nation of Israel for forty years — manna — and Aaron's rod that budded to validate his divine call to leadership. A lid was placed on the box and a crown was placed around the lid. Inserted into the crown was a piece of wood covered in gold called the "mercy seat." Blood was sprinkled on that mercy seat.

On either side of the mercy seat angels were placed, facing each other with their wings extended. The glory of God came and dwelt between the angels above the mercy seat. The presence of God was there in power.

THE PHILISTINE'S MISTAKE

Like the Devil in the wilderness and the wolves in our world, the Philistines made a big mistake. They captured the ark (1 Samuel 5). And to make matters worse they put it in the temple of the false god of the Philistines, Dagon. They closed the temple up to secure their treasure and spent the night in celebration.

The Philistines imagined the ark itself to be the god of the Israelites, and that it was an idol like theirs. They attributed the power of Israel to the box, knowing nothing of the power presence of God dwelling there.

In the morning they opened the door of the temple and the god Dagon had fallen forward and was face down in front of the ark of the covenant. It had bowed down to the ark. Actually the Power Presence of God had fulfilled the coming Word that **"every knee shall bow and every tongue confess that Jesus Christ is Lord to the glory of the Father"** (Philippians 2:10–11[41] paraphrased).

Puzzled but determined, the Philistines propped their god back up and closed the door again. The next morning an even greater surprise awaited them. This time, not only had Dagon again bowed down before the ark, but now his head, hands, and feet were broken off. The head is a symbol of plans and strategies, the hands of power and authority, and the feet of the ability to stand. Dagon had no ability to devise a plan that would stand before the ark, nor any power or authority in the presence of the God of Israel.

CONNECTING THE DOTS

Now I want you to pay close attention here. We are going to connect some dots for you so you can see the whole picture. Did the ark shout? No. Did it jump up and down and sound crazy? No. All it did was sit there, parked. It was the presence of the glory of the Lord that did the work. The false god bowed down. It had to. The victory was in the power of the presence of God.

And here is the connection, saint...**Your victories are through the same power. You are the modern-day ark.** Yes, you are!

Let's connect some more dots. Jesus took you, simple material. He formed you to contain a testimony. He covered you on the outside

---

41. [10]that at the name of Jesus every knee should bow, of those in heaven, and of those on earth, and of those under the earth, [11]and that every tongue should confess that Jesus Christ is Lord, to the glory of God the Father.

and the inside with the precious gold of His righteousness. You look good to those around you and your character is being refined through the power of the Holy Spirit.

Like the tablets of the Law in the ark, He has placed His Word in your heart that you might not sin against Him.

Like the manna in the ark reminded the Israelites of God's provision, you too have the provision of God not only for your daily bread but for the bread of life itself in Jesus.

Just as Aaron's budding rod reminded the Jews of God's power to bring life to that which was dead, God has given you the power to speak life to those who are dead in their own sins and trespasses. You have the authority in the name of Jesus to break the bondages that cripple the people whom God loves. You have the power of the rod that budded.

As a believer in Jesus you, like no people ever on the face of the earth, have the Holy Spirit of God Himself dwelling in you. **You**, saint, are God's ark of the covenant today!

He closed the box. That is, He has sealed the testimony within you by the Holy Spirit. He has rimmed the box with a crown calling you a royal priesthood, a holy nation that you should show forth His praises.

Just like the blood of the sacrifice was placed on the mercy seat of the ark, the Father has covered you with the blood of His own dear Son. When He looks on you, He sees the blood in which there is no flaw. He knows your every weakness and still calls you righteous. How great is that blood! He has placed angels on either side of you. Yes, it's true, you are a protected property, the object of His limitless love. Every demon who attempts to bring you down has to get through those two angels! Double coverage is wonderful.

He has come to dwell between those angels, above the mercy seat in your heart. Because of the blood of Jesus, God can now dwell with you and in you. His glory flows out through your eyes in His compassion for a lost world, through your hands in healing, through your mouth as you speak the words of eternal life, and through your feet as you walk the land and pray.

Just as the presence of God went with the ark releasing tremendous power, so too does His presence within you. Wherever the presence of the Lord is there is liberty. As you move about your place of work or school or home, you bring release.

THE PROTOTYPE

What the Philistines really had when they had the ark was the Attack Lamb prototype. As an Attack Lamb you can enter the gaps of your world. You can sense the presence of the wolves. You park your ark in that presence and allow the glory to flow. The forces at work there to resist the Gospel must *hupotasso* (submit) because of Him who dwells in you.

Go ahead, think of a place of tension. Perhaps you are trying to clean out your child's room. Those posters and CD's are a symbol to you of the power that is trying to capture the soul of your young one. Stand in there and gently praise the Lord. Allow the Holy Spirit in you to rise and live big. Perhaps the Lord will give you an instruction to do something. Obey it.

Did you practice His presence in that room? Imagine what you can do with this Power Presence. You could walk around your town. You could walk about the schools. You could go to centers of racial strife or public corruption and, through the Power Presence of God, you could be used of God to change your city!

You are the ark. God wants to lead you into the presence of the false gods which hold society in their demonic grip. Keep your focus on Jesus and park that ark, and you will begin to see both small and dramatic changes.

It is the will of God that every man, woman, and child have the opportunity to receive Jesus Christ as their personal Lord and Savior in this generation. This spiritual work must be done in a spiritual way. These people are held captive by the Dagons of today, and you are the ark which the Lord wants to position in the gaps to cause that false god to bow down. You will not have to shout, jump or scream. In fact, you will appear as an irrelevant or extraneous circumstance in that gap. Go for it!

....

Encouraging people to go into the problem areas of society to release anointing and overcome the evil therein could put them in a dangerous position. If the teaching was errant, they could get really messed up. And in fact, many who have sought to encounter demonic forces have indeed done so and some, who tried to be the deliverer, ended up in a bad way. These experiences have caused us to be very cautionary in the way we encourage.

We try to be biblically sound in our teaching. Balanced in the power and fruit of the Holy Spirit and do all things to give honor and glory to the Lord. A principle that has consistently been included in our seminars is this:

You should not follow after a prophecy or a dream someone else has had. God will speak to you directly. Teaching for motivation must follow several rules. They must appear in a type in the Old Testament. They must be in the teaching of Jesus. They must have been in the experience of the disciples. They must have been explained in the Epistles. They must be true to the original language. They must be consistent with the manners and customs of the time. If someone teaches you something that does not follow these rules, then do not hold onto it, and certainly, do not take action according to it.

Teaching the Ark as the type and the believer as the anti-type, or fulfillment, has been very well received in all denominational streams. The Old Testament experience with the false god, Dagon, as found in 1 Samuel 5, is a solid Old Testament teaching that has encouraged those of us who have been arrested in different nations for preaching Christianity. I am guilty and have been the guest of several nations. Seeing the power of the Holy Spirit flow to them, I have to say that the night with Dagon would have been uncomfortable, but for profit in the morning.

The experience of the seventy further illustrates the power of simple obedience. They took what the Lord gave them and walked into situations He had foreordained to bring glory to His name through them. Their names are not recorded, but His certainly is.

The teaching in the Epistles is most clear in Paul's letter to the Ephesians. This takes us to chapter 8.

CHAPTER 8

KNOW YOUR ENEMY

Pinch yourself. That's right, gently pinch yourself. Are you flesh and blood? I thought so. If you are not flesh and blood, please put this book down and slowly walk away.

Now look at the person nearest you. It could be your wife, husband, or friend. Maybe it is a close colleague or client. If you can do so without starting a riot, pinch him or her. Flesh and blood, right? If he or she is not flesh and blood, close this book and get off the bus, leave the room, or simply keep your seat and pray.

We do not wrestle against flesh and blood. Please stop wrestling with yourself. Be freed from asking if you are good enough, mature enough, tall enough, thin enough or trained enough to be used by the Lord in prayer. Anyone can pray! This is not about the ark, it is about the power. God is at work.

Look at the person you just pinched. Please do not wrestle with other people. So much time is wasted as we try to get the upper hand in relationships. Life is too short for power plays in the church and at work. We are on the earth to win these people, not to offend them. It is the will of God that they have the opportunity to receive Jesus and you are there to pray for them. Stop wrestling with people.

So many in the church today are carrying the disappointment of broken relationships. Divorce has cut deeply into the lives of two generations. Broken promises and dashed dreams have filled cities with heartsick despair. Businesses fail, contracts are broken, violence erupts, all because of broken relationships. But, good news, there is a way to defeat the devices of the Enemy and free yourself and loved ones from such darkness.

Mark praying in Singapore

THE KEY TO VICTORY

In 2 Corinthians 2:10[42] we read we must forgive in the name of Jesus. We must stop wrestling with people who have disappointed us. Can you imagine a lamb wrestling with a person? Or worse, how about two lambs wrestling with each other. If you want to be victorious in wrestling the Enemy's forces then you must first forgive those who are flesh and blood. Let's do it now.

Just pray with me saying, **"In the name of Jesus I forgive every person living or dead who ever hurt me, used me, or abused me in**

42. [10]Now whom you forgive anything, I also forgive. For if indeed I have forgiven anything, I have forgiven that one for your sakes in the presence of Christ

any way. **I release them into the hands of the Lord that they might know Him as their personal Lord and Savior. Father, I ask you to save them in Jesus name."**

As we were praying you might have thought of someone in particular. Go ahead, I'll wait while you forgive them by name. Use the name of Jesus. "Father, in the name of Jesus I forgive _____, and ask you to bless them with the knowledge of your Son. I release them to your blessing."

I call this "Rolodextm prayer." I pray this prayer every so often to make sure I'm not keeping score on anybody. If you never create an enemy or take an offense then you do not have to go through this kind of prayer; but, life is relational and we can be offended, so we must be quick to pray.

The Devil loves to create strife because, as long as your time is taken up wrestling with people, you will not be free to take on the forces which hold the world's population in bondage to darkness. To be effective in spiritual warfare, you must walk free from offense.

Good, now that we have established we are **not** wrestling flesh and blood, let's give our attention to the forces with which we **do** wrestle. Paul researched this as he moved about from culture to culture and nation to nation, and has given us a very clear list of the Dagons of today.

THE FACES OF THE ENEMY

Our King James Bible calls the spiritual forces Paul identified as:

Principalities

Powers

Rulers of the darkness of this world

Spiritual wickedness in high places

But to better understand them let's take a look at the actual words Paul used in the Greek[1].

ARCHAS

The first is the **archas**2. This word is transliterated Greek for the word which appears in the Ephesians 6:12[43] text as "principalities." It is used many times throughout the Bible. It is often translated "beginning." It carries the sense of preeminence, the "We were here first" attitude that becomes territorial. The *archas* operates through **intimidation.**

Have you wrestled with this lately? How about the home where we modify all behavior to prevent an explosion of emotion from one of the family members? Do you know any people who try to dominate their families through this force?

What about the employer or manager who cannot receive feedback from his colleagues without going into a rage? Or the teacher or coach who controls through fear. These are operating in the *archas*. It is **not** the flesh and blood, it is the power working behind them.

Your strategy, as God's instrument, is to park your ark in the gap between these folks and the Lord...and pray. As you have discerned the presence of the *archas*, you can now neutralize the impact by focusing on Jesus instead of the problem, and praying for the people.

Practice the Power Presence in that gap. If not for yourself, for the others who are under the influence of this force. Get in that place, Attack Lamb, and watch the Lord cause Dagon to bow down.

Recently I was teaching this point in a Prayer Walking Seminar in one of the great churches of Asia. Fifteen hundred had gathered and, as we shared about this point, there came the gripping realization that we had hit on a truth relevant to this people. We had touched a spiritual nerve. They shifted in their seats, nodded, smiled and I could see that their hearts were being touched.

The Asians are a very humble people with a low self esteem. Actually, I think they have a great self esteem, but by the inflated standard of the West, they appear to be insecure or intimidated. Certainly,

43 .[12]For we do not wrestle against flesh and blood, but against principalities, against powers, against the rulers of the darkness of this age, against spiritual hosts of wickedness in the heavenly places

the Asians of that city have conformed to a very legalistic society where you adapt or die.

At the conclusion of the meeting, the pastor rose to lead the people in a declaration against the *archas* to remove the intimidation from their midst. As that false god bowed down, the people began to applaud. For many minutes we were caught up in the joy of release as the Power Presence brought liberty to God's people. They were no longer bound.

In the subsequent six months they added a thousand new members to the church. It is the will of God that the *archas* be broken so that men and women, boys and girls, can receive Jesus Christ as their personal Lord and Savior.

But the Devil's bag of tricks doesn't stop with just one evil force. The next one we will consider is formidable as well.

EXOUSIAS

The second force listed as "powers" is the **exousias**[3], again a transliteration from the Greek word. This word is often translated "authority." When the scribes heard the teaching of Jesus they proclaimed, "From whence comes this teaching, He teaches with **authority**."

The root thought of the word is "**the right to speak**." Think about that for a minute. Is there any greater debate in society than who has the right to speak, to express themselves? This is the root force which has suppressed minorities and women throughout history. How many children have been aborted because they do not yet make a sound outside the womb?

This is the issue which makes salesmen, bankers, and attorneys the favored candidates for church leadership. They are appointed and elected because they can present themselves well. Sadly, many wonderful Christian people have eliminated themselves from Christian service because they do not speak well. Moses did. When God called him to be His agent of deliverance for Israel he attempted to defer saying he couldn't do the job because he did not speak well. Tradition says possibly he stuttered.

He certainly could write though. He sure could pray. He was very good at miracles. But, because of the *exousias* stronghold, he declined the call until persuaded by the Lord.

Prayer, on the other hand, is wonderful because everyone can do it. I tell you God hears the simplest prayer and, if prayed according to His will, He grants the petition. If you are praying that every man, woman, and child will have the opportunity to receive Christ, you are praying according to the will of God. Keep on praying that way and you will see people come to Christ all around you because you are speaking to the Lord.

No power above, on, or under the earth can keep you from speaking to your heavenly Father. The way has been opened for you through the blood of Jesus Christ; you have access to the throne. You are called to see heaven's vision for man. Get in that gap and talk to your Father about the souls of those around you and do not ever again wonder if you have the right to do so. The power of *exousias* is broken.

In fact, the issue has been settled forever. Look at Zechariah 3:2[44]. There you will find where God got fed up with Satan and told him to shut up. Do you see it there? Satan was standing before the throne of God and Jesus was there, and when the Devil stepped up to speak and resist Him, the Lord said to Satan, **"The Lord rebuke you, Satan!..."**

The Devil can no longer deny anyone who is in Christ the right to speak. There is neither Jew nor Greek, neither black nor white. Neither Asian nor Caucasian. There is no difference between man or woman. We are one in Christ and we all have the right to pray. We have the right to see the heavenly vision and to communicate it here in the earth. It is the will of God and the gates of hell will not be able to withstand the army of Attack Lambs going forth to park the ark and practice the presence of the power of God.

Don't you dare say you cannot speak, or that you don't have anything to say. You can pray and that is what is important. If we ask

44. [2]And the Lord said to Satan, "The Lord rebuke you, Satan! The Lord who has chosen Jerusalem rebuke you! Is this not a brand plucked from the fire?"

anything according to His will He hears us and grants the petition we desire of Him. Get out there in that gap and claim those souls and you will have the happiest day of your life!

Forgive me for getting carried away with this one, but I have seen so many wonderful Christian people exclude themselves from ministry unnecessarily because of the fear of speaking. I used to get horrible upset stomachs and nose bleeds before I had to speak. My thoughts would ramble all over the place. I would sweat and get hives. Then I realized I was wrestling with a spiritual force. It wasn't the people, they loved me. They were listening.

Once I stood against that *exousias*, I found victory. I found I was not bound by the fear of man. I found I did have the right and ability to proclaim Christ in the power of the Holy Spirit. You do too. Come on, it starts with prayer.

KOSMOKRATOS

The third force is the **kosmokratos**[4]. In English, it is "rulers of the darkness of this world."

The people who operate under the influence of this force are easy to see, they **use people to get things**. The American church has been inundated with the *kosmokratos*. About every three years I am approached by people who want me to refer them to church leaders and members so they can sell them everything from soap to mutual funds. The pitch is always the same, "We will give a percentage of our profits to missions."

I do not mean to be unkind, but to use the church as a development bed for multi-level marketing schemes is as far from the Great Commission as anyone can get. The inference that a percentage will be given to reach people who are on their way to hell's fires and eternal damnation is offensive. The truth is, unless you are giving all that you are, all that you have, and all that you hope to be to the will of God, you are falling short of the glory God intends for you.

My solution is…write the check now. Give what you have now and apply your time to prayer and the will of God. Most recently I was approached to offer "networking" business opportunities to wealthy Asians whom I have met. Wealthy Asians are those who were able to preserve money and family through the Japanese occupation of their country. They honor their ancestors in a way that few Westerners will ever understand. They did not become wealthy rapidly and they do not believe in fast friendships. My relationship with them has nothing to do with their money. To use those relationships for financial gain, even with the promise of a percentage coming to the ministry, is a form of prostitution to their way of thinking.

I enter their cities to pray. I see where the *kosmokratos* forces are operating. I walk and intercede for the people there and they are saved. My relationship to them is in the spirit, not in the *kosmos*. This blending of motive in the church is indicative of the *kosmokratos* spirit at work in our midst.

Where is the *kosmokratos* operating in your town? Some areas which come to my mind are prostitution, pornography, abortion clinics, and the drug traffic. These are areas of great commerce. We do not often look at them as spiritual force manifestation, but that is what they are.

Attack Lambs, get out there and drive off those wolves. Get the ark out there and practice the Power Presence and drive out this force of corruption. Free the people in spirit so they will hear the Gospel when you or another presents it. You could be the one who stands on the corner and prays, and gets to see a tract passer find success. Imagine looking through the cloud of the presence of God and seeing a group of youths give their lives to Christ because you have broken the peer group bondage brought on through marketing devices.

You can pray. You can park the ark with the motor running and reach heaven on behalf of those young people. They do not have to be the target of every marketing scheme. They do not have to wear certain clothes, use drugs, listen to crazy music and talk in an undiscernable dialect. You can set them free through prayer. God wants to work through you to reach them.

PNEUMA TAE PONERIAS

The fourth force Paul mentions, "spiritual wickedness in high places, is the **pneuma tae ponerias**₅.

This is the **spirit of malice**. Webster says that malice is the premeditated harm of, or the desire to injure, another human being.

This is the force which directs mass murder. In America, we kill approximately 4,000 unborn children every day. This is the biggest mass murder in the history of the human race. Our nation will decline as long as we remain unrepentant for this action. Through the *pneuma tae ponerias*, our nation and the rest of the world is being driven into spiritual, financial, and ecological disaster.

America is not alone in its bent to self-destruction. There are mobs in Korea, Skinheads in Europe, nerve gas cults in Japan, and the military in China. "Ethnic cleansing" has become the accepted term for the spirit of malice in many nations. As men brutalize their countrymen around the world, we are to believe this is little more than an expression of territorial ethnicity.

Believe that if you will, but the apostle Paul says we are wrestling with a spirit of malice. We, the Attack Lambs, the gap fillers, must take our Power Presence arks into the gaps and strategic locations of the earth's populations and, under the impact of the heavenly vision, must stand against this force.

Once, in Irkutsk, Siberia, we saw a little plant that had pushed its way up through asphalt paving to greet the Spring sun and we knew that no matter how thick the darkness, the Lord would revive Russia.

We stood against the poverty and prayed especially for our brothers and sisters in Siberia who lived in abject poverty. So many hours we had lamented over them as we traveled the Trans-Siberian region as mobile arks for Jesus.

From 1985 through 1988 we prayed, traveled, networked, and prayed again. In '88 there was a breakthrough as an attempted coup failed, and the Director of Ideology was replaced by a man favorable to the church. A greater freedom came to the church; the Dagon bowed.

Shortly, we will discover the pressure points that change a nation, the five specific places you should go to pray and bring God's Power Presence to bear. But, first we must talk about the Name that is above every name.

....

Forgiving others is not necessary if we do not take offense. This offense is nasty, subtle trickery used by the enemy of our souls to create gaps in relationships, but for it to work, you have to pick it up. See misunderstandings, and even attacks, as a device. Do not take offense.

Over the years I have learned the phrase, "I am not picking that up." Since I have lived my life largely in the gap with a very small group of close friends, I have not had many occasions to be offended but when I am, I have come to realize that the only part of me that can be offended is my pride, and I am trying to get rid of that anyway.

Offense means I am looking at myself or comparing myself to others which the Bible calls unwise. So, don't pick it up. Choose to not take offense at the words or deeds of others. And do not be an offense to others. Lambs do not offend. We are to be examples to the flock of joy and long-suffering.

So many who engage in what has been called "spiritual warfare" have done so with human aggression firing a spiritual vocabulary. The power gifts of the Holy Spirit in 1 Corinthians 12 have to be balanced with the fruit of the Holy Spirit found in Galatians 5. Power will drive off the forces, but fruit will win the soul. We must have the character of the Lamb with the power of the Lion.

CONTEXT IS KEY

The traditional teachings about our struggle with the devil are taken from Ephesians 6 where we have the naming of the four forces and the description of the Whole Armor of God. Many curricula have been written on these, most based on a hierarchical under-standing of the spirit realm. Many teachers just repeat what they had heard, but to be fair, the mainstream follows Latin teaching, which has come through the Roman church, which has a hierarchical struc-ture. There are several problems with this, especially when Satan is presented as a negative opposite of Christ.

Taking Ephesians 6, without reading the entire letter, can put us in a battle that has already been won. Unfortunately, many people have done just that; rushing to chapter six without pausing at one through five. This has unfortunately resulted in the emphasis becom-ing the warfare instead of the victory. It has given rise to a merit system and titles to levels of seeming spirituality. That is great for those who see themselves as accomplished, but fatal for the masses of Christians who, in humility, do not see themselves as victorious.

As a result, the term "spiritual warfare" has become a byword for Charismatic Extremism as opposed to a very real biblical truth.

In this second edition, we want to take a look at the whole letter to the Ephesians and seek to restore the balance. After the publica-tion of the first edition, I was referred to as one who did not believe in Spiritual Warfare. Not true; I know there was a war, I know the head of the devil was crushed when Jesus took the keys of death and hell, and I know that we are now dispossessing the forces that have been in gaps for years. I am firmly established in the absolute victory of Jesus Christ and the absolute victory of those who are in Him.

Written by the Apostle Paul to the church at Ephesus, the letter is an instruction to those who are "in Christ." When teaching the Attack Lambs Seminar over the past 20 years, we have had people read the first chapter and find how many times the phrase "in Christ" or "in Him" appeared. The opening sentence gives us the key phrase, "to the saints and faithful in Christ at Ephesus." So, our position is "In Christ" while our location is "in Ephesus."

In verse 4 we find that we were known "in Him" before the foun-dation of the world. You were known in Him. When you are facing a principality, or "Archas," in chapter 6, and the mental and emotional weapons are intimidation and argumentation based on preeminence or, "who was here first," you win because you were here in Christ before the creation of the enemy. Colossians proclaims that Jesus was before all things, and you were known in Him. Yes, you. See, if you don't read the first chapter, then you would misperceive the four forces in chapter 6. You could be chasing an illusion.

The next ten verses proclaim all that we have received "in Him." And it is most important to see the tenses of the verbs used. They are all past tense. These are not blessings you are going to obtain; these are guarantees of what Christ has done for you through His vicarious death and victorious resurrection. These are not things waiting to be accomplished, they are finished, they have been done, and they have been given to us. Jesus has won total victory over sin and the devil. He has accomplished the purpose for which He was sent. He has reconciled us to God through His blood. He has redeemed us from the consequence of sin. He has taken our shame and set us in the course that God had for us before the foundations of the world.

You are free to move into the destiny for which you were formed. Just as Jesus came in the fullness of time, so you were sent here through your parents to fulfill God's purpose for you, He is at work in you, bringing you to fulfill that purpose.

Paul understood that this is going to take some awakening in the Ephesians. Just as John on the Isle of Patmos, and the disciples on the road to Emmaus, or Peter on the Mount of Transfiguration, these believers, and we as well, need for this solid, absolute truth to be emblazoned on our hearts. Paul offers a prayer that the eyes of their understanding may be enlightened that they may know three specific things.

THE HOPE OF HIS CALLING

First, that they may understand the "**hope of His calling**" (Ephesians 1:18[45]).

---

45. [18]the eyes of your understanding being enlightened; that you may know what is the hope of His calling, what are the riches of the glory of His inheritance in the saints

Jesus came to reconcile man and God. He was the sacrificial Lamb who, fulfilling the Law, took on flesh and blood, so that, through death, He could redeem flesh and blood and destroy the one, who through fear of death, had held all flesh in bondage. (Hebrews 2:14 keyword "destroy" or make void) He entered into the gap between God and man. He was lifted up on the cross, between heaven and earth, to reconcile their differences (Father forgive them). He descended into hell, found the devil, and knocked him down (Psalm 3:7[46]), crushed his head (Genesis 3:15[47]), took the keys of death and hell (Revelation 1:18[48]), ascended through Abraham's bosom (Psalm 24), and is seated at the right hand of the Father, making intercession for us (Romans 8:34[49]).

Jesus was sent to be an intercessor.

As you hunger to continue in the calling of Jesus, you too will find yourself entering in between two with a view of reconciling their differences. Whether at school or work, on a vacation or an outing, you will feel the prompting to participate with Jesus in His calling. You will be an Attack Lamb declaring to powers and principalities (Archas and Exousias) the manifold wisdom of the calling of Christ. He knew you before the foundations of the earth. At the right time for you, he sent you forth, through your parents, to be walking with Him in fulfilling that calling of reconciling people to God. You are an ambassador of Christ sent forth from Glory destined to return to glory having fulfilled your purpose.

Just as Jesus did not speak His own words or create His own ways, so you will stand in the gaps of your world; talk to God about the people until He gives you something to say to the people. Following the example of Jesus, walking in His calling, you will never be separated

---

46. [7]Arise, O Lord; Save me, O my God! For You have struck all my enemies on the cheekbone; You have broken the teeth of the ungodly.
47. [15]And I will put enmity Between you and the woman, And between your seed and her Seed; He shall bruise your head, And you shall bruise His heel."
48. [18]I am He who lives, and was dead, and behold, I am alive forevermore. Amen. And I have the keys of Hades and of Death.
49. [34]Who is he who condemns? It is Christ who died, and furthermore is also risen, who is even at the right hand of God, who also makes intercession for us.

from the presence of the loving Father. You will always have all of the authority of heaven with you and in you. The Attack Lambs are confident because they have had the eyes of their understanding enlightened and they know the hope of their calling in Christ Jesus.

THE RICHES OF HIS INHERITANCE

The second thing the Apostle prays for is that they may understand the riches of the glory of His inheritance in the saints.

Jesus endured the cross looking forward to the joy that was set before Him. His inheritance was about to be obtained. He stayed on that cross until the last drop was shed, the last agony felt, the full price paid for our redemption. We are His inheritance. Every soul that comes to know Jesus is an addition to that inheritance. It fulfills His calling; it costs an immeasurable price.

His inheritance is multiplying in the saints. You and I are part of that inheritance. We are joint-heirs (Romans 8:16-17[50]) with Jesus in His inheritance. A joint-heir has an equal share. We get an equal share of the inheritance in Christ. So many have made this a material inheritance, and while I do believe in a literal heaven and earth and a New Jerusalem, I also believe that the inheritance can be enjoyed today in the true meaning of the Body of Christ, the Church.

Once our eyes are opened to the fact that the inheritance for which Christ died is sitting in the service next to me, and the way to multiply that inheritance is to pray for and reach out to all mankind, then we are never going to divide the church. We will drop all reproach against the church, refusing to take up any offense, and rather, see it as our inheritance. To divide it, to take up offense within it, to speak evil of it, is to diminish the multiplying power of the inheritance.

The Attack Lamb does not take offense (Father forgive Them) and does not create or support division in the inheritance.

---

50. [16]The Spirit Himself bears witness with our spirit that we are children of God, [17]and if children, then heirs—heirs of God and joint heirs with Christ, if indeed we suffer with Him, that we may also be glorified together.

THE POWER OF HIS RESURRECTION

The third thing the Apostle wants us to understand is the hyper-power that the God of our Lord, Jesus Christ, the Father of Glory demonstrated when He raised Christ from the dead and seated Him far above all principality, power, might, dominion, and every name that is named, not only in this age, but also in the age to come. And He put all things under His feet and gave Him to be the head of all things to the church, which is His body the fullness of Him that fills all in all.

Now that is some power. Power over death. Power for the resurrection. Power to destroy the works of the enemy.

When Jesus gave up His spirit, His body was placed in the tomb. But that was not the end of the story. He burst forth from the tomb and descended into hell on a mission to crush the head of the devil. To destroy the devil, for it was for this purpose that the Son of God was manifest. Having found the devil, Jesus knocked him down, breaking his jaw, and breaking out his teeth, then crushed his head. Jesus then turned to ascend.

We see in the story of Lazarus and Dives (Luke 16:19-31[51]), that there was a place called Abraham's Bosom where those who died

---

51. [19]"There was a certain rich man who was clothed in purple and fine linen and fared sumptuously every day. [20]But there was a certain beggar named Lazarus, full of sores, who was laid at his gate, [21]desiring to be fed with the crumbs which fell from the rich man's table. Moreover the dogs came and licked his sores. [22]So it was that the beggar died, and was carried by the angels to Abraham's bosom. The rich man also died and was buried. [23]And being in torments in Hades, he lifted up his eyes and saw Abraham afar off, and Lazarus in his bosom. [24]"Then he cried and said, 'Father Abraham, have mercy on me, and send Lazarus that he may dip the tip of his finger in water and cool my tongue; for I am tormented in this flame.' [25]But Abraham said, 'Son, remember that in your lifetime you received your good things, and likewise Lazarus evil things; but now he is comforted and you are tormented. [26]And besides all this, between us and you there is a great gulf fixed, so that those who want to pass from here to you cannot, nor can those from there pass to us.' [27]"Then he said, 'I beg you therefore, father, that you would send him to my father's house, [28]for I have five brothers, that he may testify to them, lest they also come to this place of torment.' [29]Abraham said to him, 'They have Moses and the prophets; let them hear them.' [30]And he said, 'No, father Abraham; but if one goes to them from the dead, they will repent.' [31]But he said to him, 'If they do not hear Moses and the prophets, neither will they be persuaded though one rise from the dead.' "

looking forward to the Messiah went. And there was a hell to which all others went. You could see from one to the other.

When Jesus descended into hell, those awaiting His coming could see the battle. As He began to rise holding the keys of death and hell in one hand, they cried out to the gates of heaven, "Lift up your heads oh, you Gates and be lifted up you everlasting doors that the King of Glory may come in."

The Angelic Gate Keepers called back, "**Who is this King of glory?**" (Psalm 24).

Those in Abraham's Bosom cried again, "**The Lord strong and mighty, the Lord mighty in battle. Lift up your heads, O you gates! Lift up, you everlasting doors! And the King of glory shall come in**" (Psalm 24:8-9[52]).

The Father reached down, and taking the Son by the outstretched hand, lifted him, and all those in Abraham's bosom, to His own right hand. He has the power to redeem all those from their sin, to take away their bondage. The twenty-four elders took their thrones, and the Lamb of God opened the seal. The angels cried Holy and every living thing gave glory to the Lamb.

Before we look at the truth of chapter six of Ephesians, you have to revel in the power of chapter one.

THE SWEETEST WORDS

Chapter two is about you.

"And you…"

There are no sweeter words in all the Bible. The Apostle Paul wants the church to know that we are included in the victory in Jesus Christ. In Christ, we are seated at the right hand of the Father. And what is Jesus doing at that right hand? He is interceding. He is

---

52. [8]Who is this King of glory? The Lord strong and mighty, The Lord mighty in battle. [9]Lift up your heads, O you gates! Lift up, you everlasting doors! And the King of glory shall come in.

reconciling man to God. He is imputing His righteousness to their sin account blotting out their transgressions. And who are they? They are the ones around the world who are, at this moment, finding Jesus as their personal Lord and Savior.

Imagine the joy in heaven when your prayers are answered and that boss, student, child, politician, or gangster bows a knee to the Name and asks Jesus to forgive them, and be Lord of their lives. You, as an Attack Lamb, have entered the gap and dispelled the forces by parking the ark and releasing the Spirit. You have worked together with Jesus to set these captives free and you are a joint heir with Him in this inheritance. You've got to see this and rejoice in it.

Indeed, we used to walk in their same ways. We were estranged from the body and walked in the ways of the world, but someone got in the way. When I am parked in the gap and people ask me what I am doing, I often ask the question, "How old were you when you first realized that Jesus is the Son of God?"

If they have never heard, then I have the opportunity. If they say an age, then I ask who told them. That is the person who stood in the gap. That is a person who is going to be remembered with thanks. That is a person who was fulfilling the hope of His calling and multiplying the inheritance.

Someone stood in the gap for you. And God, who is rich in mercy, heard their cry and answered it. This is what Prayer Walking is all about. The measure of success in spiritual warfare is souls saved, lives changed, churches planted. This is not about confronting already defeated principalities and powers, this is about hearing heaven rejoice as Jesus receives everyone who calls on Him.

HIS AMAZING GRACE

Chapter three is Paul's incredible testimony of how this grace could reach even him, for he had ordered the death of believers and had actually participated in the stoning of Stephen. And yet, the love and grace of God were great enough to reach Paul. And because of that impact in his life, Paul prays that we might know the love of God that passes knowledge or is beyond human understanding. When we are impacted by this knowledge of love, then we will not take offense, even at those who would kill us. We will cry out for forgiveness and we will see the Lord turn the vilest of hearts to righteousness. God is able to do more through us than we could ever imagine.

In the 20 years since the first edition, we have seen the Lord reach the unreachable. High in the Himalayas, there is a move of God going on that is simply amazing. In cities in America, there are thousands of young people coming to Christ each day. The move of God in this generation is without precedent for His mercies are new every morning.

As an intercessor, you have the ability to walk where Jesus leads and pray. If you can believe with me that prayer is the most powerful tool, then you will use every moment to look upon people and talk to God and to look to God to be able to speak to the people. Walking with God in the midst of His inheritance, calling them to Him in prayer, word and deed are the fulfillment of destiny and purpose. Paul wants us all to enjoy the walk that he has walked.

A VERY GIFTED GROUP

We are a very gifted group. We can see what others do not see. We can love when others cannot. We do not take offense. We are seated at the right hand of the Father, in Christ, and we have all we will ever need to do His will.

Here in chapter four, Paul discusses different gifts given to members of the church for the edification of the membership that is to build up the inheritance. He teaches that we are not all the same, but will have different spheres of influence. The common denominator in all these spheres is that they need prayer.

Each area of the *polis* (or society) in which we live has a particular set of unwritten laws of behavior. Anywhere you have a *polis*, you also have politics, but not here. Here we are saved by grace so we extend grace to one another. When these gifts become offices and the desire for a vertical hierarchy is manifest, politics make the lower man feel inadequate and exalts the higher man beyond reality so that people begin to appropriate titles rather than functions.

The Apostles of today rarely reflect that first group we found in Matthew 10. There is very little dust on their feet, for they hold lofty conventions with one another, or form coalitions that include anyone with $500 and a business card rather than signs and wonders, imprisonments, fasting, persecutions, and the many hours of toil. However, the apostolic function is seen in all those who step out at the commissioning of the Lord to stand in a gap and proclaim Christ without the fear and favor of man.

The Prophetic has been so compromised that no king on earth is afraid of the prophets as they were in the days of true prophetic anointing. Politics, position, and title have distracted from the One who is on the throne. The only One worthy of glory, honor, power, might, and dominion is represented by a bunch of marketeers. Paul begins here in the letter to caution the church about adopting the world's ways. He encourages hard work: pay your bills, speak the truth, give freely, support one another. Grace and the understanding of the inheritance will multiply the superpower through to calling to the purpose of God that every man, woman, and child have the opportunity to know Jesus.

FAMILIAL LOVE

Chapter five brings the idea of being in Christ and loving one another. Paul discusses the keyword, *hupotasso*, as the foundation for a successful marriage as he encourages both parties to voluntarily order themselves under the other. He is, in this letter, entering in between two with a view of reconciling their differences.

So, the presence of Jesus and the understanding of love that passes knowledge should make the couple the picture of Christ and His bride. How far we have strayed from this picture. If there is any area of life that has gaps it is in this one. How we pray for our children and their spouses. How painful it is when a marriage breaks up and the kids are left to wonder if they are the cause. So many have broken vows that youth today find it less stressful to live together without marriage than to make promises to each other.

But the good news is, as you pray, you dispel the arguments over who is in charge, the antics that attack the right to speak, so couples are finding healing of relationships by having a person in the gap praying for them. Worship in the midst releases the joy as we experience His presence. When we see Jesus, espoused to the church, and understand His love and patience, does it not make our crisis seem small?

INSTRUCTIONS FOR SPIRITUAL WARFARE

Then we come to chapter six which contains the instructional outline for spiritual warfare in verse 12.

The first two paragraphs are about submission. In the different strata of family and society, we are told to order ourselves properly. I do not think Paul advocated slavery in any way. I think he is saying that if you are an employee, domestically or professionally, you are to pray for and respect those to who you report. Over the years we have met so many who are trying to resolve on the job offense. Just don't pick it up. But if you get hit over the head with it. If the person is just absolutely against you. If life is getting so bad you dread waking up each day, then get in that gap and pray. Ask the Lord to give you something positive to think about. Find one good thing about that person and pray that it would be the seed of a great harvest in their lives. Put your faith in action through prayer. Prayer changes things.

STAND FAST

Then we come to the conclusion: Finally, brethren, stand fast in the Lord and in the power of His might.

Where are we standing? In the Lord. Whose power is being manifest through us? The power of His might.

What did that power do? Lifted us, in Christ, far above every principality, power, might, dominion, and every name that is named not only in this life but in the life to come.

See, you have to read chapter one.

So, here is the thing. Traditional teaching comes from a hierarchical perspective because of its Latin roots. Every day has a saint and a demon. The struggle is on, and man is lower than both. Of course, it would be this way; because in the middle of the hierarchy is the "Archas." So, people bind and loose, cast and rebuke and nothing happens. So, they feel like a lesser saint because they could not get the victory. They give up.

But the Attack Lamb, while fully aware of the evil presence, focuses on the throne and the Lamb. While totally understanding of the people under the influence of these forces: who was here first, who has the right to speak, who rules over the people, and malicious plans and practices, the Attack Lamb puts on the Helmet of Salvation. It is all about the Lamb.

All success in the spirit realm flows forth from an atmosphere of praise and worship. Just as Jesus did not give honor to the devil in the wilderness, he did not give title, did not give power, did not give even acknowledgment, but said, **"Get out"** (Matthew 4:1-11 NLT[53]).

---

53. [1]Then Jesus was led by the Spirit into the wilderness to be tempted there by the devil. [2]For forty days and forty nights he fasted and became very hungry. [3]During that time the devil came and said to him, "If you are the Son of God, tell these stones to become loaves of bread." [4]But Jesus told him, "No! The Scriptures say, 'People do not live by bread alone, but by every word that comes from the mouth of God.'" [5]Then the devil took him to the holy city, Jerusalem, to the highest point of the Temple, [6]and said, "If you are the Son of God, jump off! For the Scriptures say, 'He will order his angels to protect you. And they will hold you up with their hands so you won't even hurt your foot on a stone.'" [7]Jesus responded, "The Scriptures also say, 'You must not test the Lord your God.'" [8]Next the devil took him to the peak of a very high mountain and showed him all the kingdoms of the world and their glory. [9]"I will give it all to you," he said, "if you will kneel down and worship me." [10]"Get out of here, Satan," Jesus told him. "For the Scriptures say, 'You must worship the Lord your God and serve only him.'" [11]Then the devil went away, and angels came and took care of Jesus.

The Attack Lamb, heart and emotions covered by righteousness and truth (Ephesians 6:14[54]), takes up the sword of the Spirit, the only offensive weapon in chapter 6 and begins to sing hymns and spiritual songs making melody in his heart to the Lord. His focus is on the One who sits on the throne.

Out from this throne flows the anointing that drives the forces from the gap and gives those formerly oppressed by the four forces an ear to hear and a heart to receive the love of God in Christ. This is spiritual warfare. The measure of success is souls saved and lives changed. The power is the Lion and the glory is the Lamb's.

The German stream of theology, of course, protests hierarchical thinking for grace is extended to all. The four forces are represented as competing with one another, a pack of ravenous wolves that combine to hold mankind captive. But the Lion is the King.

Trite, simplistic, but profound. How do you pull down something you are above? Good question, don't you think? When the eyes of our understanding are opened to know, as were Peter's, Paul's, and John's, then we too cry, "Worthy art thou, oh Lamb of God."

And then, in verse 18, is the key to victory, "**Praying always with all prayer and supplication in the Spirit…**" Our communication with the Father releases those for whom we pray.

Jesus has prevailed to open the scroll. Jesus has defeated the devil above the earth, on the earth, and under the earth. From our position in Him, we participate in that victory. Ephesians is a fantastic letter to you and me about the glorious victory of Jesus and how to live in its glory. Ministry, life principles, marriage, the church, the nations, it is all there in Ephesians.

---

54. [14]Stand therefore, having girded your waist with truth, having put on the breastplate of righteousness

CHAPTER 9

NAME ABOVE ALL NAMES

Prayer walk team with monks they had met

The fragrant fumes of burning joss sticks filled the temple with a mystical haze. The Tien Fu Gong Temple is a worship center for thousands. From my position to the left of the rear altar, I could see the tourist buses unloading their curious crowds.

The fortune tellers called out. Spiritual hucksters. They displayed their diagrams and tools before them and offered to plunge into the depths of the spirit realm to tell these Europeans something of their future.

Inside the temple the medium was asleep, the result I think of the combination of the smoke and our little group of intercessors. He always takes a nap from noon till closing we found out. A very scary fellow with long lashes and a totally stoned expression on his gaunt little face. He often reminded me of a hobbit perched on his stool.

A tourist couple in their thirties approached me, "Excuse me," the lady said, "do you work here?"

I was indeed working there. My ark had been parked for several hours at that point. "Yes, I am working here." I responded, wondering how the Lord was going to reach these two.

"Could you tell me where I could find a kitchen god?" she asked with such earnestness I was startled. Looking at their size you could see her cooking was neither bad nor lacking.

"That would be at the altar surface level," I answered, "among the domestics."

I motioned toward the altar which had three levels: the *heaven-lies*, the *earthiest*, (or surface level) and the *nether world*. They are the representation of the structure of the ancestral worship system which has evolved in all of Asia.

"You may not take the idols," I told her, "but you might want to talk to the medium if he wakes up." I hoped his appearance would dispel her interest.

At that point her husband entered the conversation. "What do you do here?" he asked. "I am a Christian missionary," I began to explain.

He was startled and a bit confused. "Well, what are you doing here then?"

Well, since you asked, I thought. Here was my God-provided opportunity.

"I am here praying for the Chinese that they will be set free from the power of these forces. I am declaring to them that Jesus has defeated the Devil in the heavens, on the earth, and under the earth, and that He has a name that is above all names. That at the name of Jesus every knee shall bow."

My answer was made more effective by the smoke and stench of idolatry which filled our lungs and eyes, causing them to water.

Their curiosity was aroused. They had never heard anything like that. We stepped into an open courtyard and continued our conversation. They assured me they were Christians, traveling on an Asian tour package. This temple was part of their itinerary and they were fascinated by the diversity of culture. They didn't really want a kitchen god, they just wanted to see one, and had not realized how deeply their host nation was bound by spiritual forces.

With a reaffirmation of their faith in Jesus, they boarded the bus and continued the tour. I returned to the gap which the Lord had assigned for the day. I placed myself beside the altar and once again began interceding for the people as they came to offer sacrifices to the idols. How my heart ached for each one that they might know the joy of life with Jesus.

The Dagons of today are operating in many temples. You and I, as the modern day ark of God's covenant in Jesus, must go to those places and establish the lordship of Jesus, invoking His name and speaking what the Holy Spirit gives us to say.

THE DEFEATED FOE

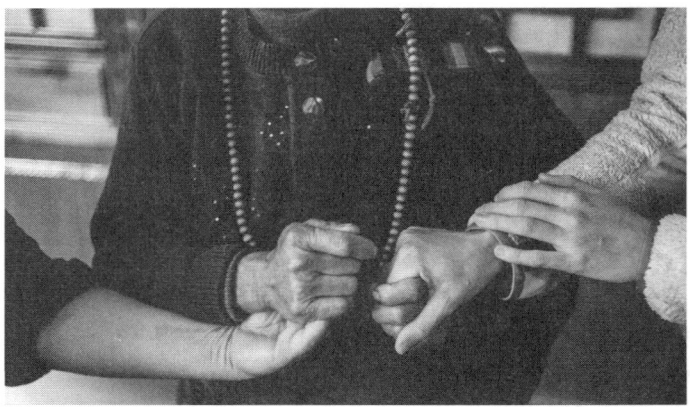

2016 prayer team praying with Tibetan woman

Ezekiel 28:11–20 tells us the Devil was an "anointed cherub" whose job was to convey praise and worship to God in the heavenly service. But iniquity was found in him. He attempted to ascend to the throne of God and was cast down.

He will be placed in fire which will come forth from him and will be utterly destroyed before those through whom he used to traffic.

Isaiah 14 makes the point that Satan was cast down from the heavens. Remember, Jesus told the disciples He had seen Satan fall like lightning. **Jesus has defeated the Devil in the heavenlies.**

Then, in Matthew 4, Jesus went into the wilderness after He was baptized and defeated the Devil on the earth. What great news this is! How we rejoiced when the Lion of the tribe of Judah commanded the Enemy to "get thee hence." **Jesus has defeated the Devil on the earth.**

Finally, in Ephesians 4 Jesus descended into hell and, for three days, sought out the Devil. Having found him, Jesus put His foot on his head and took the keys of death and hell away from him. Then, with the battle won, the Holy Spirit caused Christ to rise, and passing through Abraham's bosom, He led those captive there to freedom. **So Jesus has defeated the Devil under the earth.**

You see, Jesus, as the Attack Lamb Prototype, defeated the Enemy in all three areas of temptation. The victory of Jesus Christ is complete in the heavenlies, in the earth, and under the earth!

The third part of our acrostic **S-I-N-G** is the **name of Jesus**, the **Name above all names**.

Paul describes the Lion of Judah emerging from the Lamb of God.

Wherefore God also hath highly exalted him, and given him a name which is above every name: that at the name of Jesus every knee should bow, of *things in heaven, and things in earth, and things under the earth*; and that every tongue should confess that Jesus Christ

is Lord, to the glory of God the Father.
Philippians 2:9–11[55] KJV (emphasis added)

HIS GLORY...OUR GLORY

September 2011 prayer walk team

The glory of God which dwells between the angels above the mercy seat in our lives, dwells there because of the name of Jesus. Had Christ not come, the blood would not have been applied and His powerful Presence would not have been able to abide with men. Through His death on the cross, Jesus made it possible for the will of the Father to be accomplished and God's desired fellowship with man was restored. He does not want any to perish. Therefore, He has commanded a spiritual people to bear His Presence in the earth in such a way that it will cause the Dagons to bow down and the souls of men to be released.

Romans 8:5–11 clearly states that to be effective in the purpose of God we must be spiritually minded. This is possible only when

---

55. [9]Therefore God also has highly exalted Him and given Him the name which is above every name, [10]that at the name of Jesus every knee should bow, of those in heaven, and of those on earth, and of those under the earth, [11]and that every tongue should confess that Jesus Christ is Lord, to the glory of God the Father

the Spirit of Christ dwells in us. Those who are "in the flesh," that is, having their thinking oppressed by the influence of the *archas*, *exousias*, *kosmokratos*, and *ponerias*, cannot please God.

The focus of an Attack Lamb must be Jesus, the Lamb sacrificed for us. It is from Him we receive the patience, love, mercy, and compassion to endure the assaults and contradictions of the four forces of the Enemy mentioned before.

Paul goes further to say that you are not in the flesh if the Spirit of Christ is in you (Romans 8). Bold statement that it is, it stands nevertheless.

When we name the name of Jesus and accept Him as our salvation, the *archas*, *exousias*, *kosmokratos*, and *ponerias* must bow down in our lives. The more we forgive in Jesus' name, the more free we become to love others and to reach them with the good news of the Gospel. The name of Jesus will set us free to set others free. This is the Christian experience. There is power in His name!

PULLING DOWN YOUR STRONGHOLDS

Second Corinthians 10:1–6 gives a description of the "strongholds" in our lives. The only use of the term in the New Testament, this verse is a key in understanding the Power Presence of God, and His flow through us.

Now I Paul myself beseech you by the meekness and gentleness of Christ, who in presence am base among you, but being absent am bold toward you: but I beseech you, that I may not be bold when I am present with that confidence, wherewith I think to be bold against some, which think of us as if we walked according to the flesh. For though we walk in the flesh, we do not war after the flesh: (For the weapons of our warfare are not carnal, but mighty through God to the pulling down of strong holds;) casting down imaginations, and every high

thing that exalteth itself against the knowledge of God, and bringing into captivity every thought to the obedience of Christ; and having in a readiness to revenge all disobedience when your obedience is fulfilled.

2 Corinthians 10:1–6 KJV

The warfare in which we are engaged as Attack Lambs is the neutralization of the tactics of the *archas, exousias, kosmokratos,* and *ponerias* as we see them lift themselves up in our minds and in the culture in which we live. How do we do this? By bringing the thoughts stimulated by these four forces into subjection to the knowledge of Jesus Christ.

Let's say that tomorrow you go to work, and there is competition between two divisions to see who is going to get an award. This is a carnal way of stimulating production. The incentive is a three-day trip to a beautiful island where you can just lay around in the sun and feel good about your employer.

Both divisions are asking employees to donate time to productivity so that the prize can be won. You know you are going to be pressured to do your share for your division. How do you bring this *kosmokratos-archas* force in subjection to the knowledge of Christ?

You set apart time in the morning and you pray. You ask the Lord to give you the courage and grace to serve your company as a good witness, but to be free from the manipulations. You then invoke the name of Jesus against those strongholds of imagination and manipulation. You remain in prayer until you feel a release in your spirit that the warfare is accomplished and you go off to work. You do your regular excellent job and ask the Lord to give you greater productivity throughout your normal day.

This sounds so simple, yet time after time I have seen it work. **Prayer which combines God's ultimate purpose with the invocation of the name of Jesus is incredibly powerful.** Your being at that place of work is God's design to neutralize the four forces as they try to operate. Why? So that those around you will be able to receive Jesus Christ as their personal Lord and Savior.

Already, before even going to work, you are able to praise the Lord for the outcome. You have a witness in your spirit He has heard your prayer and, leaving the arm-twisting to Him, you begin to give Him praise. Remember, all successful spiritual endeavor comes forth from an attitude of praise and worship. The name of Jesus has been invoked, the Dagons will bow.

How do we know what the Lord wants to do in that office? Romans taught us we are led of the Spirit to fulfill the purpose of God. First Corinthians 2:9–16 goes on to tell us how. Let's look together at this very exciting passage.

> **But as it is written, eye hath not seen, nor ear heard, neither have entered into the heart of man, the things which God hath prepared for them that love him. But God hath revealed them unto us by his Spirit: for the Spirit searcheth all things, yea, the deep things of God. For what man knoweth the things of a man, save the spirit of man which is in him? even so the things of God knoweth no man, but the Spirit of God. Now we have received not the spirit of the world, but the Spirit which is of God; that we might know the things that are freely given to us of God. Which things also we speak, not in the words which man's wisdom teacheth, but which the Holy Ghost teacheth; comparing spiritual things with spiritual. But the natural man receiveth not the things of the Spirit of God: for they are foolishness unto him: neither can he know them, because they are spiritually discerned. But he that is spiritual judgeth all things, yet he himself is judged of no man. For who hath known the mind of the Lord, that he may instruct him? But we have the mind of Christ.   1 Corinthians 2:9–16 KJV**

Wow, that is a lot to read and understand, and yet it is very simple. You are an Attack Lamb. On the outside you are the most natural of all people. You are free from the four forces, you do not look like the world, but you do move about in it. As an Attack Lamb, you are led by the Lord's purpose. You approach your profession differently than those around you. You realize you are where you are so the Lord can reach others in the environment. You stay tuned in to the purpose of God in your life.

You know what the Lord is doing in that place because you are there in the name of Jesus. The others around you identify you as a Christian. You become a standard of right and wrong, and they are quick to let you know if you have transgressed their expectations. You set the standard for the place.

As the ark in the presence of Dagon, you are not invited to participate in many of the things which go on there. You are left to yourself and are able to gain tremendous leverage through kind words and prayer. When people have very real problems, they come by and drop them in your lap. You are God's point of contact for the people. He has brought you there to display relationship with the Father for them; to be the salt which makes them thirsty for Him.

You bring the things you see and hear into subjection to the word of God. In so doing you become a filter through which the devices of the *archas, exousias, kosmokratos,* and *ponerias* cannot pass. You are in the gap. In fact, when some approach your place of work, the worldly spirits in them will see the Lion in you and flee.

As you see those forces assault one of the flock God has given you there, you pray and they flee. That is why you are there. You are an intercessor. When you see the people as God sees them you will learn to love them as He does.

In Matthew's gospel Jesus defines His disciple's role, and ours, in that place of His Power Presence.

And I will give you the keys of the kingdom of heaven, and whatever you bind on earth will be bound in

**heaven, and whatever you loose on earth will be loosed
in heaven.   Matthew 16:19**

Why was the name of Jesus to be concealed at that time? Because
He was still to go into the depths of hell and take the keys away from
Satan. He still had to pay the price for our salvation. He was instruct-
ing the disciples in the power that would be theirs, and ours, **after**
His resurrection from the dead.

Now, Jesus is risen from the dead. It's OK to shout as you read
that. Now, Jesus is risen from the dead! He has defeated the Devil
above, on, and under the earth. The keys work!

Remember in Zechariah 3 how the Lord told the Devil to be
quiet. What power we saw as Jesus rebuked the Devil for your sake!
Now He has given you the power to enforce on the earth His declaration in that text. Bind it and it is bound, loose it and it is free.

I do not know where you work. It may be an office or school.
You may keep a lovely home or work in the church. You may be a
Christian minister. I have no idea where the Lord has put you to serve
Him, but I know this: you are there to stand in the gap for the lives of
those who are around you.

SHARING THE BURDEN

I work in Asia. It is a land filled with idols and ancestral worship.
My particular burden is for the Chinese people. Several years ago
Wang Ming Dao of Shanghai laid his tortured, withered hands on
my head and consecrated me to a work among the Chinese. My life
has not been the same since.

In the temples where I work there is the altar of the immortals,
and in the back or to the side is the place of the ancestral tablets.
On these tablets are inscribed the generations of the Chinese families
who pertain to that temple. It is here that offering is made to make a
better harmony for departed ancestors.

The worship system involves the Goddess of Mercy and the eight immortals. It is believed they direct the affairs of every Chinese. I have spent days praying over the heads of young men and women who come to seek the will of the goddess. She never speaks. She cannot.

It is through these altars that the generational curses and familiar spirits operate among the clans. It is not unusual to hear curses invoked upon an enemy or to hear dialogue with an ancestor over business matters. Several years ago the Lord led me to "park the ark" in the gap between these altars and the people. I am not praying to the idol, or addressing it in any way. Neither am I lifting up my voice to draw attention to myself in some display of seeming spirituality. In a quiet way I simply stand there and pray in tongues.

When someone prays in an unknown tongue, they speak mysteries unto God (1 Corinthians 14:2[56]). They build themselves up in faith (Jude 1:20[57]) and they flow in intercession, praying the perfect prayer of the Spirit. As the Lord leads, I bind the familiar spirits of the families of that temple and loose the people to know Jesus as their Lord and Savior. I am happy to report that in the three years in which we have been doing this, the Body of Christ in our test city has doubled.

But, what if you have not yet received the spiritual gift of the baptism in the Holy Spirit with the evidence of speaking in tongues? Can you still be an effective Attack Lamb? Yes, of course you can. It is Jesus in you who is seen by the four forces. It is not the vessel that puts powers to flight, but the One who dwells in you. I encourage you to continue to ask the Lord to give you this very valid gift, but do not disqualify yourself from being the ark just because you do not pray in tongues. Press into Jesus and He will give you all He has for you.

As we stand in the gap and park the ark with the motor running, the evangelist, church planter, outreach coordinators and all the Christian workers are experiencing a great harvest in the city.

---

56. [2]For he who speaks in a tongue does not speak to men but to God, for no one understands him; however, in the spirit he speaks mysteries
57. [20]But you, beloved, building yourselves up on your most holy faith, praying in the Holy Spirit

As you work in the gap the Lord has given you, you will be effective to loose the people who pertain to that place so they may hear the Gospel and understand it. You will receive from the Lord, through the Holy Spirit, the specific ways to pray and you will hear of souls saved.

Go to that work place as an Attack Lamb and neutralize the power of the four forces. You have been given the freedom to use the Name that is above every name. God has adopted you into His family to direct you into His purpose. He has given you the ability to discern the thoughts and intents of the four forces set against man. He has given you the ability to understand His plan to neutralize their power in every situation, and He has authorized you to use the name of His Son, our Savior Jesus. All that is left for you to do is to convert your place of work to a gap, park the ark, take the key of faith and get your motor running.

CHAPTER 10

SPEAKING OF NAMES

In the twenty years I have been involved in Christian ministry I have been called many things. Never tall and thin, but many things. My parents were very strong Christians in the Presbyterian church. Father was an elder and Mother played piano, led women's circle groups and taught Sunday School. Our home was, by today's standards, quite strict: short hair, no loud music and morning and evening devotions.

Even as kids we accumulated titles at an early age. We were, of course, in the youth and senior choirs and were expected to shoulder responsibilities in the youth group. As a result, positions and titles were not strangers in our home. We knew how to "do church."

The charismatic movement of the early seventies brought a revision of titles. It still amounted to sincere people doing the service jobs of the church, but now they were called shepherd, undershepherd and so forth. Again I began to accumulate titles. In the twenty-five years I have been involved in charismatic circles, I have been called "Apostle," "Prophet," "Evangelist," "Teacher," and "Pastor." I have been an "Elder," "Deacon," "Home Group Leader," "Worship Leader," and more. By the end of the first fifteen years I had somewhat of an identity crisis. I was called so many things that none of them seemed real. Worse, while I could "do church," I wasn't growing any closer to the Lord.

I sought the Lord concerning this because it seemed to me I should be getting closer, and He led me to the book of Acts.

But you shall receive power when the Holy Spirit has come upon you; and you shall be witnesses to Me in Jerusalem, and in all Judea and Samaria, and to the end of the earth.   **Acts 1:8**

AMAZED

I was amazed. All God had empowered us to be are witnesses. I thought about witnesses. A witness is someone who has seen something happen. He can report only on what he has actually and personally seen. He cannot testify to something someone else has seen. So a witness is someone who has seen something happen, and says what happened.

My immediate question was, "Why do we need the power of the Holy Spirit to be a witness?"

The Lord impressed me with this thought. *Spiritual work must be done in a spiritual way.* That's right. The Holy Spirit is the One who reveals to us the things of God. He is the One who knows the deep things of God and shares them with our spirit even to the realization of who we are in Christ. Jesus gives us identity by the power of the Holy Spirit.

Fair enough. As we walk about our place of work, do we not want the Holy Spirit to lead us? As we make decisions and pray in the gaps of our families, don't we want the Holy Spirit to give us faith for their souls? Of course! As we see our own weakness, we want more of the power of the Holy Spirit.

What about the telling? As this witness power descended upon the disciples, they had the experience of speaking in tongues. This was a language they, the ones speaking, did not understand. True, the business men out of every nation heard understandable languages, but when a person speaks in an unknown tongue, he speaks mysteries unto God. A mystery is something **you** do not understand.

I have found that when I think I understand what my heart is telling me to pray, I am often limited or just plain wrong in my feelings. I begin to tell God what I think about the situation from the very limited experience I have. For every one point of which I am certain, there are an infinite number of things about which I know absolutely nothing. I thank God that He has given, through the power of the Holy Spirit, the ability to speak in a language of witness or prayer language that I cannot understand. My tongue can communicate the perceptions of my divinely enabled spirit in a way that I cannot alter through intellect, will, or emotion.

That paragraph had a ton of doctrine in it. Maybe we better chew on that a second. What I am saying is, if I view a situation without the power of the Holy Spirit, I will see it according to or in the light of my own accumulated life experiences. I will process the information and formulate a prayer accordingly.

OPERATING WITH POWER

With the power of the Holy Spirit I look at the same situation, allow it to touch my heart, and pray in tongues, not knowing what the Holy Spirit is communicating. My understanding is unfruitful, but the prayer is most effective. I am not generating the prayer content from a mind that can be affected by what my senses tell me or what I understand of the situation based on past experience. Jesus does not base His work on our lives by what we have been, but on His ability to transform us into what we shall be. In the same sense, prayer in the Spirit impacts the future rather than revisiting the past.

We pray with the Spirit and with the understanding as the apostle Paul directed (1 Corinthians 14:15[58]). As you are standing in your child's room, you may discern the presence of the four forces

---

58. [15]What is the conclusion then? I will pray with the spirit, and I will also pray with the understanding. I will sing with the spirit, and I will also sing with the understanding

attempting to keep your child from walking with the Lord. You pray for understanding in the situation. The Lord leads you to pray in an exact fashion by relating thought to your understanding. Certainly we pray in this way with great fruit.

You receive prayer requests through your church prayer chain or through a missions newsletter. You are asked to pray for someone. You begin to pray with the understanding you have received through the phone call or letter. As you pray, you are led into tongues as an avenue of prayer which reaches beyond your understanding. As an Attack Lamb you learn to hear from heaven and to speak those things which the Lord speaks or shows you. You learn not to be locked into one format for prayer, but to flow with the Holy Spirit in the fervent, effectual prayer of those who are made righteous by His blood.

Paul invites us in 1 Corinthians 14:15 to be flexible and pray in the Spirit and with the understanding. I thank God that He has made a way in which I can pray for thousands of people every day without having to know who they are, where they live, or anything about their lives except that Jesus loves them and that He has brought me to their city to pray for them. Spiritual work must be done in a spiritual way. It is God's will that the four forces be neutralized and people hear the Gospel. We are in the gap asking according to His will. The ark is parked and intercession is being made for all men.

It makes no difference if it is you in your child's room or me on the street in Beijing, the principle is the same. We can pray effectively with the Spirit and with the understanding. Please do not allow the separation of Pentecostal and Evangelical to keep you from the heavenly vision of all of us gathered before the throne of God making intercession for those who need to be reconciled to Him.

GOING "TRACKING"

I love to pass out tracts; you know, those little booklets designed to tell people about the Lord and lead them to pray to Him. In one three-day period four of us distributed 25,000 tracts hand-to-hand in the country of Nepal. I really like to "go tracking." I have often wondered why in some places people will literally knock you over to get them and in others, they will knock you over to avoid them. The answer is in Acts 1.

Jesus has a certain order to taking a city, region, nation, and the world. He told the disciples to remain at Jerusalem until they were baptized in the Holy Spirit. He wanted this witness power, the ability to see and say, to precede evangelistic outreach. The baptism in the Holy Spirit was, in His instruction, fundamental to evangelism. He did not send out a single Attack Lamb without it.

Can you be Holy Spirit-filled and not speak in tongues? Sure you can. Can you demonstrate the fruit of the Holy Spirit and not speak in tongues? Everyone who has a born-again experience **should** be manifesting the fruit of the Spirit. That is what makes us different from the world. But, the word Jesus said to them was **baptized**.

In Acts 1:8[59] Jesus tells the disciples **what** they will receive: power. Acts 1:5 tells them how. **"You shall be baptized with the Holy Ghost not many days hence."**

WHAT DOES THIS MEAN?

Jesus was talking about a baptism in the Holy Spirit which was the promise of the Father and was accompanied by these new prayer tongues. Why? So the witness which they would give through the power of the Holy Spirit would release the anointing that caused three thousand men, their wives and kids to come to Christ in one afternoon. In a proven Gospel-resistant culture a former fisherman who had denied Christ stood up in this power and declared the truth. By the same Spirit you too can declare the same truths in the same fashion. Praying in the Spirit is the intercessor's most powerful weapon.

---

59. [8]But you shall receive power when the Holy Spirit has come upon you; and you shall be witnesses to Me in Jerusalem, and in all Judea and Samaria, and to the end of the earth."

Wow! Can you see people where you work being touched by the power of the Lord because you are praying for them, not according to your feeble knowledge of their lives but in the power of the Holy Spirit, who through you is praying the perfect prayer: that every man, woman, and child on the face of this earth will know that Jesus died for him or her! I get so excited thinking of you there interceding for your boss, or your teacher, or your family member or just walking through your town in the witness power of the Holy Spirit, gently speaking the mysteries to God.

But, that's not all that is going on. As an Attack Lamb, you have the ability to see a heavenly vision. As you wait in your place of prayer, you can see the purpose of God. You are not distracted by what the Devil is throwing at you, you are focused on the Lamb upon the throne. You give praise as those apostles did in Acts 2.

As you do, the Lord gives you a word for the city, a word for a person, a specific way to pray or prophetic act to do. Now you are seeing heaven and telling earth. This is the second half of witnessing. This is evangelism. You are now involved in what the Lord had intended when he said, **"But wait for the promise of the Father,..."** (Acts 1:4[60]).

TAKING UP YOUR MINISTRY – AND YOUR INHERITANCE

In Psalm 2 we are encouraged, **"Ask of Me and I will give You the nations for Your inheritance and the ends of the earth for Your possession"** (v.8). With this witness power came the promise of God, according to His will. Devout men out of every nation were there. He had assembled them together for this great event. The disciples had spent fifty days in prayer waiting for the power of God. When that power came, the results were beyond belief. Every nation was touched. I have been blessed to follow some of the trade routes

---

60. [4]And being assembled together with them, He commanded them not to depart from Jerusalem, but to wait for the Promise of the Father, "which," He said, "you have heard from Me

which people took from that meeting to their homes. All along the way there is documented evidence of the power of the Gospel.

You are now taking up that same ministry. Perhaps you have never felt the presence of this witnessing power. Now is a great time to begin. Lift your thoughts from this page to the Lord. He has called you to see the heavenly vision. You are included through the blood on that mercy seat. He has accepted you in the beloved.

Ask Him now for that witness power and praise Him. As He touches you, He will give you that language you have not spoken before. He will touch you with a prayer language which will be yours alone. Go ahead and declare Jesus as Lord of your life; ask Him to baptize you in the Holy Spirit. We will wait here for you because I do not want you to feel rushed in this. Take your time.

See, here we are in His presence. That was a great prayer time, wasn't it? Just a beginning really as the Lord is equipping this generation of Attack Lambs as He did those who went before us. He loves us so much and wants to pour out great blessings through us to the millions who have yet to know His name. His is a love affair with us.

....

CHAPTER 9

Reviewing the first edition chapters nine and ten, I find an oft used expression, "in the Spirit." In this second edition, I think it good to take the time to discuss the Christian meaning of this expression.

John, on the Isle of Patmos, was "in the Spirit on the Lord's day" and had an out-of-body experience. Peter, James, and John were "in the Spirit" on the Mount of Transfiguration and had an in the body experience (Matthew 17). Those "in the Spirit" will not fulfill the lust of the flesh (Galatians 5); but, will have the power to demonstrate the fruit of the Holy Spirit. So, the phrase "in the Spirit" can point to many different experiences according to the will of God.

Outside biblical reference, there is a fascination today with the paranormal experiences of people who are "in the Spirit." In this second edition, we are going to take the time to fully discuss what is valid Christian experience and offer a suggestion on what I feel is an invalid or deceptive practice. I am going to share personal experiences rather than "hearsay" and share with you my journey through which the Lord equipped me to deal with the so-called "Masters" of different levels of spiritual involvement.

But, in no way am I taking the focus away from the One who sits on the throne. These events occurred over forty years of standing in the gap and my hope is they bring clarity to the phrase and confidence in the Lamb.

THE PRESENCE OF THE LORD

To discuss being in the Spirit, we must first look at the expression "The Presence of the Lord."

God is everywhere. He is omnipresent, whether we are sensually aware or not. God is absolute, that is, He does not need the affirmation of anyone or anything else to establish His existence. In our day of relativism, we struggle with absolutes. We are trained to challenge any absolute thought. This is one of the intellectual battles we face in coming to faith, walking in faith, and releasing our faith to others. The idea that an absolute God could love me is so contradictory to postmodern thinking, that if I do not bring every thought and argument into captivity (2 Corinthians 10:5), I will miss His love. You have been trained to repeat that there is no God. Those who believe in a personal god are thought to be weaker intellectually and just caught up in the extension of their fears or father image.

Further, you were trained to believe that man was here first and made gods. Certainly, if there was a god, you would never be good enough to have the right to speak to it. You are taught to be the master of your own universe. You are on the throne of your existence and it would be foolhardy to release the reigns to some supposed deity or superpower. If you have had any spiritual experience, it has possibly been through some contact with a person perceived to be able to contact the spirit realm. Comic books and video games open up thoughts to superpowers that draw spiritual power from some source. So, when we use the term, "in the spirit" we may be referring to a clairvoyant or medium Darth Vader or "The Force" an unknowable agent for good who works through a select and highly trained few.

The fact of God's existence is reflected in all religious practice as, through ritual, people try to contact what they perceive to be a "Higher Power." The idea that you can have a personal relationship with God is unique to Christianity. The concept that a perfect, absolute, all-powerful creator and sustainer of the universe seeks a personal relationship with man is just beyond all other faiths. It is "blaspheming" to most and a very coveted ideal to others. You, as an Attack Lamb, are bringing this message, seeking to reconcile man to God and God to man. As such, you stand in the gap between what God had intended for man and what man has demanded from God.

This gap is the home of many spiritual forces that are determined to prevent man from reconciling with God. When you enter the gap and park the ark, your focus in on the One on the Throne. Your decision to praise and worship Him releases the anointing from the throne and the authority of the elders and the Spirit of God is manifest, that is to say, becomes perceptive to the human senses.

WILL YOU SHOW UP?

Laurel, a missionary new to the concept of prayer walking was in Indonesia with a team led by Jeff, a very good friend with more than ten years of daily intercession around the world. They came upon a lame person on one of their walks and Jeff suggested they pray.

Laurel said words to the effect that something good could happen if God would show up. Jeff, according to Laurel's account said something like, "God is always here, He is just waiting for you to show up."

And that about sums up the Attack Lamb perspective on "in the Spirit." We walk in the Spirit. We live in the Spirit. **"In Him we live and move and have our being"** (Acts 17:28). We are hidden with Christ in God (Colossians 3:3). He is always with us, will never forsake us (Matthew 28:20).

This assurance is seen in those who, by reason of use, have trained their senses to discern between good and evil (Hebrews 5:14).

FOCUS ON THE REAL

When people are being trained to recognize counterfeit currency, they do not study the false. Instead, they focus on the real. They know how it looks and feels. Their senses are being trained by experience with the real.

Our worship service is designed to train us in the real, that is, in the actual manifest presence of God. So that we know we have been in His presence. We feel different for having sung the songs, set aside the cares of the world, and entered into a special place at a set time. Worship is a dialogue with God, and at some point, in the worship experience, we come in contact with the reality of the Presence and Power of the Holy Spirit. We can feel the presence, our emotions are touched by the presence. We enter into worship in the throne room. I am very comfortable with the broad range of worship styles from High Church Liturgical to the roll-on-the-floor-and-holler crowd as long as the presence of God is there. Are the music and the word focused on and declaring the Glory of the Lamb? That is my only question.

The issue is style versus substance. Style has changed over the ages, but substance remains the same. Jesus promised that when two or more gather in His name, He is in their midst. A husband and wife worshipping to start or end the day are as entitled to the manifest presence as much as a great crowd or throng. You can practice the presence in your home by stopping the noise and, for a moment, focusing on the goodness of God. Saying grace before dinner is intended to do this. A prayer before getting on that school bus sets the tone for the day. A moment at that cubicle or office, in the car before that appointment, invites the manifest presence into the events of the day. When you take that moment to acknowledge Christ in your life, He takes that moment to give you strength, peace, and joy in the Holy Spirit.

THE PRESENCE AND POWER OF GOD

My mentor in this seeming basic understanding was a stockbroker. He took me under his wing when I was selling insurance and four out of seven evenings my wife and I would arrive at their home after eight in the evening for an hour and a half of prayer, worship, and Bible study. Some of those evenings, we would make a field trip to a local hospital. Securing the permission of the medical staff, we would visit and pray for people who had no family or friends in the area. We learned to hear the leading of the Lord to minister and draw from the Bible verses He quickened to us.

Sunday, after a football game in the yard and dinner, he and I would take the folders of the cases we were going to meet that week. We worshipped the Lord, declaring Him to be present in every meeting and to guide every presentation. We walked between the folders and prayed for the client's wellbeing, their families, and their salvation. We spent about an hour walking back and forth and then, with a thanksgiving cheer, Ellie and I went home to be fresh for the next day.

Was it any wonder that we were both leaders in our offices? Was it any wonder that we were able to listen to clients and share the word of God with them? Worship and standing in that gap released the anointing not just for our business, but for theirs as well.

At the time of the presentation, I could feel that same calming presence that had been with me in the prayer time. Listening for the voice of God to direct the meeting, I was able to more clearly hear the voice of the client. This was wonderful training in knowing the presence and power of God.

GRACE WITH POWER

Being invited to lead worship in the Sunday service was another wonderful training. Ours was a Bapti-costal church. We had grace with power. Our style had changed from the traditional Baptist to the Neo-Pentecostal or Charismatic style. Drums, guitar, bass, and horns had joined the piano and organ and the transition had to be served with grace and patience, especially when speaking in tongues and interpretation, prophecy, and signs and wonders began to emerge. Two hymns and a responsive reading gave way to fifty minutes of what could have become mayhem, had it not been for the common hunger for the Manifest Presence and very solid Bible teaching on the person and ministry of the Holy Spirit.

Our Pastor, Ray Patterson, had graduated from Bob Jones University and was Baptist to the bone. But the Holy Spirit captured him by healing a bedridden hospital patient and Pastor Ray started to search the scriptures concerning healing. A church member took him to the Charismatic Conference in Pittsburgh, PA, and Pastor Ray remembered an experience he had while at Bob Jones. He had experienced the manifest presence. Rededicating himself to ministry in the power of the Holy Spirit, he then gently led the church into the experience and reality of God manifesting Himself in our midst.

As a part of this, he invited four men to take turns working with his wife, who was the organist and music director, to explore the release of the gifts during worship services.

Ray and Gloria Patterson were a very rare find. Solid in their Bible and Baptist persona, they craved to see the reality of what they saw the Holy Spirit do in the book of Acts and Jesus described when He quoted Isaiah 61:1-2, "**The Spirit of the Lord is upon me, because the Lord has anointed me to preach the gospel to the poor; He has sent me to heal the brokenhearted, to proclaim liberty to the** captives, and recovery of sight to the blind, to set at liberty those who are oppressed; to proclaim the acceptable year of the Lord" (Luke 4:18-19).

The service began with a few upbeat, Psalm-based calls to worship, usually declaring the awesome greatness of our God. God inhabits the praises of His people and as the congregation left behind their preoccupations, and focused on the One on the throne, the tenor of the music changed into a softer more aware type of chorus. The Holy Spirit drew us into His presence. It was manifest, sometimes so thick in feeling that breathing seemed unnecessary. Many wept, more prayed very softly, reverently either in tongues or with understanding (1 Corinthians 14:15).

It was this point that the gifts in 1 Corinthians 12 began to manifest. Our responsibility was to be certain that all was done in biblical order and pursuant to the ministries of the anointing spoken by Jesus. As people spoke out in tongues and interpretations were given, or words of knowledge for deliverance, we four were charged with validating the flow.

We met on Thursdays to prepare the music and seek the Lord for direction in the ministry time. The Pastor did not attend the meetings and did not give us the sermon topic for he felt the message would be given through prophecy and he would bring the biblical understanding. He prepared the message well in advance and stuck to it. We were awestruck at the precision and exactness of the flow of the Holy Spirit in those services. Without the patient lovingkindness of the Pastor's wife, Gloria, I am convinced that none of this could or would have taken place. We missed notes, forgot stanzas, and tried to change from song to song in different keys, but she demonstrated love in a very tangible way. She taught us, and over several years we grew to know the manifest presence of the Holy Spirit.

Reality was what we longed for. The real presence of the real God, making real and lasting changes in our lives. A salesman, a broker, an engineer, and a high school principal, all being trained to hear from the Lord, know when to be still and when to speak, and how to lead hundreds of people into that awareness.

WARNING FLARES

Seeking the reality of God became a lifestyle for our families. Hearing His voice, comparing with the others what we had heard, confirming with the Pastor the things we thought the Lord was saying to us. Around this level of God-fearing integrity, the church grew and grew. Some craziness came with new people but when they got into the rhythm of growth the Lord had established, they soon found the strength and security the ministry provided. They began to realize the manifest presence and the gifts of the Holy Spirit, they too began to prosper.

When you have the real, the false sends off warning flares before you.

A couple came to the church. Well dressed and very soft-spoken, they avoided invitations by the Pastor and the elders of the church. They began to draw people who were less established in the Bible, or who were looking for more exotic manifestations than a Holy Spirit. The leadership team observed and commented to each other, but did not speak judgment out of courtesy and humility.

Reports began to circulate of events that happened in small, by-invitation-only meetings at this couple's home. None of the leadership team were ever invited, but the number of attendees was increasing and they were all church members. Knowing that the glory of His inheritance is in the church, we finally had a chat with the couple whose declared motive for the meetings was to "help the people get in contact with their former selves so that, through prayer, hurts of their previous lives could be healed."

When asked, "What former selves?" The couple assured us that we all had been here on earth before.

That is not the Holy Spirit. We were known in Christ before the foundations of the world, but we have only one physical life on this earth. "It is appointed to man once to die and then the judgment." The couple had received errant teaching about past lives, and under the guise of "helping people resolve their issues," had brought it into the church. When we asked them to please discontinue the meetings and stop inviting the people, they put out the word that we were not on the same spiritual plane as they.

The Pastor's response: I don't want to be on that plane.

The church continued to grow and the worship services were so very rich. The presence of God and the solid Bible teaching were the perfect answer to a spirit hungry generation. Pastor would often say, "Too much Bible we dry up, too much Spirit we blow up." Balance and biblical accuracy were the two pillars of the work; the Patterson husband and wife team assured humility in both areas.

A CLEAR

The ability of the anointing to proclaim liberty to the captives resulted in our prayer for and ministry to many emotionally or mentally ill people. We as a church worked hand-in-hand with medical doctors and psychiatrists in the area and were available to them for prayer with their patients. One of these doctors, Roger Shore, brought us a man who would be strongly used by God in my life to teach me the way of spiritism. We will call him Ben for this teaching purpose.

Ben was a recluse. He was drawn to the church because of our reputation for moving in the Spirit. Dr. Shore encountered Ben, and after weeks of bringing him to church, brought him to our pastoral team to hear his story and, hopefully, to have him understand the difference between the spirit realm he served and that of the Holy Spirit. Ben felt that he lived "in the spirit."

Dr. Shore's question was, "What spirit?"

No one liked to be around Ben because he was very old and nasty, and would take off on rants laced with vulgarity and profanity that would drive you away. I, on the other hand, was as intrigued as Dr.

Shore as to the emotional makeup of this man. After a discussion with our Pastor, Dr. Shore and I decided to continue with Ben and to see how expressing the love of Jesus to him might breakthrough his mantra. We met with him on Sundays after church services.

After one very perverse tirade, Ben's countenance changed abruptly. He smiled at me and said, "You are a 'Clear'."

"A what?"

"A clear, and I can teach you to 'audit' the spiritual state of others."

I was confused, to say the least, and asked him what on earth he was talking about.

With a wry smile, he began to share with me about his long friendship with L. Ron Hubbard, the author of *Dianetics*, and the founder of the Church of Scientology. For all of the afternoon and evening, Ben told me that his rants were just a way to audit people's spiritual, emotional, and mental conditions. He could, by their response to different words or word images, read their level of conflict within the three compartments of their soul.

But, he asserted, he could go beyond that and know their probabilities of thought and action, and through suggestion, both verbal and telepathic become a guide or mentor to them. This he had learned traveling with Hubbard throughout Asia on a private ship.

I had never heard of L. Ron Hubbard or *Dianetics*, or Scientology. Ben insisted that I was the first "clear" he had found and, as the evening concluded, suggested that we have more sessions. I agreed and reported directly to my Pastor and the Doctor.

We did a crash course on *Dianetics*, and a Biblical response, and found that one of the keys to releasing the power to "read" others was taught to be held by just a handful of senior leaders of the Church of Scientology. Our question was how they did it.

These leaders had been encouraged to sign a Billion Year Agreement as the church taught that they were a spirit and would return in another body after death. They were, as such, eternal in nature but had to receive cleansing of all conflict in their souls through an "auditor" who would know the right questions to ask to release them.

Ben was an heir to a large fortune, had never worked in his life, and owned a very lucrative business along with two other siblings. To be accepted in this "higher level" eternal group, he was expected to contribute a percentage of his net worth and gains each year.

Ben had left the Church of Scientology over financial disagreements. However, he had been searching for another "clear" with whom he could communicate on that higher spiritual level. He had decided I was that person.

Sound crazy? It certainly did to me until, at that same time, my older brother offered me a copy of *Dianetics* by L Ron Hubbard. The thought of my brother becoming involved in such a crazy thing encouraged me to take the time to work it all through with Ben, responding to the issues with biblical truth.

One of his oft used expressions was, "in the spirit."

There were dangers in this exploration because you could easily be drawn into the fallacy. When he would share, there was almost a seduction going on. Biblical absolutes became the fortress of protection for my mind so that when Ben would quote one of his learned principles, my mind would respond with the Word of God. It must have been the helmet of salvation; the word of faith was more powerful than spiritism because it is absolute in nature.

When I would counter with scripture, Ben would go perverse with so much vulgarity but my spirit would remain calm as I focused on the throne and the Lamb. Hours of encounters went on over weeks of counseling. Finally, Ben declared that I was the stronger and he needed to listen to me. The Lion had come out of the Lamb.

I recall that particular session was on a Sunday afternoon. The services for the day had ended and my wife had taken our boys home. Ben and I, with two-quart jars of my wife's homemade vegetable soup, had settled down in the church kitchen. He rambled for a while as I heated and served the soup. He scowled at the soup and fed up with him I retorted, "If you don't want it, then don't take it. I personally don't care what you think of vegetable soup."

He stared, looked at me, and proclaimed that I had the higher power and he needed to listen to me.

So, we talked about the love of God in Jesus and the fact that we have one life to live and what had he done with his. He shared the hurts of his childhood and why he had sought something that could heal those hurts. He had not clearly heard the Gospel, how Jesus would put love in your heart and deliver you from fear. That afternoon he prayed and as he received Jesus, felt the false spirit leave as the real Spirit arrived.

He wept. This old codger of a man, who had been through so much falsehood and deception, wept. He had remorse for his language and actions. His mind was cleansed of the images he had rehearsed for so many years. As a member of the "higher level" group, he had seen sexual perversion and was cleansed of those images. His life began to change.

I stayed close with Ben for several years. The more worship he was in, the more his heart softened until he became a smiling old man who was always in church. His charitable foundation was required by law to donate a certain amount per quarter and we would go through many ministries and research what they were accomplishing and distribute the funds. How he enjoyed blessing people anonymously. Never drawing attention to himself, he made wonderful things possible and died a very happy man.

The things Ben taught me have never left. I learned to control my mind and emotions in encounters with spirit and intellectual forces. However, I never crossed over to the control of others, but I could really discern when those powers of the Archas and Exousias were being focused on me. As we focus on the throne and give glory to the Lamb all things become "clear."

Or as Tom Cruise put it, "Crystal."

CHI GUNG

Ben was brought to us by God to prepare us for the powers we would encounter in the Chi Gung centers of China. Chi Gung is the release of the Chi which is thought to be a life essence flowing from the bones. Release of the Chi is thought to give health, longer life, peace of mind, and the ability to control the thoughts and actions of others. This is the Archas (who has preeminence), Exousias (who has the right to speak or the word), Kosmokratos (who is going to govern thought and action), and in the extreme Poneerias (thoughts or actions that cause harm to another human) from Ephesians 6:12.

In Chi Gung, you can leave the body and be "in the spirit." The idea is to ascend through the levels of the heavenlies to receive fulfillment, enlightenment, and power from the heavenly spirit realm. This is done through meditation, self-emptying, and focus on nothingness so that the spirit is no longer under the suppression of the body and soul. Breathing rhythm is very important for the release of the mind to the spirit plane. Ben explained all of this to me giving vivid detail of the release from the three levels of will, intellect, and emotion which we define as the soul.

THE CITY ABOVE

On one of our prayer journeys to China, we went to stand in the gap for Beijing. In the center of that beautiful city is the Tiananmen square and the Forbidden City. During those years, on the third Monday of June each year, I would take a group to walk and pray for China. Our journey included the Great Hall of the People, the Great Wall, Mao's Tomb, The Temple of Heaven, and whole days walking around and praying in the Square.

On this day we had started early with a walk around the square and an hour of prayer on the four corners and then entered the Forbidden City praying for the release of the Chinese people around the world. This took until early afternoon.

Exiting the Forbidden City complex at the North Gate, we took tricycle rides to the Beihai Park, a beautiful place with a high hill in the center surrounded by a moat-like lake. It was a festive and very happy place and we enjoyed photo opportunities and Facebook exchanges with Chinese who had come from the four corners of China to see this wonder of the world. They were so very eager to meet people from the USA and loved to take pictures with us. We were, of course, observed by authorities, but who has a problem with a flock of lambs?

The central hill is capped by a stupa and a worship temple for the Spirit of Beijing. With encouragement from developed countries, China had relaxed its oppression of the Christian Church and had created Buddhist worship points. Knowing little about Buddhism, they had imported different idols and placed them in significant places for the Chinese people to enjoy the freedom of worship. The idol in this place was the many-handed Vishnu from the Indian Shiva-Vishnu group.

Walking past the statues of the traditional gatekeepers and the eight immortals, our group climbed the hundred steps to reach the second level and then ascended the third group of steps to come to the stone archway that was the entrance to the highest level. From this covering, people climbed the final stairway to stand before the idol which had been placed at the apex of the arch and was covered by another arch. From this high place, we could see the Forbidden City and Tiananmen Square and the Great Hall of the People. To the west was the garrison of special police and military headquarters.

Entering the lower arch, I encountered a Chi Gung Practitioner. Breathing deeply, with hands extended, palms up, and fingers in the reception position, he was in a trance and fully out of touch with those supportive followers around him. I stepped out of the way of the passing tour groups and waited for this man to "come back."

After some time, he opened his eyes and, with a fulfilled smile, greeted me. Through the brother translating I asked, "How high did you go?"

"What?" He asked.

"How high did you go?"

"Very high, higher than ever before, this place has great power and is a wonderful portal."

"Did you see the city above?" I asked.

"City?"

"Yes, there is a city 1,500 miles long, 1,500 miles wide and 1,500 miles high. Did you see it?"

He began a conversation with the translator about who I was and if I was a Master and is there really a city. The translator assured him that I knew what I was talking about and he should learn from me.

"How can I know about the city?" He gestured to the translator to ask me the question.

"Oh, the knowledge is in the book."

"Is it a Western book?"

"No, it is an Eastern book written by a man who was in the Spirit and caught up to the city and the throne room and the presence of all enlightenment."

"I have one here, in Chinese, and my friend here can sit with you awhile and share with you how to get to the city."

He and the translator went off to the side where there were park benches and beautiful shaded grottos. Soon, their heads were together as they excitedly explored the last book of a Chinese Bible and the revelation of Jesus Christ. I continued to climb the stairs to pray for the people of Beijing and continue to reach out to those who had come from so far.

When I climbed back down, I was met by a changed man who realized that he had a good idea, to know God, but the wrong spirit. He asked me to come to his city of Chengdu, where he was the master of a community of Chi Gung followers and to bring to them this truth: there is a God, He has a Son, His name is Jesus, He is risen from the dead, and seated on the throne in the midst of the city where He is the light.

We arranged to visit this center on a subsequent journey.

Many cults use sleep deprivation and mind control to break down the "walls of the mind" so that their followers were able to get "in the spirit." This place was no different. A former deep shaft coal mine, now portrayed as a spiritual retreat, the walls of the shafts had been overlaid with reinforced cement and filled with bunk beds. Into these chambers was piped very loud music and the lights were never turned off. With the music came the training instruction of the Masters to teach the follower how fasting from sleep would numb the senses to release the spirit for ascendency.

Once you had overcome the restrictions of the mind and body, you could live in the spirit realm. Now out of the cult, our friend could not return to the place so we just "dropped by" to have a look. Our group was taken to the master and as he stood in front of me, taking an "audit" of my spirit level, I could not help but think of Ben. This man was his Chinese cousin right down to the long eyebrow hairs and mad dog eyes.

Drawing peace from Jesus and focused on His love for this man, I passed the test and our group was invited into an ample room for further discovery. A discussion ensued which had all the questions Ben had said that spiritists would use. Finally, the man asked for a demonstration of Chi from me.

Jesus is so faithful. With a perfectly straight face and a very "spiritual" demeanor, I approached the wall where he sat. Taking time to set my feet and adjust my balance I reach out to the wall so that my fingertips barely skimmed its painted surface. With eyes closed and softly praying in tongues, I swung my arm downward and circled overhead to reach again to the wall. My fingers completed the ark about 3 inches short of the wall surface. He was amazed.

Continuing in a trance-like posture I reversed the process and the fingers returned to their original position. With great glee, the man affirmed my great power. I could, he declared, lengthen and shorten bones.

He had never been in a third-grade class in an American school where all the kids learned about shoulder rotation. This to him was great enlightenment. He guided the tour and allowed us to give "Help from Above" tracts to all the people in the center. This excellent gospel information was so perfect for those who were seeking God but through the wrong spirit.

After the tour, we stood again facing each other. "I can heal you," he said. "May I take a scan?"

"Sure," I replied, "If I may scan you after."

Assuming his "in the spirit" pose, he moved his right hand down and up in front of, but not touching me. For all the world he looked like a Chinese Ben.

"You have high blood pressure and a heart problem," he said. "I can heal you."

"No offense," I replied. "But I have neither. Now, may I scan you?"

Assuming the same posture and moving my hand in the same way while speaking in tongues I completed the scan.

"Sir," I said with complete respect and all the love that would flow from the throne. "You have a very interesting heart. You have been feeling that you are losing heart strength and in fact, there is a hole, very tiny, in your heart. It is in the shape of a cross. Very interesting shape. But, do not be afraid, when you receive the mark of the cross of Jesus on your heart, you will be healed.

"Jesus is the source of all valid healing. You have been hearing about Him and you want to know Him but you are afraid that if you leave this place, how will you live? I am here to tell you that Jesus loves you and he will heal your heart and He will make a place for you.

"Will you make a place in your heart for Him?"

"Thank you, thank you, you are so great in spirit, thank you," He went on in Chinese as he walked us to the exit.

With a hug and a handshake, we took our leave. He accepted the literature and we can only believe that the Lord spoke to him.

Power encounters while prayer walking proves the scripture, Greater is He that is in you than he that is in the world.

"In the spirit" means different things to different people.

My understanding that I would share with you is that we can live in the Spirit. With no particular sensation, we can still be assured of the presence of the Holy Spirit in our lives, so that we do not have to go through a particular ritual to increase spirituality.

A second thought on this is that we are the "temple of the Holy Spirit" (1 Corinthians 6:19). He is dwelling in us just like He dwells above the mercy seat of the ark. He lives in us and we in Him so that we are always "in the Spirit." When we focus on Him, either individually or corporately, He manifests His presence with the fullness of joy. Times of refreshing come from focused time in worship. Practicing the manifest presence, or awareness of His being there is a discipline especially in a nonmonastic setting. To be "in the Spirit" at a recital, or a dentist's office, or sports event means that while we enjoy or endure, we have a companion who is vital in our lives.

....

CHAPTER 10

Since writing the first edition of Attack Lambs, I have spent a great deal of time pondering and reflecting upon Paul's description of Spiritual Wisdom found in 1 Corinthians 2:6-16. It is foundational to his discussion of the gifts of the Holy Spirit in chapters 12-14 of the same letter. The Christians at Corinth were coming away from a culture of spiritism to a culture of spirituality. Many people, like Ben, have made this transition, nowhere more so than in the spiritual kingdom of Thailand where the King is revered as the current incarnation of the Hindu god Vishnu.

Wisdom is, by definition, the application of knowledge. How does our knowledge of the victory of the Lamb and His indwelling presence by the Holy Spirit shape our lives and calling to reconcile man to God? Wisdom tells us what actions to take, and when to take them. Wisdom tells us what words to speak and when to speak them. With the Chi Gung master, wisdom directed us to describe the destination he was seeking so that we might introduce him to the Way. In the second scenario, a child's game against a wall rather than a debate or explanation was used by the Lord to open an entire cult center to receive gospel literature. The hours spent listening to and deprogramming Ben paid huge dividends in encounters with spiritual forces and brought to life the teaching Paul gave to the church at Corinth.

THE KEY

As we pick up the flow of Paul's letter in the second chapter, **"For I determined not to know anything among you except Jesus Christ and Him crucified. I was with you in weakness, in fear, and in much trembling (The Lamb). And my speech and my preaching were not with persuasive words of human wisdom, but in demonstration of the Spirit and of power (The Lion), that your faith should not be in the wisdom of men but in the power of God"** (1 Corinthians 2:2-5[61]).

Paul stepped into the gap in the nature of the Lamb but with the confidence of the Lion. His goal for the church was to have them understand that while they were very human, the treasure they had inside was the most powerful force in the universe. The wisdom they were about to receive concerning being "in the Spirit" will result in

61. [2]For I determined not to know anything among you except Jesus Christ and Him crucified. [3]I was with you in weakness, in fear, and in much trembling. [4]And my speech and my preaching were not with persuasive words of human wisdom, but in demonstration of the Spirit and of power, [5]that your faith should not be in the wisdom of men but in the power of God.

the growth of the church to fulfill its calling. But Paul gives them the same focal instruction that Jesus gave the 70 others in Luke 10. Paul focused on Christ. This is the key to being in the Spirit, realizing the presence of the Holy Spirit and releasing the anointing of the Holy Spirit.

We are easily drawn away to tales of encounters that do not focus on the Lamb. Paul has determined to keep the church focused on the only One worthy of glory, honor, power, might, and dominion. In this cosmopolitan city of Corinth, this was as essential as it is in our globalized world. If you want the presence, power, and wisdom that goes with it, you must maintain your focus on Christ.

THE HOW AND WHY

Over the years since the first edition, I have heard many stories of people transferred in the Holy Spirit and taken into the heavenlies. I do not cast aside all the stories, but I listen to hear the giving of glory to the Lamb because everything in the vision described by John, gives glory to the Lamb. This is a subtle but powerful rule of discernment for those things that are of the Spirit of God will declare the Lordship of Jesus, but those that are not, will not (1 Corinthians 12:3[62]).

However, we speak wisdom among those who are mature, yet not the wisdom of this age, nor of the rulers of this age, who are coming to nothing. But we speak the wisdom of God in a mystery, the hidden wisdom which God ordained before the ages for our glory, which none of the rulers of this age knew; for if they had known, they would not have crucified our Lord of glory

1 Corinthians 2:6-8

Wisdom is the application of knowledge. Paul is about to tell us how the knowledge of who Jesus is equips us with the wisdom to dispel the forces that hold man captive and prevent them from

---

62. [3]Therefore I make known to you that no one speaking by the Spirit of God calls Jesus accursed, and no one can say that Jesus is Lord except by the Holy Spirit.

reconciliation with God. The rulers (Kosmokratos) of the day did not recognize the Lamb of God, for He did not fit their profile.

You have a cache of wisdom set aside to equip you as an Attack Lamb. It is stored in the word of God which you are to read each day. It is stored in the Spirit of God and will be released to your spirit as you worship. You will receive the divinely appointed and prepared wisdom God knows you will need to make decisions for your life, to impart to others as you multiply your faith in them, and to speak to the nations as the Lord gives opportunity. This has already been prepared for you, and as you come out of the multitude, serve Christ as a Believer, order your ways after His word as a Disciple, and receive anointing and direction as an Apostle, you will reach maturity and put Christ and those He loves before yourself. This is Christian maturity, to put others before ourselves.

Why would anyone leave father, mother, home, and lands to enter into ridiculously dangerous places to reconcile God and man? It makes no sense. Why would anyone volunteer to work in the childcare of the church while famous people pour forth mighty messages from its pulpit? Why would anyone set aside the procurement of perfectly legitimate toys and spend the money to help the less fortunate? Because they have learned that a mature Christian thinks of others more highly than himself (Philippians 2:3[63]).

Because they have had their eyes opened to realize the glory of His inheritance in the saints and this understanding compels them to use their time on earth to expand the inheritance. They want an equal portion of a big thing and they are willing to lay aside their privileges to obtain the greater glory.

But, as it is written: "Eye has not seen, nor ear heard, nor have entered into the heart of man the things which God has prepared for those who love Him." But God has revealed them to us through His Spirit. For the

---

63. [3]Let nothing be done through selfish ambition or conceit, but in lowliness of mind let each esteem others better than himself.

Spirit searches all things, yes, the deep things of God. For what man knows the things a man except the spirit of the man which is in him? Even so no one knows the things of God except the Spirit of God
1 Corinthians 2:9-11

When we are "in the Spirit," the Spirit is in us. The deep things of God are spoken to our spirit and from there to our mind. The Holy Spirit works from the inside out. Once you have received Jesus into your heart, He begins to, through the Holy Spirit unpack the wisdom waiting for you since before the foundation of the earth. The Holy Spirit becomes the "how" and the "why".

Now we have received, not the spirit of the world, but the Spirit who is from God, that we might know the things that have been freely given to us by God. These things we also speak, not in words which man's wisdom teaches but which the Holy Spirit teaches, comparing spiritual things with spiritual   1 Corinthians 2:12-13

HEIRS OF THE FATHER

The fruit of the Spirit we have received will authenticate the message He will give. The life of the Attack Lamb must reflect the presence of the Lion. God is love. Therefore, all things coming forth from Him demonstrate His love for man. His voice is reaching out in love, so John tells us that we love Him because He first loved us.

Standing in the gap for people caught in spiritual deception, we must reach out with love. Enveloped in the Holy Spirit, we must, through the power of His might, reach through every offense to rescue those who have been taken captive.

The gateways through which the spirit of the world operates are the lust of the flesh, the lust of the eyes, and the pride of life. If a sensation causes you to feel better, look better, or seem better than others, then it is the spirit of the world at work. We can see orchards of the spirit of the world giving fruit of the spirit of the world and enticing people to eat of the fruit and become part with the spirit of the world. The Church of Scientology is a splendid example of the organized worship of the spirit of the world. From the structure to the elitism, this group holds full control over the actions of its members and teaches that they are the saviors of mankind and the planet. With this, they infiltrate government positions to steal communications that they feel are not according to their understanding of how the world should be.

The spirit of this age is now and has always worked, in what Paul calls the "sons of disobedience," of which we were part before knowing Jesus (Ephesians 2:2[64]). But since we have received the Lord and found our position in Him at the right hand of the Father, He has given us His Spirit and, with Him, His wisdom.

But God has given us His Spirit so we are no longer under the control of the spirit of the age, but are filled with and living in the Holy Spirit. For as many as are led by the Spirit of God, they are the sons of God, and if sons, then heirs.

SPIRIT VERSUS SPIRIT

1 Corinthians 2:13[65] frames our manner of conversation with Masters of other spirits. We do not explain or proclaim the message of Jesus according to man's wisdom. Instead, comparing spiritual things with spiritual, we speak to the spirit in each person. Love is a heart language. Many aspects of love cannot be explained with more than a deep sigh. Love touches the entire being. Intellect fades in the presence of love and God is love. God loved us so much that He gave His only son that whoever would receive Him would gain the right to be called the sons of God, as many as believed in His name (John 1:12).

---

64. [2]in which you once walked according to the course of this world, according to the prince of the power of the air, the spirit who now works in the sons of disobedience

65. [13]These things we also speak, not in words which man's wisdom teaches but which the Holy Spirit teaches, comparing spiritual things with spiritual.

"God is Spirit and those who worship Him must worship in spirit and truth" (John 4:24).

Our obedience to stand in the gap between God and man releases His Spirit of Love. This is the greatest power available to man, for love never fails (1 Corinthians 13:8[66]). This is one of those absolutes. Love does not and cannot fail for it is the essence of God. All other spirits must submit themselves to the Spirit of God. We do not argue but bring argument captive. We do not confront with judgment for we ourselves are judged by God. We stand in the love of Jesus for the person and radiate the indomitable force of love.

LOVE WINS THE DAY

Mark praying for the Mahayana in Cambodia

The Sangharaja of the Theravada sect of Buddhism placed his hand in mine. We were at Angkor Wat in Cambodia and meeting for the first time. He is known as the "Gandhi of Cambodia" and has more than a million followers around the world. He attended the World Conference on Religion and Peace in 1994 and carries an amazing spiritual presence.

---

66. [8]Love never fails. But whether there are prophecies, they will fail; whether there are tongues, they will cease; whether there is knowledge, it will vanish away.

I asked for the opportunity to pray for him and he extended his hand. I started to pray when my mouth went completely dry, I could barely breathe and my head felt like it was going to burst with pain. Thank God I had spent time with Ben. I focused quickly on the Throne of God and received a burst of love. The Holy Spirit flowed through me and gave me a prayer for the man, avoiding the oppression that flowed from him in the encounter. At the end of our discussion and prayer, comparing the spiritual quest of Buddha with the Spirit of Love in Jesus, the man called the Living Buddha proclaimed, Jesus is The Way.

Love overcame the conflict. Love won the day. Definitely not any persuasion of mine. Love declared the Way. There is a great move of the Spirit of God in Cambodia today and from there it will spread throughout Southeast Asia because the key man has had his eyes opened.

A SPIRITUAL KINGDOM

Thailand is a spiritual kingdom. The King is said to be the incarnation of the Hindu god Vishnu. We have had Attack Lamb teams in every province of that beautiful nation. Because of the powers of the spirits, fortune tellers and mediums, enjoying a flourishing business, from Singapore and Malaysia come north to receive spiritual direction for their enterprises. The town of Hat Yai, Thailand is known throughout Asia as a place of spiritual intensity. In one of its temples is the skeleton of a famous mystic who was thought to be Buddha incarnate.

To receive spiritual power, mediums come to this temple, fast 40 days and sleep beside the bones. Tales of signs and wonders follow them.

Dr. Agatha Chan called and asked me to join a team of Attack Lambs led by Pastor Ho, a Chinese Methodist leader from Kuala Lumpur, who was shielding in his church a businesswoman from Singapore. We will call her Elaine for this testimony. Dr. Chan was a medical doctor with a Ph.D. in Psychiatry and a friend of Rev. Ho. She had been called in to treat Elaine and felt that there was a spiritual situation involved. Agatha, Ho, and I have formed a team before to pray in different places. We worked well together and I was very happy to join them again.

Elaine had been a very successful businesswoman in Singapore. Physically beautiful and very well known in society, she had married a very successful man and they were the talk of the Country Club. Theirs was a match for the ages.

He was doing business in China and, like many Singaporean businessmen, got involved with one of the ladies the Chinese provided as companions for their evening celebrations. His business trips became longer and carried over weekends until Elaine realized that his trips were not for business—he had taken up relations with this woman.

When Elaine confronted him, he confessed and told her that she would just have to live with it. She would be well taken care of in the public eye so that the business would not suffer, but he would not break up with the other woman.

Elaine went up to Thailand to see a medium. She had heard the reputation of a monk who had a small temple and, for a fee, could actually put a curse on someone. Others in Singapore had used the services of the monk and though expensive, he could produce.

She went to the monk and, after receiving his retainer, he went to work with all the power of Thai Black Magic. Nothing happened to the husband, but every curse that was directed to the man came back on her.

Her physical beauty disappeared in a week leaving her disfigured.

She returned to Thailand and she and the monk cut a covenant, cutting their wrists and mixing their blood in wine, drank the wine so that the power of the monk would enter her.

She began to have life-threatening internal issues and was hospitalized. The doctors, who thought her to be totally insane, treated and released her to the custody of her friends.

They contacted Pastor Ho who contacted Dr. Chan. Elaine was brought from Singapore to Kuala Lumpur and housed at the Methodist guest house under 24-hour watch, served by volunteer women of the church. The nights were filled with screams of terror as she writhed in pain. Metal needles came out of her skin as well as razor blades from her privates. Nonstop prayer was offered for her and she was embraced with love by the church.

We met as a team and felt that we needed to take her to Thailand, confront the monk, and reverse the curse that had been placed upon her. A team was formed from SEAPC affiliates with experience and Pastor Ho's intercessors, and we made the journey. Pastor Ho and his Malaysian team searched for the monk while our SEAPC team went to the temples and spirit centers to stand in the gap and release the anointing.

We were told that the monk was no longer alive. Someone had come up from Singapore and killed him and burned his temple to the ground. With this news, we had no way for the spiritual confrontation that we felt would release Elaine.

A young boy approached Pastor and told him that the monk had survived and fled to the mountains of North Thailand. He was supposed to be in a region in which we had worked previously so we contacted a pastoral team from the region, formed an international team, and headed north.

FROM LITTLE CLOUD TO POWERFUL WHIRLWIND

We arrived at the mountaintop village on a beautiful Thai morning. We had two vans and the local pastor and I rode on his motorbike. The monk had purchased a very large land and was building a spiritual center with fifty or so disciples already gathered to gain his power. The community had noticed the increased number of foreigners who came to get fortunes from the man.

With Elaine in one van with Pastor Ho and his team and our team in another, we wound our way to the high place. Deep in the valley was a little cloud that seemed to have lost its way. Often it takes till midday for these clouds to evaporate and this one was like a jewel set against the verdant hillside.

Elaine remained in the van with the church team while we approached the monk's house. The local Pastor introduced me as a Fortune Teller from America who had heard about this monk and his abilities and would like to have a session with him. They discussed it, and the monk agreed.

The disciples were called from their duties and we sat under a roof in a large circle. The monk sat cross-legged on a pillow, so his head was above mine, and Pastor Lek and I sat in front of him. We engaged stares, and he spoke first.

"You are a man great in spirit." He waited for Lek to translate.

"You will travel to many lands."

"Nothing will harm you."

"Watch out for the Muslims, they will try to kill you."

And with this and a very satisfied smile, he bowed.

I took his hand in mine and looked into his eyes. Speaking in tongues for a minute or so I said to him.

"You have been having a recurrent nightmare."

"You are spinning down a funnel toward a fire and you cannot get out."

"A man looks down on you, he is young, he has been beaten, his beard has been ripped from his face and his skin is torn. He has scars on his forehead that look like a crown."

"You know that if you can call his name, you will not go into the fire, but you do not know the name."

"Just as the heat of the fire begins to touch your feet, you wake up."

"You have not slept for days because every time you start to doze off, you start to spin downward again."

"How does he know?" the man asked Lek, trembling from head to toe, sweat beading on his brow.

"He's good," Lek answered.

"I can tell you the name to call," I said in the most loving tone I could manage, "But once you know that name you must leave all of this and serve that name only. Do you want to know the name of the man in your dream?"

"Yes," he said. "You must tell me."

"But you understand," I repeated. "Once you know the name you can serve no other. Do you want to know the name?"

"Yes, I must know the name," He said with such urgency.

"His name is Jesus," I said firmly, and in very gentle tones.

He snatched his hand free and struck Pastor Lek across the face. Leaping to his feet he ran around and around the circle screaming, "You must never say that name! You must never say that name!"

He rushed into his house and could be heard screaming from within.

A wind began to blow. It got stronger and stronger. It blew over the candles and altarpieces and finally, up from the valley, came a huge strong gray whirlwind it tore through the spirit center lifting laminated roofing in its path and rose out of sight in the blue sky.

The door on the van opened and Elaine stepped out, fear gone, beauty restored, totally set free.

We rejoiced, got back in our vehicles and spent the day praying for the region.

CHANGE IN A SPIRITUAL KINGDOM

Returning to Chiang Mai that evening, we met with our Senior Pastor in the morning. Under his arm was a copy of the Bangkok paper reporting a phenomenon of whirlwinds throughout Thailand at exactly the hour in which we spoke to the monk.

Elaine is now serving the Lord in another country and, at last report, her church had grown to 7,000 members.

We then did outreaches in the Isaan region of Thailand with teams of youth from churches in Singapore and saw thousands of young people come to Christ. The Attack Lambs first edition was translated in Thai and we have taught the material in hundreds of churches covering every province of the nation.

We do not come in the spirit of the world, but in the Spirit, who is Christ.

The spiritual man discerns all things and is discerned of none. Lambs on the outside with the Lion on the inside, we enter in or appear as an irrelevant or extraneous circumstance, just another westerner looking for a prophecy, just another fan in the stands, just another businessman, broker, engineer, or teacher. Not anything on the outside that would appeal to the natural man, but filled with the Holy Spirit and the name at which all spirits will submit themselves.

We have not received the spirit of the world.

We are "in the Spirit of God."

CHAPTER 11

CUT THE GRASS

My father loved my mother. My siblings and I grew up in the radiance of that love. We were not wealthy and my father's truck driver's salary did not enable him to give her the beautiful gifts he so much wanted to. He could not afford to buy her fancy crystal vases or flower arrangements, so we filled winter evenings planning our flower beds. We would map out the smallest detail of what would go where, how tall it would grow and what colors would look good together, etc.

Then, at the earliest possible moment, the work would begin. The result was, from early Spring to late Autumn, our yard became a floral display of his undying devotion.

Mother was just as much in love with him. Each evening when he arrived home she presented her love offering to him: a freshly cooked, hot meal of his liking. We children never had the option to decline our father's taste in food. But no matter. Mother would cook wonderful German dishes which filled the house with rich aroma. Our young mouths would water in anticipation. Spetzle was my hands-down favorite.

The garden, which my mother could view from her bedroom window, was of particular importance to my father; it was the tangible measure of his adoration of her. A continual Valentine card in flowers. But there was more than just flowers.

A gray stone walkway was bordered by carefully placed red bricks and then lined with dark topsoil. Meticulous edging, done by hand tools on the grass which grew next to the topsoil, kept a neat, straight line of contrast between the two. Then the grass was cut in patterns, also meticulously. If my father felt a plaid would be nice, or a herring bone, then it was our job to create the sensation with the hand mower and roller, gently bending the blades in his desired expression.

Never did we just fire up a power mower and tear blindly through the grass. After the lawn was mowed, the edges of the grass were trimmed with hand shears so the grass was of uniform height.

He was certain to instruct us that gray was gray, red was red, and black was black and green grass clippings did not belong on any of them.

The flowers were set in mulched beds. The deep brown of the mulch gave subtle contrast to the fresh green of the young shoots. Each plant was set in an exact spot according to our winter drawings, so, as the blooming season progressed, there was a continual cascade of love which my mother observed from the window.

DINNER TIME

The center piece of her table setting was an arrangement of flowers from his offering. Around these were set our six places. Father at the head, my brothers on his left side, Mother at the other head, my sister beside her, and me at my father's right hand.

The table was set to perfection. Each of us children had a day to set it and the precision would make the Sultan's meal look like a microwave special. Fork handles were as specifically placed as marigolds. Plates shown as the petals of her favorite roses. She responded to his love with gleaming joy and pristine passion.

My father arrived home from work each day at the same time, 6:00 PM. That was the time at which we were expected to be home from our activities, washed, neatly dressed, and ready to enjoy a family meal. We voluntarily ordered our lives around this specific hour. Our respect was made easy by Mother's example. If he was late, there was no bickering; she would take out the double boilers and keep the food at serving temperature until he arrived. We did not eat until he came.

THE LESSON OF A LIFETIME

One Spring Saturday my father woke me very early, just before he left for work, and said, "Cut the grass."

Several hours later when my teenaged eyes finally opened I remembered my friends and I had made big plans for the day. All through the long winter and early spring we had waited for the ball fields to be ready for our baseball games, and the swimming hole water to be warm enough for the daring among us to take the plunge. Today was the day.

I swept through the kitchen, baseball bat in one hand and glove in the other, and had just opened the back door to leave when mother called, "Did your father ask you to cut the grass?"

I was well and truly caught.

Knowing it was futile to attempt escape, I rushed to the garage, got out the mower, never checked to see the pattern, forgot about the edging and the clipping and tore through the grass parts of the garden, leaving a wake of fresh clippings washed ashore on beaches of brown mulch, red brick, and gray walkway. Of course I finished in record time. I grabbed up my glove and bat and dashed off with my friends to an afternoon of baseball and swimming.

I arrived home at 5:30 in anticipation of our 6:00 feast. The aroma of mother's offering was spectacular. The gentle breeze carried its sweet savors into the whole neighborhood and embraced me while still far from home. We were having spetzles.

Spetzles are these little dumplings unique to the Bavarian homeland of our family. They are more than wonderful. My father, brothers and I would always bet to see who could eat the most. We could pack away bushels of spetzles. Then we would all sit back in our chairs and tell Mother how great that batch was and pat our stomachs and enjoy the moment of sheer gluttony.

Passing through the kitchen I verified that we were about to consume my favorite meal. I could taste it as I washed and put on a clean shirt. My mouth was watering as I went to my place at the table. I had to sit on my hands to keep from sampling the feast before me.

My father had arrived from work. I heard the sound of the car as it entered the drive way. His voice was pleasant as he called to my mother. I heard the familiar sounds as he washed off the grime of another day on the road and heard the steady pace of his footfall as he climbed the steps to the living area.

Their greeting was always the same. He smiled at her and she came to him and they gave a little peck. They never embraced in front of the children, but the intensity of their eyes set the standard for each of our marriages. He then checked the stove top and expressed his appreciation for her labor of love.

A LESSON LEARNED

When Father came into the dining room it was our signal to assemble. We four children never had to be called a second time. From my place at his right hand I watched the others as they came to the table. Each one had been involved in something but dropped it immediately when my father signaled that the time had come. Our worlds revolved around his timing.

We joined hands and he prayed. It was the same at every dinner I can remember. He always humbled himself and our family to acknowledge Jesus as our Savior and Provider. My left hand disappeared in the giant gentleness of his right hand. The strength of that bond was to hold me to Christ for all time.

With the close of prayer, he continued to hold my hand and said, "You may leave the table."

I was in shock. The blood drained from my face and breath came in gasps. The flood of anticipation in my mouth was replaced by a desert of despair. A waterfall of emotion began to gather behind rapidly blinking eyelids and I looked to my mother for support. She was very busy dishing out long-anticipated servings to my sister.

"Sir?" It was more a plea for time than an attempt to respond.

"You may leave the table," he repeated.

The repeated instruction gave me no more information than the original. I didn't understand.

My eyes flew to my brother's faces for some clue as to what the problem could be, and for any kind of help they could offer. Whether it was the tone of his voice or the realization they were going to get to eat my share of spetzles that caused them to look away I cannot be sure, but one thing was certain, they were not going to get involved.

"May I ask why?" I squeaked out.

My question caused complete silence. I think the world stood still for an eternity. I know our home did.

"I told you to cut the grass."

His voice was steady, secure, non-negotiable. He knew he was just and right in his decision. He said no more.

I knew he was right as well. He had asked me to do just one thing and I had not done it. He was not being cruel, he was right. I had broken relationship. The silence was devastating as I slipped from my chair and went slowly to my room.

Mother did not bring me any food that evening. There was no grace in this. We were taught to obey our father or pay the price, and she was not going to undermine that teaching in any way. When she was asked why, she told us she felt she owed it to our future wives to make good husbands for them.

It was the lesson of my life. I have never forgotten it, and it has motivated me when nothing else could.

JESUS SAID...

Our Lord and Savior has similarly given us a command, our own "Cut the grass." Jesus said, **"...All authority has been given to Me** in heaven and on earth. **Go therefore and make disciples of all the nations,...**" (Matthew 28:18,19). The command is simple, "Go."

Our going out is based not on the need of the world, but on the authority of the Lamb upon the throne. He said "Go." It is commonly understood that to go one must get up from where he is and move in some direction toward a new location. People ask me to pray for them and give them a "word of direction." They want me to tell them where the Lord wants them to go so if they have a hard time they don't have to take responsibility for the decision. They can blame it on me or, worse yet, God speaking through me.

I won't do it. The first law of direction is motion. For centuries the Church has sat in one place and said, "Lord, direct us." That is like a child pretending to drive a car. Until the thing moves there is no point in asking for direction.

Jesus has already said, "Go." That is very plain. Because He knew we wouldn't want to hear it, He wrote it down. In the Greek it says, "Go." In other words, get into motion. Everyone in the Bible is in motion. Abraham, Isaac, Jacob all moved about. David, Jesus, Paul, they all moved about. In fact, the one time David did not go out when he should have, he got into sin with the girl next door.

THE CHARISMATIC "MOVEMENT"

If you want to know where all the sin came from in the charismatic movement, consider this. It wasn't a movement because the people never went anywhere.

They all played games, swam in streams of anointing and had a great feel-good time, but they never did the one thing Jesus said to do. They never cut the grass. The two-thirds of the world which has yet to hear the name of Jesus in a way it can understand is evidence to a just God of the rebellion of His people.

Yes, they were baptized in the Holy Spirit. Yes, more money flowed than ever has in the history of the Church. Yes, great buildings were built. Yes, great music was written. Yes, there are more books and book stores than ever in the history of the Church. But the unharvested fields are still standing there. The uncut grass stands there, a silent witness.

The fields are still ripe unto harvest and the Church is still playing games and looking for a fresh pool to plunge itself into. Jesus **is** coming back. When He gets here, the grass had better be cut or there are going to be some pretty shocked people leaving the table.

UNDER COMMAND

Jesus has made you an Attack Lamb. His plan is to put intercessors on every corner of the land and neutralize the Enemy's four forces through His Power Presence. He said, **"Go…and, lo, I am with you always,…."** (Matthew 28:19,20[67]). We have the ability to use His Name which is above all names. We go in His authority. He has given us the power to witness, the ability to see and say. Now, the choice is ours. Will you do it?

As we read on I will share with you the five pressure points that will change a nation. I'll teach you what to do when you park the ark and why it is important to keep that motor running in the spirit. But you must decide to go on. Will you make the choices that align you with God's purpose on earth?

I believe you will join the millions world wide who have said to the Lord, "Jesus, I am sorry that I have lived so much for myself. I give my life to You. Lead me in paths of righteousness for Your Name's sake. Redirect the affairs of my life that I may respond to Your love for me. I accept Your love offering of the nations, and will enter in with You to Your inheritance."

There, now can't you just smell that dinner?

---

67. [19]Go therefore and make disciples of all the nations, baptizing them in the name of the Father and of the Son and of the Holy Spirit, [20]teaching them to observe all things that I have commanded you; and lo, I am with you always, even to the end of the age." Amen

CHAPTER 12

WAR

We had come to Moscow on the train from Beijing. Our trip had been a real eye-opener. We had gotten off the train in several places: Ulan Battur, Irkutsk and Novosibirsk. We were now focused on the seat of power for the communist regime.

Now I found myself walking through the Kremlin asking the Lord for a strategy to free the Soviet people. It was 1985 and the USSR was in full bloom.

For two days I sat in the replica of Lenin's office and practiced the Power Presence of the Holy Spirit. I asked the Lord for insight into the power of the *archas* which was emanating from that place. "What," I asked, "would break the power of the lie that there is no God?" The Lord impressed me that the word of truth would break that power.

From Lenin's office, I walked the two blocks to his tomb. Rather than join the line to enter the tomb, I took up a location opposite the front door. I began to softly declare, "There is a God. He has a Son. His Name is Jesus. He died for Me." I walked about the entire Kremlin complex repeating this same declaration. Each time I repeated those phrases I experienced a greater sense of freedom.

For the next few days I stood in the Kremlin garden, an Attack Lamb on location, and softly spoke the declaration, "There is a God. He has a Son. His name is Jesus. He died for me." All too soon our scheduled time ended and it was time to move on.

For the next several years whenever we went prayer walking in parts of the Soviet Union or sent teams there, we continued to make this gentle, confident declaration. We mobilized Attack Lambs from Beijing to Berlin, and today the former Soviet Union walks in more religious freedom than it has in decades. The simple declaration of the Word of God's truth established the reality of what we declared.

AN OPEN DECLARATION

We have declared war on the Devil's four forces. We are determined to touch every nation according to the command of our Lord and Leader Jesus, and to do it according to His plan. And as we do, one thing we know for sure. We are not wrestling with flesh and blood. We are wrestling with four concentrations of power. They were defeated in heaven, defeated on the earth, and defeated under the earth. The disciples reported that in the power Jesus gave them, the four forces voluntarily ordered themselves under the name of Jesus. It's our job to enforce that victory.

We have seen, as we are faithful to the purpose of God in the earth, these four forces can be neutralized since we have the same power the disciples had. We can share their experience. The four forces are no match for an Attack Lamb parked in front of a Dagon of today, and as long as we are living to present Jesus to every man, woman, and child on the earth in our generation, it will ever be so.

OUR NEXT ACROSTIC

In the next three chapters, we are going to follow this acrostic… **WAR**.

WORSHIP

ANNOUNCE

REJOICE

All successful spiritual endeavor comes forth from an attitude of **worship**. When the disciples returned to the Lord in Luke 10, they reported to Jesus that even the devils were subject to them in Jesus' name. After centuries of bondage in the nation, this was incredibly good news. Jesus declared they had authority over all the power of the Enemy, and that nothing would in any way harm them. Sounds like a pretty secure war zone to me.

As fabulous as that truth was, and still is, Jesus responded by making one of the most startling replies of His entire ministry. He called them to a priority of focus. He commanded them to rejoice not in who was submitted to them, but rather, to rejoice in Him to whom they were submitted.

If we depart from a focus on Jesus and begin to focus on the forces which oppose us, we give them a place they are not entitled to.

How about the one who prays and rejoices in Jesus? They are filled with joy, and rather than focus on the works of evil, they overcome evil with good.

20/20 VISION IN THE 10/40 WINDOW

The 10/40 Window is the part of the world in which are found the least evangelized, mega-people groups. If they are to be reached, Attack Lambs are going to have to go forth and "park the ark" with the motor running until the Dagons of today bow down, releasing the people to hear the name of Jesus.

Second Chronicles 20:1[68] illustrates how King Jehoshaphat faced the challenge of the children of Ammon, Moab, and Mount Seir, using power worship as an instrument of warfare.

The Moabites, the Ammonites and those from Mount Seir had come against Jehoshaphat to do battle. The war was on! These peoples, conceived through incest, were the descendents of Lot and his daughters. The same forces the Lord engaged in battle at Sodom and Gomorrah were now at it again.

In this case, those forces are the *pneuma tae ponerias* and the *archas* combination. How do we know? The history of sexual perversion tells

---

68. [20]It happened after this that the people of Moab with the people of Ammon, and others with them besides the Ammonites, came to battle against Jehoshaphat

the tale of malice. Sexual perversion destroys the individual. It corrupts body, soul, and spirit. According to Romans 1 it will render the mind incapable of rational thought. First Corinthians 6 says it will cost you your ability to function in the kingdom of God and, worst of all, it will cause spiritual union with the Enemy.

Those who entice and involve others in corrupt sexual practices are malicious in nature. They are driven by a spirit of malice, which is a Dagon of today. You and I have the power of God's presence to stand in quiet confidence and see them bow down. When the children of sexual impurity solicit our families, we can stand in the gap. Our victory is assured if we stand in faith. We can lift our hearts and eyes to a heavenly vision, and see the glory flow from the throne, as we declare victory over the Devil's forces.

The war-loving "*archas* of Seir," who likes to ride upon the high places and intimidate, is the force King Jehoshaphat has to battle. The sexually impure love to intimidate the rest of society saying, "We will get your daughters and sons for our pleasures."

In America today there is a spiritual movement accusing 98 percent of the population of having a fear of homosexuals. Two percent is saying to 98 percent, "You are afraid of us!" That is ridiculous! It is the same ploy attempted by the demons who try to get you to forget there were two angels who remained obedient to God for every one who did not. The implied superiority of evil is fed through the force of the *archas*. We wrestle with this force for the salvation of others.

FOCUS, KING JEHOSHAPHAT, FOCUS

Now these two forces had come up against King Jehoshaphat. In verse three he finds his proper focus,

> **And Jehoshaphat feared, and set himself to seek the Lord, and proclaimed a fast throughout all Judah. So Judah gathered together to ask help from the Lord; and from all the cities of Judah they came to seek the Lord.**
> **2 Chronicles 20:3–4**

Proper focus in time of trouble is demonstrated by the king, and all those who followed him. They did three things necessary for victory.

First, they set themselves to seek the Lord. They did not look to neighboring armies for help. They did not appoint a committee but became a prayer group to handle this. They all sought God. Every person looked for a heavenly vision.

Second, they fasted. They denied their appetite for things of earth to create a greater appetite for the Lord. They turned off their senses to seek His face. Through fasting, they sealed off the Enemy's access to them. In all times of warfare there is special training to prepare the warriors. Fasting is vital to successful spiritual warfare.

Third, they gathered together. The way of the world is separation, and Satan's strategies often include isolation. Hitler, Stalin, Kruschev, and Mao are the most recent examples of leadership developing exclusive rather than inclusive practice. It is through this exclusive attitude that the archas invades the hearts of nations.

"Not forsaking the assembling of ourselves together, as the manner of some is;..." (Hebrews 10:25[69]) was not written to insure a large attendance or a large offering. It is the directive of the Holy Spirit, knowing that as we gather together Jesus is present in the midst of us, and His wisdom and power will be manifest. By gathering together, these people affirmed their faith in the king and his direction to fast and seek God. They rallied to the call of leadership. They were faithful to the principle of submission.

ATTACK LAMB INTERCESSION

Jehoshaphat's prayer of 2 Chronicles 20:1–12 contains several very important lessons about Attack Lamb intercession.

First, he stood in the midst of the people before the new court of the temple to pray. He was in the gap. He was between the people

---

69. [25]not forsaking the assembling of ourselves together, as is the manner of some, but exhorting one another, and so much the more as you see the Day approaching

and the Lord in a position to make sacrifice if the problem was the sin of the people. He did not lord his kingship over them, but **identified with them**.

Isaiah was in a similar position when he said, **"Woe is me!... I am a man of unclean lips, And I dwell in the midst of a people of unclean lips;..."** (Isaiah 6:5[70]). He identified with the people in their sinful state.

Paul was identifying with the prisoners as he called out to the jailor not to kill himself saying, "We are all here." This principle of identifying with the people is vital to the ministry of intercession. We cannot stand aloof from the crowd to avoid being touched in our hearts with their sin. Remember, we too have fallen short of the glory of God at times.

As a witness you have the ability, through the Holy Spirit, to identify with the sinner in the consequence of sin without becoming a doer of that sin. You do not have to do drugs to feel the pain of the drug addict. If you are willing to walk among the lepers, God will allow you to pray until their pain lifts. You will feel as much as He allows to keep you in prayer.

I have often experienced the feeling of total helplessness of the Buddhist as he stands before an image that cannot see, hear, or touch him and cries out for his ancestors. My identification with the ethnic Chinese grows in depth each time I stand and pray for them. So by the grace of God I am no longer a foreigner in their midst.

Jesus became our sin. Through this experience, He is touched with our infirmities. His heart is our heart. His feelings our feelings. He bore our griefs and carried our sorrows. And now, He ever lives to make intercession for us. He is still identified with you. When He moves in your life, He causes you to have the grace to identify with those for whom you are praying. You are not alone in the gap.

---

70. [5]So I said: "Woe is me, for I am undone! Because I am a man of unclean lips, And I dwell in the midst of a people of unclean lips; For my eyes have seen the King, The Lord of hosts."

Second, King Jehoshaphat proclaims who God is. His proclamation in verses six and seven establishes that God has brought them to this point in time, and dwells among them. It is vital to success as a leader that we **maintain the focus** of those around us on the fact of the sovereignty of God. Should the people look to us, the enemy, or themselves, we are headed for disaster. The king directs the attention of the people to the person of God.

Third, he **declares the promise** of God. Look in verse nine at the power of this declaration, **"If, when evil cometh…we stand before this house,…and cry unto thee…then you will hear and help"** (2 Chronicles 29:9 KJV). What strength there is in the promise of God. What comfort there is in His presence. What joy in the realization of His Person.

Fourth, he **reminds the Lord** that the entire situation is the result of a sovereign decision made at the time Israel came up into the land. Moab and Ammon exist because God had given orders not to destroy them. He had been giving them time to repent. He is faithful to the heart of Abraham concerning Lot. The power of intercession has kept these people in the mercy of the Lord for generations, but now they are showing their true nature and will be judged.

Fifth, verse thirteen describes the scene as all Israel stands before the Lord. Men, women, and children have been fasting and seeking the Lord together. **Prayer is a family affair.** There is unity of purpose as together they call on God to defend them from the attack of their ungrateful enemy. The king leads in prayer with the agreement of the people. In their act of submission to him, and to God through him, they release the power of His presence, which will cause their enemies to submit.

GOD RESPONDS

By His Spirit, God speaks through one of the young men. He is Jahaziel whose name means "Beheld of God." He is the son of Zechariah, "The Lord Remembers," who is the son of Benaniah, "The

Lord has Built Up," who is the son of Jeil, "Jehovah Sweeps Away," the son of Mattaniah, "The Gift of Yahweh," who is a Levite, "Joined to Yahweh," of the sons of Asaph, "The Gatherer." The names are very important as the Lord speaks directly, and not through an ephod or Urim and Thummim.

To those gathered together, the names became their confirmation as this young man speaks direction to king and priest alike. Imagine how the night would have gone without this confirmation. They would question his youth. His family, his position, and his spirituality would all be topics of conversation as they waited throughout that night. Imagine how the generals would feel when he said there would be no need to fight in this battle. How would those who had faced combat prepare for a nation threatening invasion if they did not have the confirmation of the names?

The Lord speaks to His people. They are not without direction. They have sought Him and He is found of them. He has responded to their prayer and fasting, their unity, and their submission. He gives them clear directive, **"Be not afraid nor dismayed by reason of this great multitude; for the battle is not yours, but God's."** (2 Chronicles 20:15 KJV).

God agrees with Jehoshaphat. He has allowed these aggressive people to flourish at this time but He will take care of them. Judah has found herself in the midst of the conflict between God and the sons of Lot. The people are in the gap interceding for the will of God to be done.

God has been trying to reach Ammon and Moab since the deliverance of their father Lot. Israel has been brought to the position of prayer through the sovereign nature of God, and their prayers have been Spirit-led. They have chosen to fight the battle in the spiritual dimension, and not in the flesh, and, in so doing have released the very presence of God to war in their behalf.

They have become…Attack Lambs!

THE BATTLE IS THE LORD'S

God tells them when and where to find the gap. In the morning they are to go to a cliff at the river's end. God issues the daily orders; there are three. He commands them to "set themselves," "stand still," and "see their salvation." These commands are our orders as well when we bring our ark into the presence of the Dagons of today. Here is the verse as a whole and then we will break them down.

> **You will not need to fight in this battle. Position yourselves, stand still and see the salvation of the Lord, who is with you, O Judah and Jerusalem!' Do not fear or be dismayed; tomorrow go out against them, for the Lord is with you.   2 Chronicles 20:17 KJV**

Set yourself. Israel has proven her ability to be in location, in prayer and fasting, with a proper focus. The families stand together and the nation stands behind her leader. They have a proper focus and are not wandering about between opinions.

Stand still. Wow! Do people have a difficult time doing this. "Don't just stand there, do something!" is a common challenge to people today. We feel physical activity is a sign of life and vitality. Once you are in the gap, there is no need for a lot of activity.

Two of my team and I had gone to a Buddhist temple in Singapore in the midst of a Lunar New Year's celebration to intercede for the families who pertain to that temple. I had positioned myself in a gap, literally, between the people and the altar, and softly mentioned the name of Jesus repeatedly.

Alongside the altar was what was called a "Money Tree." It was a huge urn over six feet across and six feet high, resting on a broad flat bottom and filled with soil. A small tree rose from the large urn, and people pinned money to it as offerings to the Buddha.

For an hour I remained in the gap softly mentioning the name of Jesus when, suddenly, this huge urn simply fell over, crashing into the altar.

We were in shock!

The Singaporeans in our team felt the controlling spirit of the temple and the city had actually bowed down to the name of Jesus.

The temple workers were even more shocked. There was no natural explanation for how the urn could even tip, let alone fall completely over. There had been no one even near it. The workers scrambled to gather the little packets of money which had been affixed to the tree and, in complete disbelief, called for help to set it upright.

There is power in the presence of the Lord in your life, and in the lives of those for whom you intercede. Stand still and trust in Him; He will cause the powers about you to submit. Let's turn that old adage around...Don't just do something, STAND THERE!

See the salvation. Stand in that gap with a heavenly vision. Be a witness in the power of the Holy Spirit. As you stand in your assigned gap you are going to have opportunity to look at the enemy, his forces, yourself, your weakness, your leadership, their weaknesses, those who stand around you, and their weaknesses. Keep your eyes on the heavenly vision! It is awesome to watch God deliver the Enemy into your hands.

AN INTERNATIONAL MINISTRY

Prayer walking has become an international ministry. There are prayer teams walking in every country. Now they are pressing in on specific people groups. The path of world evangelism has been defined by ethnicity. Any political entity may contain thousands of ethnic or people groups.

The Enemy is using this redefinition to set man against man in bloody conflict once again. The cry of the Enemy is preeminence. Bosnians say the land is theirs, Serbs say they were there first. The term "ethnic cleansing" covers the *ponerias*-driven mass murders of these times. These ethnic *archas-ponerias* combinations are throughout all the earth trying to distract people from the real conflict between God and the Devil. As we walk in the highways and byways of the earth, we bring peace because we are doing battle where the real warfare is manifest and accomplished: in the spiritual realm.

As an Attack Lamb, you are being used of the Lord to release the Power Presence of God. It is His presence alone that tears down the walls which divide the ethnic groups and cause such hatred. Only Jesus can cause man to love man.

BACK TO THE STORY

King Jehoshaphat hears the Word of the Lord from Jahaziel (2 Chronicles 20:17[71]) and falls on his face. The Levites jump and sing and shout. Of these two responses to the presence of the Lord which is correct? We are living in times when the Spirit of God is manifesting in many places with a message of peace and joy. Some places people laugh hysterically. In others the people sit quietly and in others they fall over and are in ecstasy for minutes and hours, appearing to be disoriented. Just as these groups in 2 Chronicles 20:18[72] responded differently, there are differing responses today to the presence, power, and promise of God.

Both groups are right. You cannot evaluate the presence of the Lord by people's response to Him. Their response, however, is critical. Do they embrace the Word of the Lord as truth and act accordingly?

In fact, that is what they do. In the morning they head out in an order which the king has determined after talking with the people. He sends the psalmists first. Not coincidentally, this places the young man with the Word from God right in the front row, and puts the king in the middle with the generals.

The praisers are focused on the beauty of His holiness, and they are given a song to sing, "Praise the Lord, for His mercy is forever."

---

71. [17]You will not need to fight in this battle. Position yourselves, stand still and see the salvation of the Lord, who is with you, O Judah and Jerusalem!' Do not fear or be dismayed; tomorrow go out against them, for the Lord is with you."
72. [18]And Jehoshaphat bowed his head with his face to the ground, and all Judah and the inhabitants of Jerusalem bowed before the Lord, worshiping the Lord

They do not just mill about humming whatever comes to mind. They have a definite position, a definite responsibility and a definite song.

Here is where the process of **announcement** begins. Remember our acrostic **W-A-R**. Everyone does not do what seems good to them, but it is a very disciplined march.

What happened? God gave the victory. He sets ambushments against the three armies, and they turn inward and attack each other. The preeminent arrogance of the *archas* and the treachery of the *ponerias* combine, and they destroy each other while the Attack Lambs stand and sing a very simple song.

I believe if the Body of Christ would be positive, move in the calling God has for us to step into gaps at pressure points, and do as Judah did, the forces which drive Hinduism, Buddhism and Islam would turn against each other and the masses who live under those systems would be released to know Jesus as their Lord and Savior. This is the will of God.

WINNING YOUR BATTLES

Do not argue with your family, your classmate, your colleague. **We do not wrestle with flesh and blood.** Our battle is with spiritual forces, the Dagons of today. As we move into the 10/40 window toward the least evangelized, mega-peoples, it will be hours of prayer and fasting that will get the job done. The four forces, *archas, exousias, kosmokratos,* and *ponerias* will be broken from them, just as they were in Jehoshaphat's day, and multiplied millions will come to know Jesus.

The action taken in 2 Chronicles 20 has five distinguishing characteristics:

It was Spirit-led.

It was leader-affirmed.

It included all the people.

It was gift ordered, praisers first, etc.

It was God's battle.

When the strategy for taking your city has the same characteristics, you will experience the same great victory.

Take the time to compare your prayer plans with this one. How do they line up? Here are some questions you can ask yourself to see.

Are you open to the Holy Spirit showing you the way He wants you to go?

Has your leadership authorized your going forth, or are you trying to make the forces submit without submitting yourself?

Are you including as many people in the plan as possible?

Do you allow gifted people other than yourself to be in the front or do you insist on having that place? (Watch out for the *archas* if you feel you must be in front.)

Finally, have you taken the promise of success to the cross?

Promised victory is pretty heady stuff. If it is God's battle, then give Him the glory. Keep your focus on Jesus. Keep your vision in the heavenlies.

The environment of the throne room is praise and worship. It is not a war room, it is a victory celebration. Judah went forth in an atmosphere of praise and worship. Remember: **all conclusive battles are won with praise and worship because the Godward focus of a submitted people releases the Power Presence of God from which the Enemy must flee in absolute confusion.**

Give the report to the people of the Lord, "Your warfare is accomplished. The Four Forces are subject to us as we walk in God's ordered praise and worship. Tell it in Zion and declare it to Jerusalem: there is victory in the name of the Lord!"

CHAPTER 13

AND AGAIN I SAY REJOICE

Three thousand hands clapping full force filled the renovated theater in Singapore with noise. Thunderous applause would describe it. The people had leapt to their feet in one motion. Their voices rode the thunder with shouts of joy, and tears of release cascaded over upturned cheeks. Their smiles stretched away wrinkles of fear as the Holy Spirit gave them a heavenly vision.

They were free. Man had not done it. Programs had not done it. Jesus had touched them through the power of His presence and they would never be the same.

Time stood still. Its usual hectic control of their lives was cast aside as minute after minute was consumed in the ecstasy of their release. The walls echoed their joy, sending waves of thanksgiving crashing in crescendo with their barrier-breaking bellows.

The pastor stood before them, hands raised in surrender, and his eyes closed to earthly sights. His spirit was open to heaven's throne as he waited while the Savior of these souls delivered them from generations of bondage. He had just testified that the force of intimidation had been broken. Now in his first moments of freedom, he rolled his shoulders as if to test the new garment of righteousness with which the Spirit had draped him. More than a mantle, this was an anointing to set the captive free.

A young lady came forward. Unafraid, she took a position near a microphone, yet she would not be able to speak for a quarter hour as the people continued to rejoice in victory. Arms aching, hands swelling from the pounding hand clapping, voices hoarse from shouting, they carried on. The power was not theirs. They rode with Christ upon the thunder of their praise. They were seated with Him in the chariot of God far above powers and principalities.

At last, as their bodies returned to the limits of humanity, they listened as the young lady reported, "Each time a hand clap sounded another demon of intimidation was driven from a Singaporean. Each clap released another soul from bondage." The roar began again.

DECLARATION OF TRIUMPH

Rejoicing, the "R" in **W-A-R**, is the declaration of triumph in the Lord Jesus. Paul writes to the Philippians to **"Rejoice in the Lord always. Again I will say, rejoice!"** (Philippians 4:4). How was it that Paul and Silas had been able to rejoice that night in a jail cell? They had a heavenly vision. They knew they were a part of God's plan to reach the lost. Until their last breath, they were going to announce to powers and principalities the victory that was theirs, and ours, in Jesus.

As he taught the church, Paul emphasized the power of rejoicing. He knew it to be a release point for the Power Presence of God. The earth had shaken and, when it did the jailor and his family had come into the kingdom of God. Rejoicing power had brought them from a life of death to a life without death. They were baptized and embraced the apostles, finally sending them to other unreached groups with the Good News. The power of rejoicing had taken Paul and Silas a long way.

It is the will of God that none should perish, but that all should come to the knowledge of the Truth. The angels in heaven rejoice over one sinner who repents. As you stand in that gap and pray, the angels are getting ready to party. They know this works. They know that rejoicing is a big part of successful spiritual endeavor for it is a part of worship, and all successful spiritual endeavor comes from an attitude of praise and worship.

LIFE IN THE STREET

As we walk through the nations of Asia, we realize when the rain falls, we all get wet. To people in the streets, life's showers are a common experience. There is a sort of humor we share with the people as the rains of monsoon turn the streets into rivers. Asian people love to see without being seen.

In Hanoi, Vietnam, there is a shopping district whose winding streets are lined with shops. Displays of wares have spilled out past the sidewalk barriers into the street. At regular intervals the local police come to clear a path through the mountains of plastic and cottons. Stacks of television sets yield to their cane batons. Sharp, Panasonic, and Sony all cry out. But after the authorities pass on, the vendors go back to displaying their goods as much as they can.

But at mid-afternoon the real equalizer moves in, the afternoon monsoon rains. Instantly this kaleidoscope of colors and goods is interrupted by a deluge. The big show is on. There is a mad dash to the plastic awnings in front of their shops. Vendors grab merchandise and hustle it to the safety of cover. We stand under whatever cover can be found and begin to congratulate those who make the many trips to reach common shelter. Each soul who reaches our ship of dryness is greeted with applause and the warm, gracious smiles of the Vietnamese people. Rejoicing together in the simple comfort of covering we share, we are, for the moment, friends. It lasts until the rain quits and then, still strangers in the larger arena, we go back into the now cooler streets.

There is no rejoicing that can compare with that of a freshly pressed and prim school girl who, upon reaching the cover of that shelter, realizes her hair is not going to be destroyed after all, and her skirt pleats are still quite in order. We all wait for the rejoicing outburst as school friends gather under cover and, as surely as the rain itself, they burst into the giggles which let the observer know they have been found out. Adults look to one another and smiles of joy replace scowls of complaint.

You are sent forth as Attack Lambs to proclaim spiritual shelter to those who are caught in the deluge of life's cares. Give yourself to those people. Allow your spirit to be touched with the plight of their Christless lives. See the despair in their eyes as the thunder sounds. Get into that gap and put up a shelter of His Power Presence. Give them the chance to turn away from the torrents of pressure and floods of concern and find refuge in the shelter of the Lord's Presence.

THE HORSE AND RIDER

As the conquistadors attacked the Incas, those smaller, indigenous peoples ran for caves and crevasses. The Spaniard was so large, more than ten feet tall with four hoofed feet and two heads. The larger head had flared nostrils and blood streaked eyes. It was larger than a man's, and its neck thrust forth from a powerful chest.

The smaller head was covered with metal that stones and spears could not penetrate. Fire burst out of one hand as the smaller head looked toward them. The searing pain of the fire would take the life from them.

Incan warriors attacked the unprotected larger head and, in fact, found that if they struck it in just the right spot with club, spear or arrow they could knock it down. However, the smaller-headed portion would rise up and the fire would still come out of its arm and take the life out of their bodies. Eventually, they learned the horse and rider were two and not one. Unfortunately, this discovery came after they had been conquered.

Only the Lord has the answer for both the horse and the rider. Exodus 15 is Moses' great song of rejoicing for the children of Israel who have found shelter in the presence of the Lord. The pillar warmed them by night and the cloud cooled them by day and they were able to witness the great deliverance as the horse and the rider of Pharaoh's armies were cast into the sea.

Moses had seen the fruit of his intercession. He was the first one to spend forty years in the wilderness, preparing to go back to Egypt to stand in the gap for Israel. It was he who declared himself unfit for service. It was he who said he was not eloquent. It was he who had to have the help of his brother, and who cried out to God as he suffered the rejection of the people for whom he interceded.

It was Moses who engaged in spiritual warfare as the Lord performed the ten miracles of deliverance. It was Moses who withstood the treachery of Pharaoh's magicians, Jannes and Jambres. It was Moses who saw the power of God. Now, at the mid-point of his ministry of intercession, it is he who sings this song of rejoicing,

"…I will sing to the Lord, for He has triumphed gloriously! The horse and its rider He has thrown into the sea!" (Exodus 15:1[73]). Not just the horse, and not just a thrown rider. The victory over the Enemy is complete! Both the horse and rider are cast into the sea. Moses has seen the greatest deliverance of all time. They are drowned; they are defeated! Praise the Lord!

HORSES AND RIDERS TODAY

If I say to you, "Communism is the horse," who is the rider? Think about it. The lie of communism is, "There is no God." That is the way in which the State takes the place of God in the society. So communism is the horse on which atheism rides.

If I say to you, "Hinduism is the horse," who is the rider? The Hindu embraces several hundred million gods. Polytheism is the rider of the Hindu horse. We wrestle not with the peoples of Hindu lands. They are precious, wonderful people for whom Christ died, but the horse and the rider are thrown into the sea as we rejoice.

---

73. [15]Then Moses and the children of Israel sang this song to the Lord, and spoke, saying: "I will sing to the Lord, For He has triumphed gloriously! The horse and its rider He has thrown into the sea!

If I say to you, "Buddhism is the horse," who is the rider? The followers of Buddha believe there is no heavenly reward. There are reincarnations, but all of the hereafter is spent in another life form in the here and now. So the rider is the lie, "No heaven." Hear the song of John Lennon after marrying a Buddhist, "Imagine there's no heaven, it's easy if you try..."[1] I rejoice daily as I walk and work in Asia that the horse and the rider have been thrown into the sea. Not just the religious system, but the spirit behind it all is defeated through the blood of Jesus. As we go to our points of prayer, park the ark, praise the Lord, gain His perception, and pray with His Power Presence, we too shall see horses and riders worldwide fall into the sea and be defeated.

Permit me one more example. If I say to you, "Islam is the horse," who is the rider? Is it not the false prophet who denies the virgin birth, the miracles of Christ, the fulfillment of Abraham, and the death and bodily resurrection of the Son of God? Do we wrestle with the horse? No. Do we wrestle with the people under this dominion? No. We wrestle with the *archas* and *exousias* which operate through this system. We go to strategic locations and call upon the Lord.

Standing in the shade of the same cloud with the heat of the same fire, we speak to the *archas*, *exousias*, *kosmokratos*, and *ponerias* which operate in these places. We maintain God's Power Presence, and see the souls of men delivered. We sing with Moses, **"...I will sing to the Lord, for He has triumphed gloriously! The horse and its rider He has thrown into the sea!"** (Exodus 15:1).

IS IT WORKING?

We were recently in a city in western China. Our team had been praying up from Pakistan, and had come through the mountains on the Old Silk Road. The team was walking about in a mosque when one of the teachers invited them to come in and visit. They did and upon entry, this old man closed the door securely behind him and asked in earnest, "Did you bring it with you?"

Quite uneasy, the leader responded, "Did we bring what?"

"The Gospel," the old man replied. "We have been praying for five years that someone would bring us the Gospel." This man knew the sound of the horse; for him it was Buddhism. He knew the emptiness of the rider; no heaven. He had heard from the radio the good news of Jesus Christ and had been praying for five years that someone would bring him the book of the One whose Word is true! Because we had agreed to step into that gap, we were allowed to be the ones to bring it to him.

The world is waiting for you to put on your Attack Lamb mentality and get out there. Do not fear the horses. Do not worry about the riders. God is in control. Give your life over to Him and join in the victory song. The horse and the rider are thrown into the sea!

Think it through. How many horse and rider combinations can you perceive in your community or place of work? In the USA it has been thirty years since the Lord's Prayer was declared illegal in schools. Many efforts have been mounted to restore prayer, but to no avail. Many horses have been slain, but the rider has yet to be destroyed. Can you think of situations in which you have been unsuccessful in unseating the rider?

Ask the Lord to show you the instances in which you have been successful in neutralizing the power of the horse, only to have your hopes dashed as you realize the rider is still at work. List each one. Pray that the Lord will show you how they work together. Remember, you are not to get involved in struggles with people. Behind each of these combinations you will find one or more of the four forces set against salvation.

ROCK MUSIC...REALLY?

Five-tone rock music is often the repetition of musical scales which have their root in Hindu or Buddhist chants to invoke spirits. These repeated scales were learned by the pioneers of rock music during their sojourns to the East. The sounds were novel and sold a lot of records. However, they brought with them their accompanying spiritual riders. Just as the Lord dwells in the praises of His people, demonic forces dwell in these rhythmic progressions.

Many parents have become heartsick at the changes in their children as they open their spirits and minds to these songs. The kids say that they don't even hear the lyrics, they just like the music. When the parents attempt to regain control, frustration sets in and they become angry. Well, guess what? That is exactly the point of the music. Music from Japan is used to invoke Shinto spirits of anger, and music from India is used to invoke Kali, the goddess of destruction, of the Hindu people.

The result is global. The horse is controlled but the rider is killing the kids. This is the number one weapon the Enemy is using against young people. How are you, the ark of the covenant, going to stop this onslaught on your home? Through the power of rejoicing.

The first proclamation of a worshiping warrior is, "The Devil is defeated." Jesus defeated him in the heavens. He has defeated him on the earth. Jesus has defeated the Devil under the earth. Jesus is Lord! This proclamation defeats the work of the Enemy in three areas.

It defeats the *archas* through the declaration of the preeminence of Christ. He alone is before all things. By Him all things consist. It pleased the Father that in Christ all fullness should dwell (Colossians 1:19[74]). There is no room for the Enemy or any other disorderly, rebellious thing. Jesus has established order and since you are born again, you are a part of that order. You have been set in a position in Christ which is far above all *archas* and *exousias*. You are the righteousness of God in Christ Jesus, the head and not the tail. You have authority over all the power of the Devil (Luke 10:19[75]).

The *archas* cannot intimidate you. It cannot tell you that you are going to lose your child or friend to the ways of the world. You have the agreement of heaven for the salvation and maturation of that soul. You have lived a witness. You have trained up that child. Do not

---

74. [19]For it pleased the Father that in Him all the fullness should dwell
75. [19]Behold, I give you the authority to trample on serpents and scorpions, and over all the power of the enemy, and nothing shall by any means hurt you

throw away your joy because of a few months of difficulty, reach out to that kid and tell them you love them. The *archas* is not in control of your life or of the lives of those who pertain to you.

Paul told the Philippian jailor, **"Believe on the Lord Jesus Christ, and you will be saved, you and your household"** (Acts 16:31).

The jailor did a brilliant thing, he took the ark home with him. He did not leave his new-found friends at the jail, he took them home. He brought God's Power Presence into his home. Bring it in to yours. Do not bow the knee to the *archas*, rise up in righteousness and wrestle with that thing. Put it down in Jesus' name.

Go to your child's room and pray. We will be with you in spirit. Call upon the Lord to show you the ploy of the *archas* and announce that Jesus was here first. He has claim to your family through your prayers. Go ahead, rejoice.

Yes, you do have the right to go into that room! You have every right to stand there and to proclaim the Power Presence of the Lord. You have every right to speak to that child in the name of Jesus! Yes, you do have the right to speak into his life, to bind those forces set against him. Take it on in the spirit. Do not back down! You do have the right to embrace that child.

The *exousias* would try to defeat you by telling you that you have no right to rejoice. *"Who do you think you are to come into this place and proclaim Jesus?"* is the thought this force uses when it realizes it has been found out. Go get it! Blast that thing in the name of Jesus. You have every blood-bought right to rejoice in the face of the Enemy. Sing the song of Jehoshaphat. Sing the song of Moses. Get that rejoicing going because you are driving the Enemy into the sea and it shall soon close over its head. Drive the devils out with the sound of praise!

The *ponerias* has been trying to bring destruction to your family through this type of rock music. Look at the videos, the posters, the styles. They destroy the people who make the music and the people who listen to it, but not yours. You are in the gap. The wolf has grabbed the wrong lamb this time. Through you, your family and their friends will be delivered. Take it on in the Spirit.

The *ponerias* operates through terror. Call it what it is, a defeated foe. You are not going to believe the lie that your loved one will be involved in drugs and violence. You are going to think according to your prayers and relate to that person according to the Word of the Lord. Hear from God. Rehearse the promises over that bed and in that room. Anoint their CD's and tapes with oil and call upon the Lord to deliver them.

DEFEATING FEAR

There is no fear in Christ because perfect love casts out all fear. As a parent I know what it is like to see your child head for the world and have to be prayed back. As a teenager, I rebelled against my godly parents. My mother prayed herself to sleep many nights as I wallowed in a drunken stupor. The longer my hair grew, the longer she prayed. She did not back down from my ugly words and deeds, but took on new determination in prayer.

My return to the Lord's ways took seven years. My mother never gave up. She interceded with great love, often refraining from any correction. Her silence spoke more than any angry outburst. She did not wrestle with this flesh and blood, but she did a spiritual work in a spiritual way. Many nights I could hear her singing herself to sleep with the hymns she knew so very well. At first it would make me very angry, as the *ponerias* raged through me, and then I would gain comfort in knowing that she loved me.

You can, through rejoicing in the face of the forces, deliver your entire home, office, or school from the devices of the Devil. You do not have to cringe in fear. You can rise up and proclaim the victory of Jesus, because all successful spiritual endeavor comes forth from an atmosphere of worship. Rejoice in the Lord always and again I say rejoice. His promise is greater than your problem!

Moses realized with the closing of the sea that Israel had been redeemed. He had cause to sing as the Lord had shown him the defeat of the horse and the rider. They were cast into the sea!

The song of Moses came from a heart encouraged with the fulfillment of a vision. Moses held God's promise that, as he entered in before the people and Pharaoh, God would move to set the people free. The cry of the people had come up before God and He was going to deliver the people from their hard bondage. Moses had to enter into the situation in order to work that deliverance.

ENTERING IN

Entering in is the action word of intercession. To step between a rebellious teen and his course of action isn't often pleasant. One father of five suggested to me the proper word picture for such an action is "velvet steel," that is, very soft to the touch, but very difficult to bend.

Moses had to face pressures from family, Pharaoh, and those he was trying to serve. Each one rejected him. The family rejected him because of the circumcision required by the covenant conditions (Exodus 4:25[76]). Pharaoh rejected him because of the *archas* which had possessed him (Exodus 7:13[77]). Until his royal highness became his broken lowness, Moses was an unwelcome visitor to Egypt. Even Israel rejected him because he called them to God (Exodus 20:19–21[78]).

Moses still stood in that gap. He faced rejection as Christ would have, with a discipline of going to God. He found his fellowship in the One who had promised. He took solace in the One whose voice was as thunder and whose presence was as the spring rain. Moses became the friend of God, His prayer partner on the earth, the one on whom God could call for fellowship. He became the disciple of the true and living God.

---

76. [25]Then Zipporah took a sharp stone and cut off the foreskin of her son and cast it at Moses' feet, and said, "Surely you are a husband of blood to me!"

77. [13]And Pharaoh's heart grew hard, and he did not heed them, as the Lord had said

78. [19]Then they said to Moses, "You speak with us, and we will hear; but let not God speak with us, lest we die." [20]And Moses said to the people, "Do not fear; for God has come to test you, and that His fear may be before you, so that you may not sin." [21]So the people stood afar off, but Moses drew near the thick darkness where God was.

He was a walking warrior. Each day he had to discipline himself to walk in the ways of God. Each day he heard the complaints of thousands who refused to enter into the promised rest. Each day he entered into that place between a rebellious people and a loving God, and when the sea closed and the horse and the rider breathed their last, a song began to flow forth from his spirit.

It was a song inspired by the Holy Spirit. A song of triumph. A song of joy. In it was the faith which had carried him in that space and, as he sang, his faith was renewed. The Lord who had been his strength had now become his victory. God had manifested His victorious power.

How our heart rejoices as we see prayer answered. How the joy floods our soul when that rebellious one starts to renew relationship. How the joy floods our soul when the prodigal returns. Strike up the band and prepare the feast, we are going to rejoice. I stand with you right now in faith for that one for whom you are praying. Yes, the Lord will do all we need to see them restored. As surely as the horse and the rider were cast into the sea, He will deliver the one for whom you are praying.

Worship. Announce. Rejoice. The weapons of our warfare are not carnal, but mighty through God for the pulling down of strongholds (2 Corinthians 10:4[79]).

When we **worship** we see the throne of God.

When we **announce** we initiate the enemies of our loved ones in to the understanding we have received from the throne.

And when we **rejoice** we govern the thoughts of our minds and bring captive every thought through the knowledge of Christ.

Yes, it is a war, but the advance intelligence report has been received...We win!

....

---

79. [4]For the weapons of our warfare are not carnal but mighty in God for pulling down strongholds

CHAPTER 12

This section of the first edition of Attack Lambs was developed along three keywords: Worship, Announce, and Rejoice. In the 20 years of practice since the first edition, we have found that we cannot overemphasis these three words.

All success in the spirit realm flows forth from an atmosphere of praise and worship. You cannot control the outcome, but you can control the atmosphere.

Announcing to powers and principalities according to Ephesians 3:10[80] has become a wonderful experience for us as we determine who is the "kosmokrat," or worldly leader, of the people and pray our way into seeing them. At that time, we proclaim the word the Lord has given us, His wisdom to their problem. The outcomes God has given have been wonderful.

Our heart of rejoicing in the victory of Jesus has kept us from focusing on self or Satan. Indeed, the gaps are polluted with remaining forces that need to be dispelled; but, at the declaration of the victory of Jesus, they flee.

THE DIALOGUE OF WORSHIP

Worship is a dialogue. There are two voices involved in every worship experience.

We bring a sacrifice of praise. Like Paul in prison or David in a cave, Daniel in the lion's den or John on the Isle of Patmos, we decide to focus on the throne and bring praises to the Lord. Habakkuk said, **"Though the fig tree may not blossom, nor fruit be on the vines; though the labor of the olive may fail, and the fields yield no food; through the flock may be cut off from the fold, and there be no herd in the stalls, Yet I will rejoice in the Lord"** (Habakkuk 3:17-18b).

---

80. [10]to the intent that now the manifold wisdom of God might be made known by the church to the principalities and powers in the heavenly places

Praise is the first voice of the dialogue and it is offered by us, by choice. You have to decide to praise the Lord, to focus on Him, no matter what your situation. Praise is born in the human spirit and released by choice. I will enter His gates with thanksgiving in my heart, I will enter His courts with praise, I will say this is the day that the Lord has made, I will rejoice for He has made me glad.

The release to enter into worship is God's Spirit calling to those who praise Him. Recorded in Isaiah 1 is the dialogue between the prophet and God. The Lord asks, "Who has required you to come into my presence with sacrifices of the earth. If I wanted these, I have a limitless supply. I want your heart. Yes, we are separated by your sin; but, come let us reason together, though your sins are scarlet, I will make them white as snow" (Isaiah 1:10-18 author's paraphrase).

Worship is born of the spirit of God and can be initiated only by Him. We cannot make a sacrifice of worship because we do not own worship. Just as John was called to "come up here" so we must be called to worship. I appreciated Rick Warren's diagram of the worship experience very much, in which he taught his worship teams to begin with praise songs, setting the atmosphere for invitation. The contemporary song "Here as in Heaven" by Elevation Worship totally captures this thought in its opening line, "The atmosphere is changing now."

OMNIPRESENT GOD

God is omnipresent. He inhabits the praises of His people. He manifests, or shows Himself, to our senses as we focus on Him. When a person sets their heart upon the true and living God, He will open the gates of heaven and the eyes of their understanding to manifest himself to them. Their response to His voice of invitation will determine the outcomes.

Prayer is born of the human spirit. We have our prayer guides and our prayer lists and they most often are in the physical or material realm. And that is fine, I certainly encourage such prayer. I encourage all forms of prayer because we are declaring the nature of God by coming to Him in prayer.

Worship is born of the Spirit of God and by invitation. Intercession is born of the Spirit of God. In intercession we enter in between God and man to reconcile their differences. A mediator is not a mediator of one, but God is one (Galatians 3:20[81]). To know His deep thoughts on a situation, circumstance, or even in the life of an individual, we must be in the presence of the Spirit who searches the deep things of God. Yes, if we yield to Him, trust Him to be the rewarder of those who diligently seek Him, then He will show us His perspective on people and situations. But we must yield to Him, we must not, in fact cannot, barge our way into His presence with a shopping list of needs and wants.

FELLOWSHIP IN CHRIST

He wants fellowship. He wants us to see from His perspective and time table so that we properly represent Him in the dialogue with people.

So often in our worship services we come to this point. There is a stillness. The people realize that God is present in the place. He waits. Are we going to yield to Him or are we going to ask Him to yield to us? He asks us to be still that He may speak.

If we can focus, not be distracted by agenda or time pressures, relax and trust Him, He will speak to us through the gifts of the Holy Spirit, but we must yield to Him. We cannot move onto the announcements, youth video, or offering until we have waited on the Lord for His message and purpose. He is ready at this point to release the Wisdom we need. He is ready to give those Words of Knowledge that are so desperately needed. There are people in the midst who are crying out in their hearts for release from oppression and addiction. God wants to save, heal, and deliver in this moment, but so often the digital clock at the back of the hall tells us to move on.

---

81. [20]Now a mediator does not mediate for one only, but God is one.

It is awkward to wait upon the Lord. But He has waited quite a while for us.

When God speaks, His voice causes the impossible to be possible. He knows the thoughts and intents of the hearts of all assembled. He loves each and every person in the room with equal and impartial love. His presence brings release and fullness of joy. God is present, we must yield to Him to hear His voice.

This is the training ground of the Holy Spirit. As we come together, and He is in our midst, we are being taught by Him for the moment when we are in an important meeting and we need that same Word of Wisdom or the Word of Knowledge. Then we will speak prophetically to individuals and nations to set them on the course of blessing the Lord desired for them. At this moment in our corporate worship, the Lord is preparing the church to lead the community in their God-given destiny. **"But those who wait on the Lord shall renew their strength; they shall mount up with wings like eagles, they shall run and not be weary, they shall walk and not faint"** (Isaiah 40:31). We must learn in the school of the Spirit that standard of submission and practice that lifts us to the position of world changers.

How my heart breaks when someone takes the place of God in the conversation of worship. What could have been? Who could have been healed? What did not happen because a person needed to do something, say something, or stick to the agenda instead of waiting on the Lord? This has really impacted our ministry in a very big way. So, each street corner, each gap in the midst of humanity, has become a place of dialogue for us. We focus on the throne and wait for the Lord. He is there, and as we wait on Him, He manifests His presence. God is always here. He is waiting for us to show up.

Since understanding this dialogue with the throne, we have had doorways open to impact nations. Each meeting with a General or a Prime Minister, a Mayor or Police Chief, has become an extended worship service having no personal agenda, but waiting on the Lord for His. He has a plan for every person and our role is to make that plan understood.

FAITHFUL IN THE MATERIAL

God speaks through His gifts and we respond with our tithes and offerings.

Why is this a part of the dialogue of Worship? Because to be entrusted with the spiritual, we must first be found faithful in the material. Why would God entrust to you the souls of people when you don't even participate in the minimum in the material? How could a just God give someone into your watch when you are Biblically a thief? And how could a righteous God ever mislead a person to trust you when you steal from Him?

Indeed, our next step in the dialogue is to continue to worship the Lord with our tithes and offerings. Abraham knew this without a Pastor encouraging him to tithe. Our Father in the faith ran to get 10% of the spoils of victory to exchange them with Our Father in the Spirit there in the plain. Melchizedek, the King of Peace brought forth bread and wine of the covenant and made an agreement with Abraham that His Spirit would come over Abraham's daughter and a child would be born who would be called the Prince of Peace. When we bring our tithes into the storehouse, we affirm the covenant that through us, the inheritance of God will be expanded.

BE FRUITFUL AND MULTIPLY

His next voice is the preaching of His word through an anointed servant, dedicated and trained specifically for this purpose. God is speaking to us, and the anointed Word, mixed with faith in our hearts brings forth eternal life and causes us to be able to multiply. It is through this voice from God that souls are saved.

He commissions us to ministries in the church context and with this blessing comes a responsibility.

Our response to the entrustment of people's lives is what I refer to as the Wave Offering, for it is here that we see pride. This sense of pride, accomplishment, or title, causes us to call the ministry "Mine." Humility wins the day when we say we are serving the ministry of the Lord. When we declare that the Lord has done this, we are praising Him and the dialogue continues. From the first-fruits, He gives us the nations.

When we declare Him among the nations, we are bringing praise and glory to His name which causes Him to call us to yet another place of prayer and service. Those who are faithful over the few will be charged with the many, towns, cities, and nations.

And so, the dialogue goes on, walking and talking with God in a constant fellowship. As many as walk in the Spirit, they are the sons of God.

....

CHAPTER 13

In the dialogue of worship, the voice of the Lord is heard in the proclamation of His word; the announcement to powers and principalities of the wisdom of the Lord. These powers (Exousias) and Principalities (Archas) are about the right to speak and who was here first. They have clouded the minds of generations until the world now wonders if God is dead. When we step into the gap between God and man, it is with the proclamation that there is a God, He has a Son, His name is Jesus, and He died for us. The power that makes it believable, is the presence of God flowing out from our hearts.

The manifold wisdom of God is a fascinating combination of Greek words as we find it in Ephesians 3:10[82]. Wisdom is the common expression, "Sophia" it is the standard word for wisdom and, as we have examined in chapter 10, is available to us as we seek the Lord.

---

82. [10]to the intent that now the manifold wisdom of God might be made known by the church to the principalities and powers in the heavenly places

The adjective, "Manifold" is the Greek word "Polupoikilos" which means variegated or "of many colors."

EQUAL OPPORTUNITY SAVIOR

Jesus is the equal opportunity savior. He is certainly not color-blind. Sin is not black, it is scarlet. Jesus sees every person as he made them. Each is a unique and wonderful gift of God sent to earth at a set time for a purpose. When we understand the riches of the glory of His inheritance in the saints, we are going to see that He has an impartial love for every race on earth and the even greater fact that human life is sacred.

That is right, He knew each person before the foundation of the earth. Each was secretly and wonderfully made the womb. Each has in them the faith to receive Jesus. We, as Attack Lambs, enter into the gap, dispelling the forces there, and proclaiming the love of God is for every person.

If anything has obscured the wisdom of God and led the way for people to decline the gospel, it is racism. The white, Anglo-Saxon, protestant church (of which I am one) has gone so far as to make evangelistic materials using the color black for sin and sinners. These bracelets and books are banned in our ministry. Sin is not black, it is scarlet and to be made white, it must be covered by red blood. White privilege and position have so permeated the cultures of Africa and India that two-thirds of the world thinks they cannot have a personal relationship with God through Christ. Mission posters of a white hand handing a meal to a black hand are also banned in our ministry. Until the British left, Hong Kong was divided according to color.

"God is Light and in Him is no darkness at all" (1 John 1:5b). Light contains all colors. Light, when viewed through a prism ranges from infra-red to ultraviolet. People of all colors are accepted in the Beloved and heirs of the inheritance of Jesus. How we have gotten so far from the truth is amazing to me. Throughout Asia, people are avoiding the sun so that their skin will be lighter. They use face creams and whiteners, special toothpaste, cosmetics, and hair straighteners. Why do they do that? Because they have been taught that darker is lesser.

The right to speak in the church has been kept from them. The right to marry cross caste has been kept from them often by killing their intended. The proclamation of the manifold wisdom of God speaks right in the face of this racist, caste-oriented, demonic bondage.

But, if we walk in the Light as He is in the Light, we have fellowship with one another and the blood of Jesus Christ cleanses us from all iniquity.

GROWTH IS THE GOAL

In every place to which we have been called, now 122 nations, the question of "Who was here first?" and "Who has the right to speak?" has been the strongest force we have had to overcome. Behind every conversation, we can hear the echo of the past. Nations now emerging still follow the old ways of mission where payoffs and special favors were common. In such conversations where we are approached to play the old game, we assert that the 6,500 promises of the Bible are the same in every language.

We do not own land in developing nations; but rather, empower the local people to own the land. We build millions of dollars of buildings as a gift to the local schools and churches with the mandate that they must advance the people by adding value to them.

We teach that today you are a recipient nation but your goal is to become a donor nation for it is more blessed to give than to receive. We stand on the promise that if any man opens the door to Jesus, He will come in and make His abode there.

A PROCLAMATION FROM THE LORD

I entered Cambodia in 1994 during the war against Pol Pot. It was a mess. Pol Pot had killed fifty percent of the population in the Killing Fields. Another twenty-five percent fled to Thailand and other nations leaving the lame and the elderly. At one point, the capital of Phnom Penh was void of humanity, its buildings and streets without human sound.

I walked and prayed along the National Highway 6 which goes from Siem Reap to the Thai border of Poi Pet. The road was pockmarked with land mine and bomb craters and, in those years, was a pathway of escape to the Thai refugee camps. Cambodia was devastated.

As I prayed in those villages and saw the result of the latest conflict over who was there first and who would speak for Cambodia, who would rule the mess left behind, and the work of the malicious spirits that drove Pol Pot to such tortures of his own people, the Lord gave me a proclamation to make.

"In His resurrection power, Jesus will raise up from these minefields and killing fields a generation that is Christ-centered, Bible-based, Holy Spirit-filled, and academically excellent that will lead Cambodia into its future as a witness to His Power, in Cambodia, ASEAN, and the Nations."

The prospect was so dim that people would laugh when I said it, but each time, a few believed. Orphanages were established, schools built, lives changed, and we were noticed by the Deputy Prime Minister. As the Lord would have it, it was he who led the troops in the defeat of the armies of Pol Pot so he had great influence. On the morning that he first heard me proclaim this Wisdom of God, he stood to his feet and agreed saying, "Amen."

Not a Christian at that time, but a leader in need of a vision, he began to learn the proclamation. Now, he has repeated it to the Prime Minister, who has repeated it to the cabinet, and the manifold wisdom of God is coming from a Cambodian face to Cambodian faces declaring that Jesus is doing a great work in the nation. And He is.

The government has released millions of dollars to cleanse the education system of its old caste ways and the farmer's child has an opportunity to rise up to the professions. Young Cambodia has caught the vision for academic excellence and thousands are receiving Christ as the Center of their Being. The Word of God is going forth in great power and they too are picking up the proclamation.

The ministry we serve has been invited into the public schools of all Cambodia, Thailand, and Laos as the proclamation goes forth.

YOUR PROCLAMATION FROM THE LORD

How do we get a proclamation for our region of service? Enter into the dialogue of worship. Bring a sacrifice of praise, not a litany of complaints, before the Lord. Proclaim His worth so your ears, heart, and mind are reminded of His greatness. As He draws you nearer, maintain your focus, do not allow yourself to be distracted. Wait for the word from Him, He is speaking and will open the eyes of your understanding. Rehearse the word you receive in His presence. Speak it to Him. Keep it in your heart until it is fully developed and He gives you a place to say it.

When He gives you the right to speak, speak it simply. Do not make a big deal about yourself, God used Balaam's ass to speak to the prophet. Be sure the word is about Him and not you.

Take action according to the word, giving glory to God and not to yourself. When people say that your vision or proclamation is ridiculous or impossible, grin and do not take offense.

Racism, and the division of the church as a result, is a great sin in America. As we pray about this, we realize more and more that we have lost sight of the sanctity of human life and the value of every person. I have as much cultural bias and try to use my white privilege for purposes in the kingdom. I certainly bear no guilt for having been sent to earth in a white body.

None of us choose our race, family, location, or gender; but, each of us was sent by God.

This announcement needs to be made. It needs to be proclaimed around the world. Jesus loves each of us, and through Him, we can love each other.

CHAPTER 14

A FRESH WORD

We were in Cam Low, Vietnam, with a returned American Marine. During the war he had been stationed here, and had come back to resolve his personal conflicts. He and his wife had joined our team to prayer walk in areas of former conflict. We were the contact team for the Prayer Through the Window initiative for unreached peoples groups in the 10/40 Window.

As we were praying at what used to be the gate to a large base where he had been stationed, he began to flash back. This was the moment his wife and I had been waiting for. As his mind flashed back and forth from then to now and back to then again, his eyes took on a very strange and distant look. He could not get his bearings on time and location. Fear overtook him and he started saying, "Where is it? It should be right there. Where is it?" He was looking for the gate which had meant safety so many years before, and indeed it was not there. The pavement which had entered the gate was there, but the gate itself was long gone.

"You're right," his wife said. "**Old things have passed away, all things are become new**" (2 Corinthians 5:17[83] author's paraphrase). The Word reached down into his heart. His mind cleared and his eyes focused. "You're right, all things are become new!" he announced. A joyful laughter bubbled out of him, and he announced that scripture over and over again to the forces trying to oppress him. "Old things

---

83. [17]Therefore, if anyone is in Christ, he is a new creation; old things have passed away; behold, all things have become new

are passed away, all things are become new." That word was for him, and announcing it set him free.

But the story doesn't end there. We continued our journey for several days, visiting the place where he had been wounded and med-evacked. We stood at the first place where he encountered enemy fire. We walked the trails where he had led patrols, and in every place he said, "It has all changed, old things are passed away, all things have become new."

What we needed in that prayer walk was a fresh word from God. The Lord provided it, and it became the anchor for our souls. Throughout Hanoi, and in every other part of the country, we received friendly greetings because we had the positive attitude that it is the will of God that every man, woman, and child in Vietnam will have the opportunity to receive Jesus as their Lord and Savior in our generation. We were no longer fighting a previous war, we were declaring His victory in a new one!

At this writing, we have heard reports from throughout the country of a sweeping revival which is reaching the mountain people as well as the city dwellers. It is changing the look of Vietnam as another extension of the lie of Moscow comes tumbling down.

THE ANNOUNCEMENT

Ephesians 3:10[84] says the Church will announce to principalities and powers the manifold wisdom of God. The Greek word *gnorizo* means "to initiate into knowledge" according to W. E. Vine1. This is the role of the church. To initiate *archas* and *exousias* into the knowledge of the manifold wisdom of God. What is that wisdom? It is that Jesus was before all things, created all things, and will be worshiped by all things. Those things can be in heaven, on the earth, or under the earth but it doesn't matter because Jesus is Lord in all arenas of existence.

---

84. [10]to the intent that now the manifold wisdom of God might be made known by the church to the principalities and powers in the heavenly places

You are then to go forth into all the earth and declare that Jesus is risen from the dead and has vanquished the Enemy and all his forces. As an Attack Lamb, you go to the five pressure points and you initiate the *archas, exousias, kosmokratos,* and *ponerias* into the understanding that they are defeated. The battle is won, you are the announcer, "Four Forces, we have a decision. The winner and still Champion is Jesus Christ. You are dismissed!"

All conclusive battles are won with praise and worship. Worship is a dialogue with God. It is the language of intimacy with the Holy Spirit which releases confidence in us, and an earthly agreement with Him. It is imperative for every Attack Lamb to maintain a worship discipline. This dialogue with Jesus is the heartbeat of Christian experience.

As we celebrate our salvation in a worship service, we praise Him. This is the sacrifice of praise. Then, when you park your ark on some totally corrupt corner and choose to praise the Lord, you initiate a dialogue. Speaking in the power of the Holy Spirit, you give witness to what you see. That witness is true because it cannot be contaminated by intellect and emotion.

Praise is what opened the prison door for Paul, and it will break the yoke of bondage on those around you. As you praise, you definitely serve notice to the *archas* and *exousias* that there is someone present who can speak mysteries to God. They are dreading the moment just as the demoniac in Mark 1 dreaded the arrival of Christ.

We must dialogue with Jesus about His will in a place. In the history of King David, he asked about every movement. He did not presume that yesterday's plan would bring today's victory. Instead, he sought the Lord for every move. We must also ask the Lord for perception. "What is going on in this place from Your point of view?" is our operative question.

He responds according to His promise, **"If any man lack wisdom, let Him ask of God who freely gives and does not upbraid."** (James

1:5[85], author's paraphrase). He shows us what combination of the four forces are at work in that place. As we wait on Him, He will give tremendous insight. Chinese leaders in many countries have expressed their amazement at the insight which I have been given concerning the clans and power structures in China. Only a Chinese should know these things. In discussions with Taoist believers, they have expressed amazement at the way the Lord has instructed us to pray. A Westerner should not know these things.

This perception has been gleaned as a result of hours of intercession in the five pressure points of these nations. God will show you as you seek Him. Ask the Lord to give you perception into the power structures of your community. Ask Him as you walk through the place where you live just how the four forces are preventing your loved ones from hearing the Gospel. Get the insight from Him.

PRAYING WITH GOD'S PERCEPTION

Next, we pray according to the perception the Lord gives us. I shall never forget sitting in the replica of Lenin's office and realizing the man had, with the help of the *archas*, persuaded nearly two-thirds of the world there was no God. When the Lord showed us that the lie was empowered by the four forces, it became defeatable. I did not have to defeat them again! Jesus has already won that battle! I just had to announce that there was one person in that place who knew Jesus Christ in a personal way. One word of truth defeated the power of the lie. This is *really* praying with the understanding.

Jesus will then give you the word to speak. He has promised if we will say what we hear from Him, and will do what He shows us to do, we cannot lose. We are not leaderless as we stand in that gap. We are in dialogue with the Commander. He has direct access to our spirit as we pray.

---

85. [5]If any of you lacks wisdom, let him ask of God, who gives to all liberally and without reproach, and it will be given to him

THE WORD FOR NOW

So many people make a list of "warfare scriptures" and at this point in their prayers begin reciting the long list. Now, I do believe the Word of God which He sends forth will not return void, but will accomplish that for which it is sent (Isaiah 55:11[86]); but I also believe we are to hear from the Lord in every situation with a current word which He would have us speak.

In our work in Asia, there are many times when what opens the door of utterance to a monk or a temple leader is not a statement, but a question. I ask the Lord to bring to my mind the right question to lead this man a step closer to Christ. Understand, sinners live a hopeless existence whether they are part of a religion or just free thinkers. In either case they have no hope. The Lord gives me the questions, and they plumb the depths of their understanding of their own hopelessness. They invariably come to the conclusion that they need Jesus.

Try this, instead of presuming to speak to a situation, ask the Lord to give you the *rhema* word, the now word for the place.

Recently in Saigon a group of Attack Lambs related to me the story of a prayer walk which they had taken to a center of education, one of the five pressure points that change a nation. This was the center for preparation and administration of the youth movement of Vietnam, those red-scarfed young armies so visible in communist countries. The team had walked about the walled facility for several hours and then had taken up prayer watches on the four corners. The compound is about a block square with the dominant feature of an old temple in the center. The team was praising God quietly and announcing the name of Jesus.

After half hour on location they were startled by a loud crashing sound. They opened their eyes to see that the old temple in the midst of the compound had just collapsed. The next day they read in the

---

86. [11]"So shall My word be that goes forth from My mouth; It shall not return to Me void, But it shall accomplish what I please, And it shall prosper in the thing for which I sent it

local paper about the collapse. There were no injuries and officials were completely without explanation for how it happened. There were no explosives in the area. **The temple had just collapsed!** The team is certain the Lord knocked it down as a sign that He is setting the children free. Now is the time for children's workers in Vietnam.

WHAT MUST I DO?

During the same visit the Attack Lambs met with leaders from across the country of Vietnam. I was told of the experience in a northern province where the prayer walking Attack Lambs had been at a center of government. They had praised, prayed, perceived, prayed according to the perception and were speaking the word of the Lord to the building, saying, "Give up the souls of men!"

Then, from the building emerged a party leader. The Lambs were in twos and spread out so they could not be mistaken for any sort of political group. The man walked right up to one pair and asked, "What must I do to become a Christian?"

In spite of being startled and concerned about arrest, they responded, "You must repent, ask Jesus into your heart, be baptized and burn your party membership card." They were delighted to report he has done all these things, and is now being discipled in a small group. All over South East Asia the reports are the same. As teams implement the dialogue, God gives them souls.

A PROPHETIC ACT

Occasionally the Lord will lead you to a "prophetic act." This is some action which will result in a breakthrough for souls in a nation. Jesus says, "What you see me do, that do." Prophetic acts are representative demonstrations in the natural of something God is implementing in the realm of the Spirit.

I was in Brunei, taking a walk and praying. I was the guest of a member of Gideon's 300, and I was very excited to visit this small but significant country. In the course of our prayer walk, we became aware of the history of Islam on the island of Borneo.

It was explained to us that a couple had come to Borneo from Arabia. Entering the mouth of the Brunei River, they made their way upstream, past the very treacherous currents at the neck, and then to the small village of Jujugong where the Murud people live. The Murud are headhunters.

The man of the couple said, to stay alive among these savages, his wife must say she was his sister. (Sound familiar?) It didn't work. The headman of the village, who was the third Sultan of Brunei, took the woman to be his wife. They conceived a son, the fourth Sultan, and when she was sure he was healthy and strong, the woman killed the third Sultan and threw him into the river.

The woman was a fierce leader, and the son followed her example. He declared Islam to be the faith of the Brunei people; hence, the situation as it is today.

We went to Jujugong and verified the location on the river where the Sultan's body had been thrown in. It is now marked by a site which is attended only by chickens and a few teens very interested in foreign guests. The Murud are no longer headhunters, and the current Murud headman verified that, indeed, this was the place, and we had the legend right. We prayed there and asked the Lord to remove the curse from the land and the people, and to open them to the good news of Jesus.

As we were praying with this perception, the Lord showed us we should take up the Brunei River by the tail as Moses picked up the serpent. Our location near the head waters of the heavily siltladen stream was in fact the tail. As we stood on a jetty, one member of our team took the place of the lady, and a Murud pastor the place of the man. They led in prayers of repentance for Islam coming to the island.

Then we took a bottle of drinking water and, praying the Lord would remove the curse from the river, we poured it in. We sang and danced to the joy of the local teens and then went on our way. We shared the experience with several prayer warriors and I returned to Singapore.

Several months later, we wanted to hold a Prayer Walking Seminar in Brunei. Again, the Gideon's 300 member was volunteered to try to use his influence to make the arrangements. But to have an open meeting there would require an invitation from the Bishop of Kuching. This dear brother has the incredible responsibility of maintaining an open door for Christ in the middle of a Muslim nation. His faith is tremendous.

Weighing the decision, and thinking that people who dance about on jetties and pour water into rivers might be a bit extreme for the delicate balance he has to maintain, he was reported to be a little reluctant to endorse us to the Religious Affairs Bureau.

The time for decision had come and he committed it to much prayer. We too asked the Lord to do something which would confirm the Seminar. On the morning of the last day in which the decision could be reached, the Brunei Bulletin headline read, **"Clear Water Phenomenon Occurs in the Brunei River."** It just so happened that on that day, from a jetty at Jujugong to the mouth of the river, the water ran completely clear!

This was the first time anyone could remember such a thing happening. Children swam in the river and new species of mature fish were caught by fishermen. The Sultan invited specialists to come and examine the river to see what had, in fact, caused this to happen, but they were totally at a loss to explain it.

The invitation came and we had a wonderful seminar which was climaxed by a visit to the *istana* (palace) of the Sultan of Brunei. We also received his personal handshake and greeting! The Lord loves him. It is the will of God that the Sultan and his family enter into a personal relationship with Jesus and be saved and healed. Jesus loves the Sultan enough to change the nature of his river.

I tell you that as you go into the gaps of the world and announce to *archas* and *exousias* the manifold wisdom of God, Jesus will change rivers to open doors for you.

THE REAL ACTION

Prophetic actions are a part of prayer walking, but the real action is in the dialogue. Through worship you have the ability and calling to walk with God on this earth and to participate with Him in His purpose of bringing the Gospel to every person. You can speak life where death has reigned. You can be a way of provision to people who have less than nothing. People, whose spiritual poverty makes their earthly poverty look like riches, become sufficient in both realms because the *kosmokratos* had to flee the Lion in you.

In the course of this dialogue between you and Jesus, there comes a time when the Lord gives you a release in your spirit that the purpose of your prophesying has been accomplished. Some refer to it as a "release," others a "peace," some a "breakthrough." For me it is a secure knowing that Jesus has heard my prayer. Not unlike the resolution of a conflict in the home, this peace releases torrents of love. It is the product of intimate relationship. There is a vast difference between reading a scripture from a list and claiming something has been done, and actually praying until the release is manifest in your spirit, and then humbly proclaiming what the Lord has done.

You are an Attack Lamb. Jesus has sent you forth as a sheep among wolves. Those wolves are in big trouble. You go to those pressure points where the Dagons of today are and park the ark. Keep that dialogue going.

We praise Him and He opens our hearts to worship. We pray for perception and He gives us understanding. We pray according to that perception and He gives us the word or action for the time. We speak the word of the Lord in the anointing of the Spirit, and He gives the release. We proclaim the victory which is to come, and Jesus watches over His Word to perform it.

THE KEY TO PRAYER

Thanksgiving is the key to prayer! There is nothing greater in life than to walk and talk with the Lord, to celebrate in His great joy, and to know the fellowship of His broken heart for the nations. To see the world from His point of view is a maturing thing. It allows no room for anger with man. It gives no place to the work of the Devil. It calls unrighteousness sin and sees millions under the pain of a hopeless existence.

Through dialogue with Jesus we enter into a selflessness which no longer claims the means to soothe the emotional, but cries for the reality of the Spirit through which the yoke is broken and the captive freed. You are called as was John to enter into that heavenly scene and to dialogue with Christ, to hear Him say, "Who will go for us?" Live your life in the impact of His powerful presence.

Go ahead, get in the action. Give yourself to it. Rivers will change, temples will crumble, your enemies will walk up to you and ask to be saved because you are in a dialogue with Jesus, and He never fails.

Announce it to your world! There is a God, He has a Son, His name is Jesus, I know Him personally and you can too.

....

My nephew was one of those typical high school football players who took the game very seriously and prepared for each game as though it were the Super Bowl. He is half-hearted about nothing and has loved the Lord since his childhood. While he was playing for the local high school team, the schedule presented a way for my family to attend his game. So, with coats and blankets, gloves and caps, we drove the few hours with joy anticipating a Pennsylvania tradition, Friday Night Lights.

It was during a time when there was a bit of controversy about football coaches continuing to have their teams kneel before the start of the game to pray together. This was public school and some black-robed people in the Supreme Court had decided that public education could go without Jesus for a while. Several coaches had been reprimanded and a few fired because of their stand for prayer.

Finding our bleacher seats and arranging our blankets, we adjusted to the breeze coming out of the North and began to identify the players. My sister was up on the family events of each of them and gave us a complete background so that we would better enjoy their success. Indeed, several had overcome personal hardship to be on that field.

After some stretching and running, our nephew's team gathered at one end of the field and all knelt together to ask the Lord's protection and blessing on them and their opponent. That is, all but one player. My nephew raised his hands above his head and began to declare victory in Jesus. He rejoiced that the Lord was there. Fifty people kneeling and one walking around rejoicing.

I asked my sister if this was a new thing and she said no, he had come to understand that if you had victory in your heart, then you should rejoice.

PRAY AND REJOICE

So, as an Attack Lamb, where does the prayer change to rejoicing, or do we rejoice in prayer? It has been heartbreaking to see so many healings declared and people not healed, provision declared and businesses fail, election winners declared and the opponent win, football games lost even though we prayed. Since writing the first edition, I have encouraged people to believe their prayers are heard and answered but to know when the Lord is saying, "Pray On," and when He is saying, "It is Finished."

There are three pieces of advice that have kept me balanced in the season of prayer and the season of rejoicing. These three are the cord of confidence that has strengthened, never broken, while waiting to see an answer.

THE DEFEATED DEVIL

First, the devil has been defeated. Hebrews 2:14-15, **"Inasmuch then as the children have partaken of flesh and blood, He Himself likewise shared in the same, that through death He might destroy him who had the power of death, that is, the devil, and release those who through fear of death were all their lifetime subject to bondage."**

The verb tense of this statement says it all. In the past, through His death and resurrection, Jesus has destroyed, made void, made of no effect, the devil. Oh yes, I believe in the devil. He is the one with the nail scarred footprint in his face, and the hands that no longer hold the keys of death and hell. He is still trying to get mankind, especially Christians, to give him familiar names and glory, honor, power, might, and especially dominion in their conversations. Even sermons and teachings lift him up. Sure, when we step into the gaps in our world, we discern evil presence. Evil has not been removed from the world; it has been left here for us to kick around.

My Old Testament companion verse for this rejoicing is Isaiah 26:12-15 KJV, **"Lord, You will establish peace for us, For You have also done all our works in us. O Lord our God, masters besides You have had dominion over us; But by You only we make mention of Your name. They are dead, they will not live; they are deceased, they will not rise. Therefore You have punished and destroyed them, and made all their memory to perish."**

I rejoice that the devil has been defeated. I rejoice that Jesus gave Himself for me. I rejoice that Jesus descended into hell, knocked the devil down (Psalm 3:7), crushed his head (Genesis 3:15), took the keys of death and hell (Revelation 1:18), and took me with Him to the right hand of the Father (Ephesians 1:20).

Just like my nephew, I rejoice before any Prayer Walk, for I know Jesus has defeated the devil and we are going to proclaim the victory, see nations change, and precious people be added to the inheritance.

HE HEARS OUR PRAYERS

My second cause for rejoicing is found in 1 John 5:14-15, "**Now this is the confidence that we have in Him, that if we ask anything according to His will, He hears us. And we know that if He hears us, whatever we ask, we know that we have the petitions that we have asked of Him.**"

I know that it is the will of God that every man, woman, and child on the face of the earth should have the opportunity to receive Jesus Christ as their personal Lord and Savior in this generation. And I rejoice that as I pray for the nations, He will hear and answer my petition. I rejoice that if I need an airfare to get there, He hears my prayer and will provide so that they may have the opportunity to know Him. I rejoice that if I need favor with a government leader, a businessman, or anyone, the heart of the king is in the hand of the Lord and He will turn it. I rejoice daily that I am just a witness of His goodness, a light in the midst of darkness, and that the darkness will flee. I rejoice that He hears me and answers my prayers.

WE'RE NOT IN MANAGEMENT

My third cause of rejoicing is found in Revelations 4:4, "**Around the throne were twenty-four thrones and on the thrones I saw twenty-four elders sitting.**" I rejoice that I am not charged with logistics, strategy, recruiting, and any other part of management. All the management positions in heaven are filled and that sets me free to yield to them and do the part I am anointed to do. I do not have to answer the "Why" and the "How," I just have to go where the Lord says to go and to pray.

Why do people insist on telling God what to do instead of listening for Him to tell them what to do?

"If God will show up, this could be a great thing."

"God is here, He has been waiting for you to show up."

I tell you this is a cause for rejoicing. We do not run the timing and the outcomes. Jesus is the healer and the deliverer. We do not control the outcome, but we do control the atmosphere and we rejoice in the promises of God. That atmosphere for miracles is an atmosphere of rejoicing in which God is, and the fact that we are His children. I rejoice in the fact that when we decided to praise Him, to rejoice in the midst of the situation, we initiate a dialogue that is going to release anointing, and the horse and the rider are going to be cast into the sea.

These are my three pieces of advice: the devil is destroyed, my prayers are answered, and I am not in management and neither are you. These three keep me rejoicing through all that life has to bring.

Rejoice in the Lord always, and again I say rejoice. No matter what the news may bring. No matter what the opinion of man may be. No matter how I feel or what I think, rejoicing in the Lord gives me power.

CHAPTER 15

DAWN OF A NEW DAY

While working in Repale, India, I witnessed the dawn of a new day for the people there. A young, American missionary had traveled from Nepal to where we were, and her journey had been extremely difficult. While working in the mountains of Nepal she had fallen and broken her leg so severely she had to be carried for several days just to get out of the mountains. An even longer trip brought her to Kathmandu for treatment. But during the time it had taken her to get there, the bones of her leg had begun to fuse incorrectly. Now her leg had to be rebroken and set properly.

By the time she arrived in India, she was acquainted anew with agony. But she had also tasted the love the Asians have for anyone who will suffer hardship to come to them. Her heart was filled with love for the Lord and the people.

We were scheduled to minister in an evening crusade and had stretched out at a friend's home to rest. This young lady sat in the room, her plaster-bound leg supporting the guitar, and she began to pick a tune and sing. Before long she had shifted over into singing in an unknown tongue. I joined with her and with full heart we sang a song in a language we had never heard. There was a sweet melody and descant. The rhythm was as foreign as the words. Time stood still as our voices filled the air with this spiritual song.

My reverie was broken by a sound at the window. We could see a crowd of people standing outside. When I went to the window and looked out I saw the house was surrounded. Other people were running to the house. We had no idea what had happened until our host exclaimed, "They have heard you sing the praises of God in their own dialect. Never have they seen a white woman or man who could play their rhythms and sing their songs. They want to know how this is possible."

She remained in India for many months, and gained such a reputation for the healings which occurred while she sang, that she was "invited" by the government to leave.

To this day you can go among those villages and they will tell you of the lady with the plaster cast who praised God in their tongue, and after whom there followed great signs and wonders. It was truly the dawn of a new day for those people.

DISCIPLE A WHOLE NATION

In these last days before the return of the Lord, the Holy Spirit is moving us to the uttermost parts of the earth and giving us strategies to disciple a whole nation.

The Egyptians and the Israelites had an interesting relationship. The Israelites were intimidated by the Egyptians because they were in power. But the Egyptians were also intimidated by the Israelites because of their great numbers. The Israelites were left leaderless and isolated by this intimidation. They felt they had no right to speak. This prevented them from hearing the word of deliverance which Moses brought.

Moses won in warfare, but he had to overcome the Four Forces which had arrayed themselves in the gap between the children of Israel and God. The Hebrews had become slaves and were being used to build the temples of false gods, and had no recourse. In their fear of the Hebrews, the Egyptians had become malicious. Each step forward for Israel brought planned retribution from the courts of Pharaoh.

Moses had to walk in three disciplines to experience his success. If they were necessary for Moses, it would do us well to adopt them for our use as well. Just as he was sent to disciple a whole nation, you have been sent by God to your gap to win too.

In the next few chapters we will be talking about the disciplines necessary for spiritual warfare, how to define a nation through five pressure points, and four keys to reaching any people. Moses lived out these disciplines and stood in the gap for Israel. You too will win in warfare as you disciple a whole nation.

THE FIRST DISCIPLINE: WORSHIP

Paul writes to the Ephesian church,

And be not drunk with wine, wherein is excess; but be filled with the Spirit; speaking to yourselves in psalms and hymns and spiritual songs, singing and making melody in your heart to the Lord; giving thanks always for all things unto God and the Father in the name of our Lord Jesus Christ; submitting yourselves one to another in the fear of God. **Ephesians 5:18–21 KJV**

Why are they encouraged to have a song in their hearts? Because the heart is desperately wicked (Jeremiah 17:9[87]), and out of the abundance of the heart the mouth speaks (Matthew 12:34[88]). And we are commanded to guard our heart because the issues of life flow from it (Proverbs 4:23[89]). To be successful in spiritual endeavor our heart must maintain its focus on the throne of God. We must discipline ourselves to focus on the throne and worship with the elders, angels, and beasts while false gods bow down. The first of three disciplines necessary for spiritual warfare is the **Worship Discipline.**

Paul's admonition to worship begins with separation from the world's source of joy. *"…be not drunk with wine wherein is excess;…"*

---

87. [9]"The heart is deceitful above all things, And desperately wicked; Who can know it?

88. [34]Brood of vipers! How can you, being evil, speak good things? For out of the abundance of the heart the mouth speaks

89. [23]Keep your heart with all diligence, For out of it spring the issues of life

Those for whom you pray are drunk with the spirit of this age. It is nothing less than the *kosmokratos* of Ephesians 6:12[90]. Emboldened by the illusion of power it supplies, children of the age declare their invincibility, self determination, right to choose, and indomitable self-will. As this generation slides down the lust-greased slope of amoral narcissism, the song playing loudly in the background will be, "I did it my way."

Paul's admonition is to those of us who will stand in the gap, reconciling the drunken and deceived so they will no longer participate in the wine of this age.

....

The **first essential** to the worship discipline is **determination** to no longer walk as the Gentiles, but walk in the Holy Spirit.

Excess is the trademark of this age. Marketing has focused more on this generation than any other. It is not uncommon to see children wearing shoes that cost more than US$100. In many Asian capitals debt is extremely high as young people spend their future on the look of the Now Generation. The *kosmokratos* is placing them under the bondage of the age, which is excess. Sultans have fleets of cars, President's wives have rooms full of shoes. One ruling Democratic family boasts about twenty percent of the nation's Gross National Product being diverted into their family businesses.

In every country homes are destroyed by spouses who determine one partner is not enough, they must have more. The drive for more is actually killing the planet as we suck the resources from its depths to feed our excesses. Excess has caused brother to kill brother and father to kill son. Excess causes women to defy all natural law and kill the life which God has designed them to birth. Men declare, "Women have the right to choose," as though that life did not start with the man.

In an age gone wild with excess, you enter the gap. You realize a man's life does not consist of the things which he possesses. You have

90. [12]For we do not wrestle against flesh and blood, but against principalities, against powers, against the rulers of the darkness of this age, against spiritual hosts of wickedness in the heavenly places

to make a determined decision to walk a separate path. You must reject the song of the world in your heart, and be filled with the Holy Spirit.

As God fashioned the ark of the covenant, so He has fashioned you with one purpose, to bear His glory into the presence of the gods of this age and see them bow down before Him. Yours is a mighty calling from a mighty God.

....

The **second essential** to worship discipline is **disembarkation.** The world is on a ship headed to hell. They are surrounded by the sirens of the sin-sick sea which sing songs of sensuality. (Whew!) But **you** must get off the boat. There is no mid-point. No compromise will be acceptable if you are going to stand in the gap. The evangelist may be able to identify with the people. The contemporary musician may be able to develop a sound similar to that of the world, but you are an intercessor and you **must** disembark. Moses could not continue in the ways of Egypt. Just as Israel was going to spend forty years in the wilderness, he did first. He had to get Egypt out of his heart before he could lead the hearts of his people out of Egypt.

Through his worship discipline Moses found that the wine of God's Spirit was preferable to the fine tastes of Egypt. The appetites which once caused him to sin were now closed to Pharaoh's temptation. Moses' passions now focused on God as he stood silently before the Four Forces. He was not intimidated, he was given God's right to speak, he could not be bought off, no weapon formed against him could prosper. The baby of the bulrushes was now the pilot of the ship of salvation charting the way of his nation through intercession.

....

"**...be filled with the Spirit;...,**" Paul continues. Spiritual work must be done a spiritual way. This nineteenth verse of Ephesians 5[91]

---

91. [19]speaking to one another in psalms and hymns and spiritual songs, singing and making melody in your heart to the Lord

gives us the **third essential** to worship discipline. We must **declare** the worthiness of God.

For Moses to declare the worthiness of God to the people, he had to first have a revelation in his own spirit. He had seen the burning bush and stood on the holy ground. His hand had been made leprous and healed again. His staff had been brought to life. His thoughts spoken back to him. He had come to realize that the Lord is greater than anything created, because He was before all things. Moses could declare the power, presence, person, and purpose of God, because they had met and walked together in the mountain.

Paul admonishes the Ephesians and us to maintain that throne room power through the exercise of the tongue in different ways. First, we are to speak in psalms. Next, we are to speak in hymns. Third, we are to speak in spiritual songs.

What is common to all three? We are to speak. When you speak, the ear nearest to your mouth is your own ear. You believe what you say. When you testify to others, you are encouraged because you are hearing one of the ways in which we overcome the Accuser...with the word of our testimony (Revelation 12:11[92]). You are listening as you talk.

The doors to the nations are open; God has opened them. You will either talk your way into them or you will tell yourself a million reasons why you are not going. You will determine what song you hear for you are the singer.

As an Attack Lamb, you control the environment around you. The song in the air will be the one you put there as you worship the Lord. How refreshing it is to hear a kind or polite word. How refreshing is a positive report. A good report from a far land is like a glass of cool water (Proverbs 25:25[93]). You will bring refreshing to your soul and those around you as you sing the Psalms.

---

92. [11]And they overcame him by the blood of the Lamb and by the word of their testimony, and they did not love their lives to the death
93. [25]As cold water to a weary soul, So is good news from a far country

THE WINNING POWER OF WORSHIP

One time in Canton, China, I was sitting in the coffee house of a restaurant waiting to return to Hong Kong. Our group had been successful in delivering a large number of Bibles to the church and we were rejoicing. As we sang, we spoke out in the song of the Holy Spirit, singing in a language we did not understand.

Adjacent to us was a table of students. In their twenties, they were very much into the new image of China. Their cigarette smoking was not as bad as their beer belching and loud shouting. As we sang they began to weep. One of them spoke to our leader, who did not understand what was said. The young man spoke again in Mandarin Chinese.

"How do these Westerners know our dialect?" he asked.

"They do not," replied our leader.

"Yes, they are singing about Jesus and His love for us, we want to confess our sins and receive Him as the song says." His tearstreaked face and remorsefully repentant voice confirmed his sincerity. The entire group opened their hearts to the Lord that afternoon.

Martin Luther declared the Spirit to be ours. Paul says to sing "spiritual songs." The Corinthians are encouraged to sing with the Spirit and with the understanding (1 Corinthians 14:15[94]). While many songs are spirited and music is used in many cultures to invoke a certain spirit, Paul is talking here about the song of the Holy Spirit birthed in our hearts.

Declaring Christ among the nations is the result of a **worship discipline**. As you practice His praise, you will see His glory. Speak in psalms, hymns, and spiritual songs, making melody in your heart to the Lord.

---

94. [15]What is the conclusion then? I will pray with the spirit, and I will also pray with the understanding. I will sing with the spirit, and I will also sing with the understanding

By exercising our tongues in these three ways, we declare Christ's worth in the Word, in the history of the Church, and today. **The worship discipline is vital to spiritual warfare.**

The word of your testimony joins with that of the Church, and the Rock of Ages calls you to His ranks of Attack Lambs. You march with Judah in the army of Jehoshaphat and watch as the Moabite and Ammonite fall before you.

Judah declared the worthiness of God. Moses and David declared the worthiness of God. You, as a worshiping warrior, must declare the worthiness of God. Moab, Ammon, and Seir fell before Judah. Pharaoh fell before Moses. Goliath fell before David. The Dagons of today **will** bow down before you as you declare the worthiness of God.

The worship discipline develops a focus on the throne of God. As you enter into the gap, you will need to maintain this focus. As it was with Moses, you will hear the sounds of government leaders, you will hear the sounds of elders, you will hear the sounds of family members, but above all you will hear the questioning sound of your own doubts. Will God really hear your prayer and save your nation?

As Moses remained focused on the sound of God, you must allow the thunder of the sound of many waters to drown out the other sounds. Government will tell you that you have the right to speak but when you try to exercise that right, you find they do not support you in your cause. You must allow the certainty of the throne to drown out the uncertainty of man.

LEADERS WORSHIPING

The leaders of churches are the hardest working group of people I know. They have my utmost respect. I can recall carrying five titles as a staff pastor in a local church. When people came to me with an idea for another area of ministry, I would feel overwhelmed. I am afraid I was not as supportive as I could have been. I thank God for the times they would patiently pray until my mind finally cleared and I could hear what they were saying.

You may encounter this type of difficulty mobilizing Attack Lambs in your church. Please pray for those who are your pastors and leaders that they will also hear very clearly and focus on the throne of God.

Each time I inform my family members of travel plans, I know, while they support the work I am doing, they would rather I remain at home. Just as Moses' wife had to make major adjustments to the idea of covenant relationship and going down to Egypt, our families may have to adjust to the call on our lives.

Many fine Women's Aglow officers have had to walk this tight rope of submission. They have had to maintain their focus on heaven's throne and speak its peace to the throne of their home. The joy of worship has paved the way for them.

Worry wars against worship. "O what peace we often forfeit, O what needless pain we bear, all because we do not carry everything to God in prayer,[1]" the old hymn says. As an "A" type self-motivator, I can easily fail in the worship discipline and begin to worry about management decisions in the Kingdom. I have to remember, **I'm not in management…I'm in sales.** The worship discipline begins with a sacrifice of praise, and I am not always adept at giving it. I am asking the Lord to make me faster with the worship, and eliminate the worry.

Moses maintained his focus on the throne of God. The voice of Pharaoh was silenced. The voice of the elders of Israel received a new song of thanks to our God. Moses' sister took up the tambourine and danced before the Lord, and Moses' own doubts were stilled as the Red Sea closed. The worshiping warrior had learned the delivering power of the discipline of worship.

Moses' dialogue with God teaches us an Attack Lamb strategy. You will one day stand before important people, seeking the freedom to declare Christ in your schools, towns, and places of business. Just as Moses did, you will need to hear the voice of God in the midst of the pressure of the gap. Just as Moses did, you need to practice a conversational relationship with God.

THE FOUR VOICES IN WORSHIP

The first voice in the dialogue with God is your **praise**. You offer it. It is birthed in your desire to proclaim Jesus as Lord of your life. We bring the sacrifice of praise in the face of opposition. Praise causes you to focus on the throne in the face of the Four Forces.

The second voice in the dialogue is the release to **worship**. This is different from praise. Worship is initiated in your spirit by the Holy Spirit. It is the inclusion of the Attack Lamb in the timing and anthem of heavenly expression. True worship is occurring as you allow the Holy Spirit to set you free from the preoccupation caused by the presence of the Four Forces. You are giving all trust to the Lord as you worship.

Flowing with the Spirit, you begin to declare the worth of God. This is initiated in your spirit as the depth of devotion divulges the desire of the born-again heart. This draws open the curtains of intimacy with Christ. This worship invites His participation in further dialogue.

The third voice is that of **blessing**. He will speak a promise to your heart. In corporate worship, the gifts of the Spirit will manifest. Jesus is blessing the believer or congregation with an answer to their needs. Because He is manifest both in corporate and private devotion, we must develop the discipline of worship to release the blessings He has for us.

The fourth and final voice is returning **thanks** to Him, which is a form of praise. The conversation is complete as we return thanks, and the process begins again. When we have this dialogue as a discipline incorporated in our daily experience, we begin to hear the heart of God for our family, our church, our city or our school. The discipline of worship is God's school to teach you His voice.

He speaks today, as always, to give direction to the deliverers of this age. Those who are His children hear His voice, and enter into dialogue with Him for the benefit of the nations.

··············

"All authority has been given to Me in heaven and on earth. Go therefore and make disciples of all the nations, baptizing them in the name of the Father and the Son and of the Holy Spirit, teaching them to observe all things that I have commanded you; and lo, I am with you always, even to the end of the age."

Matthew 28:18b-20

In our book, *A Faith to Die For* we developed the five steps of Christian growth set forth in the reference section of the Thompson Chain Bible and defined the steps of discipleship as Multitude, Believer, Disciple, Apostle, and Martyr. In our Attack Lambs first edition, we defined what a disciple is and gave three essential disciplines that must be taught: Worship, the Word, and Work.

In this second edition I would like to set forth another discipline, but this one does not start with "W."

N+1

We live in an impoverished world. No place is worse than Cambodia. I entered Cambodia with the sole intent of praying for the place. Now, 25 years later, I am an advisor to the government on international affairs. This non-paid position gives me access to the decision makers. Not that we have great influence, but we are able to bring "those things I have commanded you" into discussions on health, education, youth, and economic development. We have this "right to speak" to the "Kosmokratos" because of the demonstration of the love of God.

When we began working in the education sector, we were asked to bring our "N+1" education system to a rural school and raise up a model that, if successful, could be replicated across the nation. Our model is the current national system (N) plus the teachings of Jesus (1). We complimented the existing system, calling it "excellent". We implemented the word of God, teaching them what Jesus has commanded and making a "more excellent way" (1 Corinthians 12:31[95]). The result is a partnership of church and state with defined goals of academic accomplishment.

When we began working there the schools were staffed with volunteers who had survived Pol Pot or had returned from refugee camps in Thailand. They were paid one dollar per day, thirty per month. They taught five hours per day for six days per week. However, the rice farmer in their village, whose children   they were teaching, earned $200 per year or $0.55 per day. This is poverty by any scale.

We began to subsidize the teachers by giving them an additional dollar per day but demanded a higher standard of attendance and preparation. They joyfully responded to our quarterly "in service" weekends where we would add value in teaching methods, math, and science. They were very happy and worked very hard to make us the number one rural school in Cambodia. The "+1" and the teachers incentives raised the standard.

With doubling their income, we gained the right to speak about finances. It is never wise to criticize, so we complimented their coming up from the Killing Fields and their dedication to the children and we taught them one of SEAPC's core values, "Today you are a recipient nation, but soon, you will become a donor nation for it is more blessed to give than to receive."

We held an assembly for all teachers and administration and taught the principle of Seed Time and Harvest. I chuckle to think about a city boy teaching this to rice farmers. They know more about seed and yield, and the factors that determine the ratio than I ever will. Of course, they got it.

Then we made application in finances of sowing seed into another and how much yield that would make.

Our Cambodian friends have a delightful habit of carrying just a few paper bills of the smallest amount in their left front shirt pocket.

---

95. [31]But earnestly desire the best gifts. And yet I show you a more excellent way.

After teaching to give to one another, and taking a time in prayer, I instructed them to go to a person in the room and give them some small amount as a gift. With a great deal of shyness and giggling, they did it.

In the same meeting we explained tithing as a covenant with God (Genesis 14:18-20[96]) for people to be born into the inheritance. We serve the Lord by teaching the young people. We add value to them through our faith and the education they receive. Our trust is that they will be Christ-centered, Bible-based, Holy Spirit-filled, and academically excellent. By adding value to them, we multiply the value Jesus has sown in us. As a result of this sowing, we will reap a harvest. God is the rewarder of those who diligently seek Him (Hebrews 11:6[97]).

In anticipation of the blessing we would receive, we established a tithe fund that would be overseen by representatives from among the teachers to be distributed to families in need. Thereby, relativizing need to scale at village level.

With great rejoicing we concluded our time and I moved on to the next post.

About six months later I returned to this school and was invited to a very important meeting. A month after the beginning of giving, the education department had raised the national school teacher's salary to $250 per month, an 800% increase. They presented me with a beautiful letter saying, "Thank you for helping when we had nothing, now please do not give us any more money, but use it where it is needed in another country."

So, I am adding the discipline of giving to this edition of Attack Lambs.

---

96. [18]Then Melchizedek king of Salem brought out bread and wine; he was the priest of God Most High. [19]And he blessed him and said: "Blessed be Abram of God Most High, Possessor of heaven and earth; [20]And blessed be God Most High, Who has delivered your enemies into your hand." And he gave him a tithe of all.
97. [6]But without faith it is impossible to please Him, for he who comes to God must believe that He is, and that He is a rewarder of those who diligently seek Him.

THE TITHE DISCIPLINE

Tithing is a covenant declaration in Worship. Giving takes us to a new dimension, it releases nation changing power. There are many who say, "I don't give to receive. I do not believe in sowing finances to gain finances." My response?

You must not be a farmer.

Every farmer I have ever met knows exactly how much seed must be purchased and sown into how much acreage to produce how much harvest to be sold at what price to make a return on the seed sown. This is the business of farming. As I drive from the East Coast of America to the West Coast, I spend days driving past fields that are perfectly groomed and producing marvelous crops. On one prayer journey among Native Americans, I stopped on a rise in Wheat County, Montana. The view was so vast it actually made my eyes hurt. It is called Wheat County for a reason. It is not Corn County and it is not Soybean County. They sow wheat and they harvest wheat. You get what you sow. I burst into praise and thanksgiving for this land and the bountiful harvest. Seed sown had been multiplied into such a yield that men and machinery worked into the long summer evenings gathering the harvest.

One year we mobilized prayer on university campuses. I traveled to 42 schools in 40 days criss-crossing America by car. Seed time and harvest is a God given principle by which America feeds the world. The abundance and beauty of these farms in absolutely breathtaking. Kansas, Iowa, and Nebraska have more acreage under cultivation than the total land mass Cambodia, Vietnam, Laos, Thailand, and Myanmar combined. Prosperity in the heartland of America is determined by the God given covenant, "**While the earth remains, seedtime and harvest, cold and heat, winter and summer, and day and night shall not cease**" (Genesis 8:22).

But, giving is a discipline. Very few Christians meet the minimum of the tithe. It is a shame that tithing is taught as a law and not a natural flow from the heart of Abraham. Abraham knew instinctively to gather 10% of the material spoils of victory and to meet in the Valley of the Kings with the King of Peace. He knew it. Moses and the law would come centuries later and reestablish the standard with the Children of Abraham. But, Abraham knew it. It was in his heart to give glory to the Lord for the victory he had received. He had gathered materially; but, more importantly, he had recovered his family member from captivity. Genesis 14 should be taught by every pastor and missionary in the body of Christ. It certainly should be taught in the business community. A marketplace ministry without tithing is moving in the wisdom of man, not the manifest wisdom of God.

The King of Peace did not need the tithe to keep the lights on in Jerusalem. He was the Light of the city.

And His Son, the Prince of Peace, doesn't need the tithe for His city either. He is the Light of that City.

FOUR PROMISES

Tithing releases four very special promises to the believer. That is why I feel it is a discipline every Attack Lamb should develop.

The words spoken in Malachi 3 are a message of reconciliation in which the Lord is calling to mankind to remove curses and poverty. They have become part of our teaching to lift people from poverty into the blessings of God. We teach tithing, but do not require it, for the discipline of tithing and offerings must be formed in the heart of the believer. Our premise is that if we are the seed of Abraham, then this will also be in our hearts.

The first blessing that is promised to those who have the discipline of giving the tithe is the opening of the windows of heaven and pouring out a blessing too great to be contained. God even says, "**If I will not open for you the windows of heaven and pour out for you such blessing that there will not be room enough to receive it**" (Malachi 3:10b). When we began the ministry, I could keep the financial records with little difficulty. We tithed and increased so much we had to hire a bookkeeper. We continued to tithe and grew big enough that an external audit was required. We tithed and now have a department and staff just to keep up with the daily cash flow into the ministry. By God's grace we have kept administrative costs under 7% all these years. We now invest 95% of every donor dollar into fields around the world.

The second blessing to those who develop the discipline of tithes and offerings is, "**I will rebuke the devourer for your sake**" (Malachi 3:11a) The compound interest demon of debt shall not touch you. Sickness, which consumes your budget, will not rest upon you and your family. You will be protected from every device of the devil. No weapon formed against you shall prosper. Those who set a snare for you shall fall in it themselves. Now retirement age, I am sustained by the fruit of a lifetime of tithing. The Lord is taking really good care of me through the fruit of seeds sown many years ago.

The third blessing, "Your vine shall not fail to bear fruit for you in the field." At the beginning of our experience with the tithe we were practically funded by a handful of people in the US and especially in our home area. As we "extended our vine" to the nations of Southeast Asia we began to see that these people, particularly Chinese, began to hand us money. We saw that as the vine extended into the field, the fruit in the field began to not only pay all costs, but make significant increase in our seed bag. The Lord gave us sufficient for the worker and abundance for the work and increased our bag of seed as is promised in 2 Corinthians 9:8-15. So, we not only tithed, but sowed significant seed into the work. Our fruitful vine continues to grow as we work in the field God has given to us.

The fourth promise to the tither is, "All nations will call you blessed, for you shall be a delightful nation." Indeed, we are seen as those who can help in every situation. We are approached constantly by ministries and governments to help in our fields of prayer, healthcare, education, parenting, and micro-economic development. This global reputation is a gift from the Lord and gives us the right to speak to nations. We are able to teach at a governmental level the things the Lord taught. We are able to step over the separation of church and state to bring Jesus's words to the ears and hearts of policy and decision makers.

Four promises, made by the Lord of Lords, to all who would walk in the covenant of Abraham and, from the heart, worship Him with tithes and offerings.

THE GENEROSITY FACTOR

What has to happen for this discipline to become part of your Attack Lamb lifestyle? S. Truett Cathy is the founder of Chick-Fil-A, one of America's fastest growing quick service restaurants. He co-authored wrote a great little book called *The Generosity Factor*. I suggest you get it and read and reread it. This book has been a guide to me for over 15 years.

Cathy says that there has to be a **HEART** change for a person to become generous. Until this **HEART** change we are bound by what we will receive and not free to give when the opportunity presents itself.

HE OWNS IT ALL.

The **H** in his acrostic is to remind us that God owns it all. He purchased us and He owns not only our sin, but also our success. So whatever funds I handle in this life are His, not mine. Generosity does not think in terms of mine and His, it is all His and I am His.

EVERY DAY IS AN OPPORTUNITY.

The **E** is to remind us that every day is an opportunity. Wayne Myers, the Apostle of Faith, has, from his Mexico City base, blessed every nation on earth. For over 70 years he has been used of God to fill gaps in some of the most remote places on earth. He was used greatly in my early years concerning prayer and giving. His favorite verse on giving is Luke 6:38, "**With the same measure that you use, it will be measured back to you.**"

Wayne and his wife, Martha, set a discipline of giving something to someone every day. It may be a dollar, it may be a thousand, but they start each day looking for the God sent opportunity to give something to someone.

This discipline causes us to be concerned with the cares of others. It frees us to enter into the gap with a view of reconciling people to God. It causes us to be cheerful as we see a small seed grow into a big plant that reaches around the world.

ACTION MUST BE TAKEN.

The **A** is to remind us that action must be taken. You might be nodding your head in agreement and saying to yourself, "I will start tomorrow." No, start today. You have the means to sow a financial seed right now and get in the flow of this marvelous discipline. Use your phone or computer, go online, find Every Home for Christ (ehc. org/give-now), and sow a seed. Transfer funds to them. They are one of the unique ministries that reach every nation. Go ahead, action must be taken.

RECALL WHAT THE LORD HAS DONE FOR YOU.

The **R** is to remind us to recall what the Lord has done for us. Generosity has a momentum. God has blessed us in so many ways. When we stop to reflect on His goodness to us, it inspires us to be more generous with His abundant blessings. Generosity is a relational power which, once set in motion, produces a stream of God's provision that can be directed, through prayer, to points of need. God blesses us to be a blessing to others.

Psalm 112:3[98] teaches us that wealth and riches will be in the house of the man who fears the Lord. The fear of the Lord is to abstain from evil. Evil is anything that acts against the nature of God, the wellbeing of mankind and is detrimental to the environment.

---

98. [3]Wealth and riches will be in his house, And his righteousness endures forever.

Wealth and riches will dwell in our house. Riches are what you have, wealth is what you give. Riches testify to the faithfulness of God to His promise of blessing, wealth is the measure of our return to Him by giving to others. Many rich people are not wealthy and many wealthy people have chosen to use their riches to benefit others.

The problem here is that the more you give, the more God gives to you. So, riches and wealth will both be in your house.

TAKE TIME NOW TO THANK GOD FOR YOUR BLESSINGS

And the **T** is to remind us to thank God for all we have and all He is doing through us. The attitude of gratitude is the heart of the Attack Lamb. We do not work to be saved; we work because we are redeemed. This relationship we enjoy with Jesus is absolutely the most wonderful value we have. Related, a joint heir, child of the King, we must give thanks to Him with a grateful heart, and let the poor say I am rich in the power of His love.

The financial disciplines of tithes and offerings releases the full provision of God to go where He sends us, to be effective there in prayer and the release of the Holy Spirit, and to make disciples of the nations by teaching them financial discipline according to the Word of God.

GIVE

After the publication of the first edition of Attack Lambs, I was approached by a Financial Development Director of a sister ministry. She was very keen to know what our system of fundraising was, for the Lord was pouring out blessings upon us. We met in our rented office space and I really enjoyed listening to her approach to marketing Christian ministries. Always ready to learn, I gave her over an hour to speak and she was quite good.

Then she asked me what our system was.

I responded in one word, "Give." Luke 6:38[99] gives us very clear instruction that we are to give to start the flow and to keep on giving to sustain it. I encouraged her that day and you today, don't look for the place you can receive, look for the place you can give. It is more blessed to give than to receive.

Working as a consultant in missions, I have been approached by several churches concerning the raising of funds for their ministries. I just ask for the church checkbook and in about 20 minutes can give direction. Their expenditures tell me their priorities. Are they a giving group? Do they thank God for abundance? As Pastor Jay Passavant told North Way Christian Community in the face of a large building payment, "We do not serve the God of Get By, we serve the God of More than Enough." He then increased their mission giving and the Lord poured out a great blessing, meeting the need and beyond.

Get this discipline of giving deep in your spirit. Live to give. Ask the Lord to give you the heart of faithful Abraham who knew instinctively what to do.

---

99. [38]"Give, and it will be given to you: good measure, pressed down, shaken together, and running over will be put into your bosom. For with the same measure that you use, it will be measured back to you."

CHAPTER 16

THE WORD OF LIGHT

The second discipline necessary for spiritual warfare is the **Word Discipline**. It is through the soul-saving, incorruptible seed of the Word that we gain a place of ministry and the ability to perform it. By the strength and light derived from this discipline, we have the power: to dispel darkness from the peoples of the earth, to establish the government of God in all we do, to exercise the ministry gifts God has bestowed, and to manifest His Power Presence.

God said, "Light be," and light dispelled the darkness. We used to play a little game with our children who were afraid of the dark. We would turn on a light and try to find where the darkness would hide, because the darkness is afraid of the light. Together with the child we would look under the bed, but when we shone the light under there, there was no darkness. We would look in the closet, but when we opened the door, we could find no darkness for the light had dispelled the darkness. When we looked deep into the toe of the last pair of discarded shoes deep in the corner of the closet, we could see a little darkness, but that was certainly not enough to keep us awake, and we certainly would not be afraid of something hidden that deep in the toe of an old shoe. In fact, if we threw out the shoe, we could throw out the darkness at the same time.

While this is a child's game, it has truth for us. The darkness is strong only until some Attack Lamb starts to shed light on it. The light will dispel the darkness.

When Jesus asked, **"Will you also leave me?"** Peter replied, **"Lord, to whom shall we go, you alone have the words of eternal life"** (John 6:68[100] author's paraphrase). Attention Attack Lambs: to bring nation-changing revival, we must first study to show ourselves approved unto God. Until we are disciplined in the Word, God will not entrust the lives of those for whom He died to you.

NO ONE IS HOME

So often I look into the eyes of those around me when I travel to foreign countries, only to realize there is no light in the soul I am seeing. Often I comment, "There is no one home." The real shock comes when the person is someone I think highly of. Until they know Christ, the light will not shine forth from those eyes. It is my daily prayer that the darkness will be dispelled and light will fill the void.

In the Genesis account of creation we find that darkness covered the face of the deep. And then…"God said." God spoke to the darkness. Man, is that ever a power principle! God spoke, David spoke, Moses was supposed to speak, Jesus said…speak to the mountain… We are really onto something here!

God said, "Light be," and there was. Isn't this what we want to see happen to those around us? Isn't this the cry of your heart, you who have entered into the gap to intercede to reconcile man to God? Isn't this what you want to see for your parents and children?

WHEN THE LIGHT COMES ON

Can you imagine the light coming on in your school or place of work? Just think how it would be if this afternoon the light of the Gospel came on in the minds in Jakarta or Beijing. Imagine the light coming on in the United Nations when they realize only Jesus can bring true peace to the world. Imagine OPEC when the light comes on!

---

100. [68]But Simon Peter answered Him, "Lord, to whom shall we go? You have the words of eternal life

It works the same way in our lives, beloved. As we exercise our Word discipline, we dispel the darkness in our lives.

Often I'm asked where a person should go to prepare for ministry. I tell them the first place to go is to their own Bible, and study. When they assure me they are ready to launch out, I gently ask them to name the books of the Bible. Then I ask for the theme, time, and setting of each book. By then the would-be Attack Lamb realizes what I am saying. The Word discipline must be established for the darkness to be dispelled.

ATTACK LAMB LIFESTYLE

So many Christians have a sense of salvation but little, if any, idea of the Attack Lamb lifestyle. They are always asking directional questions. They have no lamp for their feet. They certainly are not equipped for spiritual warfare because they lack discipline.

Matthew 10 teaches the lifestyle of the Attack Lamb. It is this lifestyle which separates the disciple from the believer. In the Sermon on the Mount, Jesus indicates the impact those who walk in the power of His Word are going to make on the community and the globe. Darkness is dispelled from their minds as He teaches them how to relate to Him and to each other, and to the world around them. He is very clear they must love each other, as well as those whom they hope to reach.

In like fashion, He instructs the disciples they are not to be encumbered with the cares of this life as they go out to those who are in those fields ripe unto harvest. They are to bring healing and deliverance and proclaim the Kingdom of God. The government of all affairs is to be seen in the light of the Gospel.

YOU – A LIGHTHOUSE

When you enter into the gap and face the Four Forces, they are dispelled by the light of truth. You have become the "lighthouse" to direct your friends and neighbors away from the rocky shores of this age and into the safe harbor of Christ's love.

Imagine how the shadow of **intimidation**, the first force, must flee when the light of the perfect love which casts out all fear shines from your eyes. You are not afraid of the terror by night or the destruction at noon day (Psalm 91). The love that Jesus has placed in your heart allows you the freedom to dispel the darkness from your environment. You have become the indomitable force upon whom the threats of ungodly Goliaths have no effect.

The **right to speak** is the second force you can now dispel from the security of your "lighthouse." As you enter into the space between your community and Christ there will be forces who will say, "You cannot talk about Jesus here."

They will threaten to sue you. They will challenge the legality of your personal witness for Christ. They will try to cause you to lay down your God-given commission to name the name of Jesus. The light of the Word in your "Lighthouse" will drive them off.

I recently produced a TV special on "Christ in the Public Schools." The American Civil Liberties Union (ACLU) responded by threatening the school board of that community with lawsuit. Thank God for a principal and superintendent who responded with the light of the Gospel saying, "Do not threaten us. If you are going to court, go; but, be prepared for the battle of your life." The ACLU blinked first and backed away from the battle.

THE FEARLESS FIGHT OF LOVE

The third force you will dispel is that of **using people to get things**. As you demonstrate the love of Jesus through acts of kindness you dispel this power. The Lord, finding you interceding in the gap, will allow you to become aware of information. He will speak to you facts about those in the area so you can pray for them. As you pray for them, you will feel the love of Jesus beginning to flow out from you. His glorious Power Presence will accompany you to activities in the community, and those you have been praying for will be drawn to you.

Remember, they are used to being used. They will have their guard up and defenses at the ready. Be gentle. A kind word is often appreciated. You will notice that as you bring a cheerful greeting, a kind gesture, or a warm handshake, the *kosmokratos* will be dispelled. I have seen it time and again.

The counterattack will be the invitation to use your freedom in some kind of community action which uses people for their money or influence. Be careful. Do not take up the idols of the land. Let the governing principle of the Lord's provision keep you from opening the door of your Lighthouse to the *kosmokratos*.

The fourth force which the light shining from the windows of your eyes will dispel is **malice**. When Jesus looked into the eyes of the rich young ruler, the man began to be drawn to the government of God. When Jesus looked into the eyes of the woman taken in adultery, she too was drawn to the government of God, finding it far more gracious than man's. So it is with those around you. As you pray for them, there will be a time when their eyes will meet yours and malice will flee.

There is so much talk of racial division in our age. "Ethnic cleansing" has become the phase replacing "genocide." In the modern-speak of our one-world-government age, malice is justified by family planning and overpopulation. Genocide in Europe and Africa now spreads into the Western world as hatecrimes increase. Governments trade in horrible alterations of God's creation so that the wonder of atomic structure and genetic order now becomes demons of agonizing destruction, and the systems to deliver them are big business among the nations.

THE POWER OF ONE

Who are you in the face of such global power? Once while sitting in the gap for the Soviet Union, I had the most wonderful experience.

I was in the replica of Lenin's office in Moscow. Our prayer team had been walking and praying in that city for several days. It was the Spring of 1985.

The tour group had passed on but, with permission from the guards, I remained to contemplate the overthrow of Communism. How was this manifestation of malice to be removed from the earth? Two-thirds of the globe was at that time under the forces emanating from that place. As an intercessor, I had entered into the gap to hear the Word of deliverance from the Lord.

The Lord quickened to me that communism was just the horse. The rider was atheism. Marx, in rebellion to his Jewish parents, had never addressed the subject of faith. Into this void the State had entered so young people were trained to call on Lenin for provision. Our team had a very meaningful encounter with Jews in Siberia on our way to Moscow from Beijing and the thoughts of Stalin, the ethnic cleanser of his age, were still very fresh in my mind. He had determined to wipe out faith in a generation.

As I sat there praying, I asked the Lord for insight. "What will dispel the darkness of the lie of atheism?"

I was startled with the speed and clarity of His response, "One word of truth."

That was it. I left the Lenin museum and crossed Red Square to the famous bell tower gate of the Kremlin. There the tower clock set the pace for several hours of prayer walking. I walked around that bastion of atheism declaring, "There is a God, He has a Son, His name is Jesus, He died for me."

As I walked and prayed, I had the distinct sense that the fountain of atheism was being sealed by the Rock of Ages. I tell you, it was a marvelous feeling to know that the *pneuma tae ponerias*, the spirit of malice, was being dispelled from millions under the repression of communism. I felt that, for my purposes, the axe was laid to the root that day.

Not too many years later the entire enterprise of the USSR came to a screeching halt. For me and the many teams we accompanied and sent into the Soviet Union, as well as the millions of intercessors around the world, the day the Berlin wall came down was one of the sweetest victories ever. Intercession is the key to release for millions in darkness today.

A SPECIAL MINISTRY?

Is this a "special ministry?" Are those who walk the earth in prayer called with a "unique calling?" No! In recent years the prayer movement has grown larger than any one organization. Even with the wonder of the Internet and global communication capabilities, the answers to prayer are happening so rapidly they will be recorded only in heaven's throne room.

I have noticed a common thread in those whom the Lord is using in this great time of prayer. They all demonstrate three characteristics.

First, they are all **filled with the Word of God**. Their conversation is the Word. They encourage each other from the Word. What they do not do is sit around and tell war stories and demonstrate the arrogant one-up-manship of previous groups. These prefer to remain irrelevant, giving all glory to the Lord.

Second, they are **humble**. They realize their identity is hidden in God and He has given them their area of responsibility. Their attitude is one of being in awe of His grace at even having been included. This humility is the foundation stone of their ministry. Most intercessors only become famous after their death. The purity of selflessness is thus maintained. Man may never know you have invested a lifetime of prayer for your city. But, heaven knows.

Third, they are **avid students of the Word**. God measures our lives by His own standards. Second Timothy 2:15[101] is the common doorway through which those working in the various continents have

---

101. [15]Be diligent to present yourself approved to God, a worker who does not need to be ashamed, rightly dividing the word of truth.

come, **"study to [show] yourself approved unto God."** There is no short cut to ministry.

Much study is indeed an aggravation to the flesh. The thought that after years of service the Lord could be calling you away from the business of the church to seek His face and study so He might prepare you to be with Him in the gaps of the globe is so radical very few enter in.

IT'S THE WORD

Developing the discipline to dig in the golden veins of God's Word is as difficult as becoming a brain surgeon. But to whom will that surgeon turn when he has done all he can, if not that one whom the Lord has led into the situation? Standing by bedsides I have learned the Word of God takes precedence over all the instruction man can have. Faith is paramount. How does one prepare for the life-walk of holiness that is God's pathway to power?

STUDY THE WORD!

As I participated with a great team in birthing the Unreached Peoples movement, I often wondered why the Lord had not entrusted these peoples to us before this. An interesting question was, why now? Why us? Why Dr. Barret? Why Dr. Winters? Why Peter Wagner? Why Dr. Foltz? Why Eric Watt?

One day George Otis Jr. left my home with manuscript in hand and I wondered, *"Why not his father?"* As I sat and watched Dick Eastman carry people from the couch of complacency to worldchanging intercession, I wondered, *"Why such a mild mannered gentleman as he?"*

One morning in 1984 I was scheduled to speak at Christ for the Nations in Dallas. I arrived early and was so fortunate to hear Dr. Jonathan Chao deliver an update on the need for prayer for China. Then I spoke concerning teams for Nepal.

The next speaker was Loren Cunningham, so I waited to hear him. He spoke of the need for mobile ministry teams to cover the earth. Little did I know I would stand with him at the southernmost point of the Asian continent eight years later and ask the Lord's forgiveness on behalf of all missionaries for the colonial attitude we have had toward the native populations, the "locals."

COMMON DENOMINATORS

As I continued to observe these men, several common denominators shone through. Humility and holiness were the first two; the third is they are all men of the Word. Each one is governed by the Word in his heart. Each is a man of discipline. Each is a man of prayer. Each keeps his emotions governed by the Word. Each has prioritized his life to be found where God wants him, and to be doing what God wants him to do. And, finally, each is willing to wait for an eternal reward.

Two particular meetings with Dick Eastman have affirmed and illustrated the value of keeping the Word in one's heart.

We met at the train station in Canton, China. He was so excited because he had been able to bring some Bibles into the country without being detected. Then, I watched as his first act in this success was to pause and give thanks to the Lord. An act of humility from someone whose emotions were being governed by the Word in his heart.

The second meeting was in Warsaw, Poland, the week after the Chernobyl nuclear incident. He was aware of the cloud of radioactivity that shrouded the city of Warsaw that week. But he flew into that cloud anyway, just to keep an appointment with me which he believed God had ordained. As a result, the Change the World School of Prayer was translated into Polish and became a guiding light for prayer for the Catholic youth who wanted desperately to dispel the darkness of communist atheism from their land.

The common denominator of those involved in the global prayer movement is the deep treasure of the Word in their hearts. They live it out among the nations. They demonstrate its wisdom as they fill global gaps and pray. They are entrusted with ministry for they have studied to show themselves approved unto God.

These men have some common experiences. Each has taken a stand for the ministry to which they have been called. They have not always had the approval of man upon the directions they have chosen to go. While they have sought to be at peace with all, there have been times when God's approval has caused them to take a step beyond their peer group and, in so doing, have redefined leadership.

I shall never forget John Dawson preparing to write the great book, *Taking Our Cities for God* (Creation House). We were at a board meeting in Kansas City when John asked our pardon from meetings that year. He explained that he was going to be out of circulation for a year because the Lord was calling him to write. Here was a young man at the helm of a world-changing ministry, who was going to draw aside to the Lord and write. That book would become a tool of mobilization through which millions would come to Christ. Because of the Word discipline in his life, he was free to make such a decision and walk it through to fruition.

Because he spent time in the Word, the apostle John was able to define the practical directions necessary to dispel the darkness from a population center, Ephesus. We too can move in nationchanging effectiveness, when we have a Word discipline in our lives. God governs His actions through His Word. When we do the same, govern our actions by His Word, we bring ourselves into alignment with His purposes. Then we will have the wisdom to know when, where, and what to do, as He directs.

PRACTICAL SUGGESTIONS

Here are a few practical suggestions which will help you develop your Word discipline. First, select a Bible of a size, weight, feel, and typestyle that is as comfortable to you as though you had owned it all your life. It seems strange, but my Bible has a certain feel to it I really like very much. Like a gunfighter's Peacemaker in the Old West, your Bible has to feel "just right." I learned this from watching two men as they handled their Bibles.

Dr. Lester Sumral would take up his Bible to teach and heft it in his hand. He had a certain way of holding it; you just knew it was his Bible. It rested in his hand as a trusted friend, a constant companion.

When Dr. Costa Dier opened his Bible to teach, some of the pages were so worn you could no longer read the text. As he taught seventy-five points of leadership, those following were unaware he was not reading from the text. He had read those pages so much the ink had worn off them. That is a Word discipline.

Next, find a tool that will lead you through the Bible over a prescribed time period. Many intercessors I know, including myself, use the *Youth With a Mission Personal Prayer Diary* (Youth With A Mission Publishing). It combines Old and New Testament readings with some really good material on the nations. It's been my faithful Word companion for years.

Many pastors have found strength in their church reading through the Bible in a year. As the people develop their Word discipline, they move in common faith, which keeps the light on in the house and heresy out on the corner.

One of the things I do to keep current in the Word is to read the chapter of Proverbs that corresponds with the date. There are thirty-one chapters so most months it fits. I also multiply the date by five and read those chapters of Psalms so in a month the 150 Psalms become a part of the light in my house.

Pastor Peter Raphgi, a Tibetan, taught me to read a text and then ponder it by asking myself these questions:

What does this text tell me about God?

What does it tell me about unregenerate man?

What does it tell me about regenerate man?

What does it tell me about me?

Peter found the Lord while still a Buddhist monk. He had been under a vow of silence for seven years when one day the Lord appeared to him and led him through the Himalayas to Kathmandu, Nepal. There he heard the Gospel and was saved. He excitedly shared his deep joy that he could now speak and study the Word of God daily.

The Lord wants to speak to you through His Word. He wants to daily affirm His great love for you. As you prayerfully take up His Word, you demonstrate your love and respect for Him. It is to those who are faithful in the Word they have, that He will entrust the ministry which they do not have. This is the relational testing ground for the Attack Lamb. The Word discipline is essential to spiritual warfare.

....

To intercede is to intervene between two with a view of reconciling their differences. Abraham was an intercessor. Moses was an intercessor. Jesus was an intercessor and, in fact, still is as He is seated at the right hand of the Father interceding for us (Hebrews 7:25; Romans 8:34).

To Intervene means to enter in or appear as an irrelevant or extraneous circumstance. Abraham walked with God and negotiated for Lot because of the covenant relationship and promise. Moses described himself as the meekest man on earth; relevant to God but disrespected by those he came to deliver. Jesus was despised and rejected, a man of sorrows and acquainted with grief. Yet, all three appeared before the Almighty crying out for the souls of those same people who mistreated them.

Love, which cannot fail, overcame personal pain and rejection and put Abraham in the path of God, Moses on the mount of God, and Jesus on the throne of God.

What will it take for us, Attack Lambs, to understand the magnitude of the love that Jesus has for the lost? This is something with which I wrestle daily. It is a very simple thing to say, "If I go out today for one hour or so and walk around the high school releasing the anointing of the Holy Spirit, something good will happen at that school. The one hour invested could bring a harvest of righteousness that would touch our community for generations."

It is not such a simple thing to go over there and do it.

One of our good friends and a real Attack Lamb, Hubert Chan, has covered more ground praying for countries along the Mekong River than anyone else I have met in the past 20 years. I have no idea how many pairs of shoes he has worn out covering jungles, mountains, flooded plains, and dust bowls. Hubert lives all that you have read so far in Attack Lambs. Of the many things he has said about the teaching, the one I think of most often is, "This is simple, but not easy." Something has to drive him to continue.

CONSTRAINED

My own experience has been beautifully captured in 2 Corinthians 5:14-15, **"For the love of Christ compels us, because we judge thus: that if One died for all, then all died; and He died for all, that those who live should live no longer for themselves, but for Him who died for them and rose again."**

The word "compel" is an action word. Love requires an object and we know that God loves the world so much that He gave His only begotten son that whoever believes in Him will not perish but have everlasting life. When that love hits your heart, you have no choice but to leave all others and cleave to Christ. This is our compulsion, to take that love to neighbors and nations. We are compelled to do so.

The NIV agrees with "compel" from the NKJV above; but the KJV, the old text, carries this a bit further. It translates the word as "constrains us." Our steps are guided by the Lord. He keeps us on the straight path. We are constrained to righteousness, governed in His will and direction. Lead us not into temptation and, Psalm 37, the steps of a good man are ordered by the Lord. He has a pathway for us and along the way, we become aware of gaps between where society is and where they could be. Our eyes are opened to understand why things are the way they are and not the way they should be. We discern but are discerned of none. An Attack Lamb carrying the presence of the King of Kings into places that do not recognize Him.

Jesus guides us by the Holy Spirit to bring His manifest presence into the places He has chosen before the foundation. His knowledge guides us and His wisdom flows through us to those who desperately need Him. We are "constrained."

The NAS uses the word, "Controlled" in this verse. We are controlled by the Love of Christ. God is love and the essence of every word of God is love. He will not take action or word that contradicts His essence. Love will flow to us, and through us to others, when we are controlled by the Spirit.

HE CALLS US TO HIMSELF

Christian maturity is getting beyond ourselves so on that prayer day, we say, "Lord flood me with your love. Give me the desire, courage, anointing, and love I need to go to that prayer point, focus on you, release the Holy Spirit through worship, and see lives change."

The Lord has worked all these years in my life by saying, "Go to this place and I will meet you there." Honestly, and all glory to Him, I get very excited when I hear it because I am going to have a personal meeting with the King of the universe. He and I are going to be involved together in something spectacular. I am anointed to be a witness of the good things of God. I am going to see something happen that only He can do, and He loves me enough to call me to go and do it. He goes before me to make a way for me and then He calls me to Himself.

That is the key, He calls me to Himself so I am compelled by the Holy Spirit living in me to go to the place and see what the Lord is doing. So many times, in these 20 years, people have asked, "Why would you go there?"

I have simply responded, "I have a meeting to keep."

God is always there to manifest His presence with a gentle touch and to direct my attention to a situation or an individual and the game is on. The devil loses more souls; people and nations are changed. Joshua had to show up daily for a week. Sometimes I walk around in His presence for a week or more, watching. And then, it comes to pass.

Jesus gave us the direction to love the Lord with all our heart, soul, and strength, and to love our neighbors before ourselves. Love is an active force. It cannot be kept from performing its purpose, to draw people to Jesus. When we step into that gap, compelled, constrained, and controlled by the love that is in Christ, nations change.

Abraham was compelled by covenant, Moses by relationship, Jesus by love. We are compelled to participate in the purpose and plan of God by His Spirit of love who abides in our hearts.

CHAPTER 17

IN OTHER WORDS...WORK!

Jesus selected net menders as disciples. These fisher-men were hardworking people who fed their families from the labor of their hands. They fished at night, cleaned and repaired their nets in the early morning and spent the heat of the day resting. In this way they made a living for their family. The nets were vital to their existence, and more care and meticulous time was spent on them than on the fishing itself.

The work of repairing the nets required great discipline. Each knot had to be inspected and tested. In case of a frayed end or a tear, the damaged parts had to be cut away and new fibers tied in its place. Undisciplined work could mean hunger for that man's family, and perhaps the entire village.

The Body of Christ is also a net, a global network of cooperation to harvest that most precious of riches, the souls of men. You are reading this book to become equipped to fill one of the spaces in that network of intercession. As that net grows, and we become more skilled in using it, people are coming to Christ in unprecedented numbers. Don't be surprised to find yourself being knit together with believers you don't know in an ever-growing net of prayer.

Those who have studied and shown themselves approved unto God become "workmen." As intercessors, our work is clearly defined: we are to "enter in" between two with a view toward reconciling their differences.

THE THIRD DISCIPLINE...WORK

To be successful in this we must develop our **Work Discipline**, and add it to the disciplines of worship and the Word. Nowhere in Scripture is the importance of work and reconciliation and restoration more clear than Galatians 6. Here Paul clearly defines several aspects of the work of reconciliation both for believers as well as in reaching the lost.

> **Brethren, if a man is overtaken in any trespass, you who are spiritual restore such a one in a spirit of gentleness, considering yourself lest you also be tempted. Bear one another's burdens, and so fulfill the law of Christ. For if anyone thinks himself to be something, when he is nothing, he deceives himself. But let each one examine his own work, and then he will have rejoicing in himself alone, and not in another. For each one shall bear his own load.** **Galatians 6:1–5**

This apostolic instruction describes the fruit of the work discipline.

MENDING YOUR NETS

Jesus is still calling net menders. Here's how it works. The other day I took my son to the orthodontist. He is in the last stages of completing that American teenage ritual of braces to straighten his teeth. The patient following my son was a young girl who was also accompanied by her father. Now the doctor is a wonderful man and a real **net**worker. He introduced the girl's father and me to each other as "religious men." That term always makes me nervous because I never know what to expect. But in this case I was glad to find my new friend was a pastor and a prayer walker. We even found out we had prayed in the same places on different days.

Now he and I have a decision to make. Are we going to make the effort to keep in touch with each other? Are we going to do whatever is necessary to set aside the time to get together and to pray? It is going to require work to use this divine appointment to catch the "fish" who live in our common waters. Each of us is a new section of net for the other, one that has to be carefully woven in.

So it is with each of us. We can either put forth the effort to mend nets, or let them rot through neglect. The fibers the Lord uses to create, mend, and clean His nets are believers. But some of us suffer from being too busy to make these connections or keep them in good repair by speaking the Word, with its cleansing power, to each other.

It's easy to say, "Well, there aren't any fish to catch anyway." That's sour grapes. That person is a net destroyer. He is interested in something other than catching fish. Most of the time he is looking for personal recognition or another notch on his spiritual gun. His next move is to insist on fishing alone rather than surrendering his individuality to become a part of the net mender's team.

THE APPEARANCE OF IRRELEVANCE

The most effective intercessors are those who are content to appear irrelevant or extraneous to the situation for which they pray. The great labor for intercessors is to maintain this humble approach to their role of apparent irrelevance. This attitude walks hand-in-hand in unity with other workers in God's kingdom. The objective of the intercessor is reconciliation and restoration. They want those who are frayed or torn restored to the net and tied once again to the whole.

ON A LARGER SCALE

The power of unity in the Spirit was demonstrated to me during the Russian occupation of Poland in 1985. I was walking in a section of the old city. Unknown to me, the Lord had shown my face to people with the Light and Life movement of the Catholic charismatic youth in a vision several days before. They were astounded when they actually saw me. We had a divine appointment! As a result, I was invited to return to Poland and teach on the Person and Ministry of the Holy Spirit. I was thrilled at the way the Lord had brought us together.

Later, I shared this experience with some believers in the evangelical camp. Their response was less then enthusiastic. The hole in the net was gaping. They would not join together to mend this part of the net. I was still feeling quite overwhelmed that anyone in Poland had seen me in a vision. With such a clear mandate from the Lord to proceed, I was sure they would be eager to help. I asked the Lord for wisdom.

A charismatic priest I knew, Michael Sylvangia, had served with me as an occasional host of a nighttime TV show on Cornerstone Television in Pittsburgh. We got along quite well. We respected each other and accentuated the positives through fellowship on the common ground of Christ. At the Lord's leading I asked him to go with me on the teaching trip.

The Poles were thrilled; unfortunately, some of the Americans were not. Solidarity was the key word in Poland. They could see their oppressor very clearly. He lived in their neighborhoods and dominated their affairs. He was an uninvited guest in their villages, an unseen presence at every meeting. He operated through intimidation. He restricted their right to speak. He controlled their economy and his malicious acts had resulted in the martyrdom of their leader. The opponent to the faith did not have to be imagined, he was very real.

Mike and I were blessed to spend three weeks preaching and teaching among these wonderful people. It was an exercise in the work discipline. The shadow of Chernobyl clouded every meeting. Little did we realize that the Lord was causing the Soviets to be honest for the first time in the Cold War period. The veil had been rent. By standing side by side in Christ, Mike and I were a picture of the future of Poland.

Now don't get me wrong. At every turn there were opportunities to differ. We could have filled our time with doctrinal debates. Or we could have competed for the attention of the people. Or we could have entered into striving on anything from meals to speaking order. But we worked at unity. We worked at meekness. We worked at keeping our part of the net together. And we caught fish.

THE CONSUMMATE EXPERIENCE

The consummate experience was an invitation to the south of Poland to participate in a large youth gathering. Twenty-five thousand young people were coming to the home church of the Pope to celebrate the outpouring of the Holy Spirit, and we were invited to attend. Mike sat with all the priests and I was given the great honor of being with the dignitaries. The Bishop asked if he could serve me communion as a sign to these youth and a testimony to Poland that indeed their country had not been abandoned by the pentecostals and evangelicals of the West.

I was thrilled to help restore the breach. Today in Poland we are all enjoying the fruits of the post-cold-war era. Souls are being saved across that great land. One of the reasons was the work done by a few key people in restoring solidarity in the Body of Christ.

NET MENDERS BRING ACCEPTANCE

Of the many things Dick Eastman has imparted into my life, nothing is more meaningful to me than the phrase, "He is accepted in over one hundred denominations." That takes a lot of work. It requires discipline not to offend. It also requires the wisdom of the Word to drive off the divisive forces of the Enemy and hold that net together for the sake of those who will be saved.

Did you catch that? **For the sake of those who will be saved.**

How important is that? The words of the writer of Hebrews give us insight into how Jesus felt about it. **"Looking unto Jesus, the author and finisher of our faith, who for the joy that was set before Him endured the cross, despising the shame..."** (Hebrews 12:2[102]).

---

102. [2]looking unto Jesus, the author and finisher of our faith, who for the joy that was set before Him endured the cross, despising the shame, and has sat down at the right hand of the throne of God

To succeed one must see beyond the immediate tensions of circumstances to the greater harvest to be accomplished if, in the spirit of meekness, we embrace each other across that net and hold on tight while the harvest is reaped.

THE FOURTH CONGRESS

When the Fourth Congress on Intercession in Indonesia was convened, I was asked to address the delegates. There were two hundred and fifty delegates from every mainline denomination and many of the smaller independents. These meetings occurred just a week after many had been killed in political riots in the streets of Jakarta and everyone was concerned for the future of the nation.

As I rose to speak, I could feel the Holy Spirit stirring my heart with a word for these men. I am dwarfed in ministry by their incredible success as soul winners in the face of Islamic opposition. Their educations make me an intellectual pauper. Their testimonies could fill the earth. I was as meek as I have ever been.

"Men," I spoke with tremendous restraint, "our lives will not be measured by what we could have done with what we might have had. As we go forth from this point our lives will be measured by what we did with what we do have." As they cheered, I thought, "*Great, what comes next?*"

Through me, the Lord gave a great appeal for unity and for loving one another. It takes discipline to look into the face of one who has hurt you and continue to love. It takes tremendous discipline to release the offender into the hands of the Lord. So many times we allow the differences between us to pull the net apart. When we allow that to happen, the fish in the net slip away. And our life, and life's work, slips away with them.

THE CRISIS

America's teens are in crisis. The highest suicide rate is among teens. The number one cause of death among African-American youth is homicide. There is an epidemic of death in America. Why? Because the spirit of meekness through which the net could be mended has been replaced by the spirit of malice that wants to destroy the generation who can reach the globe with the Gospel.

It takes work to stand in that gap and call on God. It takes work to walk those streets and pray. It takes work to enter that high school and pray. It takes work to rise before dawn and seek the face of Jesus to discover His ways of opening the doors to this generation.

For the American church, whose greatest labor of love is to make it to one Sunday morning church service each week, the challenge of reaching this teenage generation is overwhelming. Divorce in the Church has ripped families apart. The Church has become so much like the world that kids wonder why they should bother.

I was recently back in Singapore and noticed a young executive, who had really been growing in Jesus, wasn't there. His pastor explained to me the young man had seen the testimony of his mother compromised so many times he had come to the conclusion the whole thing was a game.

Each time a leader throws off the spirit of meekness and takes on an "I am somebody" attitude, the net gets another hole. Paul cautions us to be mindful of ourselves as we seek to restore another. In the ministry of restoration, we are kept by one thing: our work discipline.

The person doing the work the Lord has given him to do does not have time to be critical of the work of another.

OUT IN THE FIELD

Over the twenty years I have spent taking short-term teams to the prayer points of the world, I have been blessed to build close relationships with many wonderful men and women of God, career missionaries. These tireless saints give their love and lives with remarkable dignity. They open their hearts and homes to many adventure seekers giving short-term missions a try for the first time.

Part of the briefing I give each team is the admonition to refrain from correcting the career missionary. For some reason those who go once in their busy lives feel they have the liberty to correct those who have given all.

I've seen this same phenomena occur when I've been a guest speaker. Once, on the ride from the airport to the church, I was urged to address a particular issue challenging the Senior Pastor of the church where I was going to minister. Imagine that, me presuming to address the life of a person who hourly stands in the gap for his flock. I don't think so. Even elders, who should know better, have asked me to mention things to pastors...as if I am the type of fellow who would hurt those who serve God.

While serving on the staff of several fine churches, I have had all the work I could handle just completing my own job description. I have no idea how others are able to do theirs.

After a few years of this you learn to discern those who have a good work discipline and those who do not. The conversation of those who are not working is death. They speak judgment and criticism and bring division. We are to speak healing into the Body of Christ.

So often I hear comments about the church. The worship could be more of this or less of that. Pastor could use a makeover, and did you see his wife's hair? The deacons lack discernment, and the youth minister is too radical. I wonder what all the negative talk is about. Imagine if the Lord heard what some think of His Body. Maybe His response would be, "Kind of pudgy around the wallet..."

ABOUT THE FATHER'S WORK

We are to be about the work of demonstrating the Father's love to each other and the world. This is the reason we stand in the gap, to reestablish the presence of His love in situations and among people where His love is no longer evident. We are to be Attack Lambs who manifest the glory of God as we pray for reconciliation.

My wife and I recently located our family in a community with seven churches among nine thousand people. Immediately there were rumors that we wanted to start the eighth church.

Actually, the Lord brought us there to pray for the churches. My wife Ellie and a friend have prayer walked each church. They have spoken the Lord's blessing, and Jesus has given them very specific instruction on prayer for each congregation. When I return from a trip to Asia, we always have a time of sharing concerning the local churches. We believe that Jesus sees one Church in the community and that Church meets in many buildings.

We feel that it is our role as Attack Lambs to stand in the gap and pray for the pastors. We pray that the Word of the Lord comes **to them** and forth **from them**. We ask the Lord to trim the wick of the church so the light of the Gospel burns brighter **through them**. We stand against any device of the Enemy set **against them**. This means we wrestle with the four spiritual forces set against their ministry.

One evangelical congregation in town announced a Saturday night praise and prayer meeting. They have never been known much for praise and prayer, so we count that a victory. The Pentecostal work in town is new. It has grown from 50 to 400 in just a few years. They have added a second Sunday service and are looking to Saturdays as well.

The young people in the Catholic church have begun reading the Bible, and are talking about being "born-again." Imagine that. They responded to "See You at the Pole," the annual youth prayer time for the schools. And a Bible club has begun in the local high school.

The principal of the elementary school retired. The new principal is an ordained Christian minister who is actively pastoring a church in another town and overseeing several Bible studies in neighboring communities.

CHANGE IS COMING

As we pray, we begin to see the lives of those in the community turn to the Lord. In each arena we could find reason for division and dissension. We could respond to the attempts of the Enemy to destroy the net that is gathering souls. We could fall prey to attacking individuals. It is work to stay out of divisive conversation which so fills the air of small towns. But we realize we are here to labor in the work of the Lord, not to divide.

Look around the church you attend. List ten things that are wonderful. When people find fault with the ministry ask them if they are praying about the perceived problem. If they say they are, then ask them why they are murmuring rather than standing in faith for their prayers to be answered. Perhaps if they could pray as well as they can see, then there wouldn't be the problems which divide.

Find out the names of the pastors and churches within your community. Pray for them. Hear the promise of the Lord for them. Speak prosperity to them. Ask the Lord to revive the pastors as well as the churches. Become a light that drives the darkness from them.

You **can** do this. I won't kid you, it is hard work. There is every opportunity to walk away shaking your head and determine they will never get themselves straightened out. Refuse the urge. Work at that for which you have been fashioned. That is why you live where you do. Be a net mender. Reach out through prayer to your community.

THE PROMISE...OF WORK

Jesus called His fishermen with a promise, **"Follow me, and I will make you fishers of men,"** (Matthew 4:19). They had demonstrated their work discipline in the long days beside the Sea of Galilee. The net destroyers, the ones who would not mend their nets, were not there when Jesus came by. He was looking for men to whom He could teach the work discipline in the light of eternity. Jesus found men who worked for that which perishes. They would learn to work for that which would never perish.

The disciples saw Jesus work miracles and knew these were the "works of God." This prompted their question, **"What shall we do, that we may work the works of God?"** Jesus responded to them,

"This is the work of God, that you believe in Him whom He sent" (John 6:28–29).

When we see how far our nation, or any nation for that matter, has wandered from God, the area of ministry to which Christ is calling us seems very large indeed. When John Hyde went to India, the total ignorance of the love of Christ overwhelmed him. He began to pray with a fervor borne of the Holy Spirit. After several years he became ill. On consulting with the doctor, an incredible fact was discovered.

"Hyde, what type of strenuous labor do you perform?" the doctor asked.

"Why do you ask?" responded the man of prayer.

"Your heart has turned over in your chest from the strain of exertion," replied the doctor. "You must move very heavy burdens."

THE NEXT LESSON

This is the **work discipline**. There are millions left to be reached in India, but millions have gone on to eternal life through the prayers of John Hyde. Few have labored as hard in prayer for the Gospel.

With your worship, Word, and work discipline secure, you are ready to go to war. You are ready to disciple a whole nation. You are ready to prayer walk the town; but, where do you go? Our next chapter will become your road map to your testimonies of victory. You are about to learn a little about wrestling the Four Forces from the lives of your friends and neighbors.

CHAPTER 18

FIVE PRESSURE POINTS

Where do I park the ark?" Good question! My older son Sam wrestled Greco-Roman style for a time. This Olympic sport requires a very strong upper body. The object of this sport is to pin your opponent to the mat and keep him there long enough to win. In like manner we wrestle with the spiritual forces of the Enemy and exercise our power of restraint over the Four Forces they employ in their quest to interfere with the work of the Lord.

Sam and I used to enjoy practicing some of his wrestling moves in the living room of our home. Actually, he practiced, I simply tried to survive. My wife Ellie insisted we remove the furniture to give her larger male types adequate room. Having set the stage, we would wrestle to exhaustion, generally mine, in this ancient sport.

One of the first things Sam was taught was the location of several key pressure points. These are places on the body where nerves and blood vessels are very near the surface of the skin. Pressure applied to these points results in the loss of strength and force in that limb.

If you press the point of the thumb of your left hand into the flesh between the thumb and index finger of your right hand, you will experience the releasing pain of a pressure point. There is also a place on the large trapezius muscle, to the right and left of the neck, (remember the "Spock pinch"?) which is a very familiar pressure point to Sunday School teachers and all those who work with adolescent boys. One little squeeze there and attention is restored.

As we wrestle with the Four Forces of spiritual wickedness, we apply pressure to the five pressure points that will change a nation. Press hard enough and Satan will lose his grip.

CENTERS OF GOVERNMENT

The first pressure point where we park the ark is the **Centers of Government**. Think with me; how do the *archas, exousias, kosmokratos,* and *ponerias* manifest themselves at this center? Can you think of specific instances of intimidation, right to speak issues, abuse of power for gain, or malice emanating from this location in your city? Maybe it is the city hall, or the city council chambers.

Remember, as an Attack Lamb you are not relying on political power to make change. You are going to go to that governmental center and stand in the gap between this pressure point and God for the release for the people. I like to walk around the building. Maintaining my focus on Jesus, I circle the building in prayer.

When I did this in Moscow it took a full hour to walk around the Kremlin. I was not interested in discerning a specific antichrist spirit. Moscow in the Spring of 1985 was the seat of communist atheism and filled with the antichrist spirit.

On location, I began to praise the Lord. Our conversational relationship, developed through so many prayer and praise sessions, resulted in insight. The Lord brought to mind that one word of truth would dispel a lie. I repeated softly, "There is a God. He has a Son. His name is Jesus. He died for me."

Speaking such a thing in the face of the forces arrayed there evidently applied pressure. The truth negated the implied power of intimidation and I felt no fear at all. I walked and rejoiced as the Lord affirmed my proclamation of truth with His peaceful Presence. He sent the blessing of peace.

Encouraged by the closeness of His Presence, I entered the Kremlin and took a position in the rose garden across from the executive office suite. Later I found out I had been only a few meters from

Mr. Gorbachev's office. That early Spring morning, my mind was filled with the song, "I come to the garden alone, while the dew is still on the roses; and the voice I hear, falling on my ear, the Son of God discloses. And He walks with me, and He talks with me, and tells me I am his own, and the joy we share as we tarry there, none other has ever known." (*In The Garden*, C. Austin Miles, 1912)

There was power in my praise. No shout needed to be given, no railing against the Devil, just a focused faith on Jesus and the gentle declaration of His Person in that garden. My repose was interrupted by the tower clock.

MOSCOW TIME

In those years the entire Union of Soviet Socialist Republic operated on Moscow time. Even in the vast expanses of Siberia, at least one clock was tuned to the Kremlin tower. It was the pace maker of the heartbeat of Mother Russia. Of incredible significance, it now interrupted my song.

"How convenient," I thought, *"this clock can set the pace for my prayer."* The tower bell would ring on the quarter, half, and hour marks, perfect timing for the Dick Eastman hour of prayer. I sat and prayed for the first quarter hour that the Lord would send **workers** into the USSR. I prayed for those underground workers whom we had met in ministry and thought of the tremendous shock it would be to Stalin to find out he had not eliminated Christians in a generation, but in fact had only served to cause them to increase. Had he been a student of history, he would have left the Church alone.

The bell sounded the quarter hour and I shifted to the second point of the Eastman hour. "Lord, open the **doors** to this great land that the Word of God may flood in here and wash away the lie of communist atheism. Defeat the horse and the rider."

This was the Spring of 1985. The Lord met me in that garden as I parked the ark. I had a vision of a great open door to the USSR and the downfall of the government so that the Gospel could be preached in every part of the land. I claimed Ephesians 3:20-21,

Now to Him who is able to do exceedingly abundantly above all that we ask or think, according to the power that works in us, to Him be glory in the church by Christ Jesus to all generations, forever and ever. Amen.

Ephesians 3:20-21

I let my thoughts grow bigger than current events, bigger than eschatology, bigger than the Cold War, bigger than the currently available resources and began to be so very happy as the Lord again confirmed His Word with His Presence. What a rose garden experience!

At the half hour I shifted to the third part of the Eastman hour. "Lord, give **fruit** for the ministry." I knew from carrying Bibles to Siberia that there was already a move of God on the university campuses. I had heard about groups throughout Eastern Europe who were hungry for the Word and had a strong prayer life. I thought of the blood of the martyrs calling out from under the altar. The urgency of their cry gave impetus to my prayers. The fifteen minutes flew by so rapidly that I was startled by the tower bell as it pealed the third quarter.

The fourth quarter of the Eastman hour is **finances**. As I called upon the Lord to move in the realm of finance I had no idea that the chemotherapy of Reaganomics would annihilate the communist hold on these masses of people. All I knew was I had seen women with harnesses about their shoulders pulling wooden plows against the rock hard permafrost of the frozen tundra. I had seen men and women huddled together in huge, empty buildings with neither past nor future, mired in poverty's paralysis. I had seen the "black market" whose real street value bore stark witness to the lies of communism.

THE PROCLAMATION

I came away from that rose garden with a proclamation from the Lord. Communism would fall in the USSR and the Church must prepare to rush through the open doors the Lord would give. This was not a welcome message to a Church steeped in Western philosophy regarding the "Cold War." Many rebuked me as unlearned in end-time teachings. I was called aside for correction on several occasions, but continued to proclaim, "Jesus will break through in Russia; you better be ready."

We raised up prayer teams for the capitals of the Soviet republics and soon heard of many ministries mobilizing for intercession. As these Attack Lambs went out, they carried a promise that Jesus would hear their prayers. He is faithful concerning His promise. He answered their cry and, in 1991, their persistence was rewarded with open doors, fruit, and more finance than mission history has ever seen.

Intimidation fled. Right to speak was given back to the Church. The materialism of the ruling communist six percent was overthrown. The malice against Christians ceased and the weapons of malice began to be destroyed. How could such a thing happen? Christians had mobilized in prayer teams. They had followed the example of Jesus who walked from city to city proclaiming the kingdom of God.

As you enter into the center of government of your country or travel on a prayer journey to another land, know that history affirms what you are doing. Get in there. Park the ark. Praise the Lord. Hear from Him. Do as He says and you will see your prayers answered. The Lord is faithful.

CENTERS OF COMMUNICATION

The second pressure point is **Centers of Communication**.

I was sitting in the Forum Hotel in Warsaw. The trip from Beijing via the Trans-Siberian railway had left me temporarily without funds and, with the few dollars I had, I had purchased beef tartar. That dish consists of an uncooked pile of beef with a raw egg. Not the highpoint of the trip. I was distracted from my feast by the conversation at the adjoining table.

"So, we send the signal up to the satellite and beam it from satellite to satellite until we bring it down in major cities all over the world. The technique is called 'Footprinting.'"

"Which network developed the technology?"

"Actually, it was a Christian ministry who introduced it to us. They plan to use it to hold an evangelistic rally in one city and to reach the whole world with it at the same time."

A Christian ministry setting the pace in communication? I was so excited. Thank God for TBN! The Power Lifting Championships were going to be broadcast through technology invented for the Gospel!

For nine years Pastor Russ and Norma Bixler held fast to a vision for a Christian owned and operated television station for the city of Pittsburgh, PA. They prayed and walked about the land for the station. They called the Church to pray. They remained faithful to the things the Lord showed them to do. Their prayers were answered and Cornerstone Television (CTV) came to pass. Through the ministry of CTV souls are won around the world. Now, with uplink capability, they are praying for the day that they can "footprint" to the nations.

As you identify the centers of communication to prayer walk in your community, do not stop with just the radio and TV stations.

I personally believe that MTV is the Enemy's number one ballistic missile against this generation. I strongly urge you to find which of your local stations carries it, and find the location of your cable operator. Remember, gentle as lambs, go and pray. Pray as though the destiny of your children was at stake. God will meet you there.

Finally, newspapers are still most effective in small towns and the community grapevine operates very well.

Find the center. Park the ark. Focus on Jesus through praise. Pray for insight. Pray according to the insight He gives and keep it up until you sense the breakthrough. That wonderful release will come as you remain focused on Jesus.

CENTERS OF EDUCATION

The third pressure point is **Centers of Education**.

As the saying goes, "Whoever holds the children holds the future." With this declaration the red-scarfed pioneers of communism were launched. You must park the ark at centers of education. They were intended to carry the message of communist atheism into world dominance in their generation. Do you know who prevented it from happening? Read on.

We were standing in the Orthodox church in Novosibirsk. It was a bitter cold, Sunday morning, but the place was packed. This Siberian city had been created as the center for academic excellence for the emerging generation of Soviet leaders who would take Russia beyond the moon and stars.

To stave off the bitter cold I stuffed my hands deep into my pockets. I lifted my eyes to the ornate facade above the altar. There in silver and multicolored brilliance the Gospel message stood forever in the gilded characters of fourteenth-century Russia. With a sense of the abiding power of the faith, I prayed.

Suddenly my reverie was shattered as my hands were forcefully yanked from my pockets. Looking beyond the knurled finger thrust at the end of my nose, I saw the steely blue eyes of my first Russian babushka up close. This grandmother of the faith wanted me to know that in the presence of God, I had better keep my hands out of my pockets.

I looked deeply into those eyes. What had she seen? Had she been driven here by Stalin as a young girl? What was it that kept her faith so very alive? Opening her shopping bag she broke off a piece of the communion bread and offered it to me. I reached inside my jacket and took a Russian Bible and put it in her bag. I have never seen such a smile.

GRANDMOTHERS AND GRANDCHILDREN

After the service, our group was taken to an adjacent building where we witnessed several proud grandmas presenting sons and grandsons to be baptized. In spite of all the intimidation and the complete absence of a right to speak, these women were passing the fire of Christian zeal to the next generation.

We understood at the time that the Church had fifty thousand believers in cell groups. It was 1986 and faith was alive and well in Siberia. The grandmothers made certain their children and grand-children kept and multiplied the faith. What Stalin promised would happen in a generation had been reversed because of the faithful praying grandmothers of Russia. Though they were sent to die in the frozen waste, they not only survived, but also multiplied the faith.

By the time Russia opened the door to the Gospel there were over a hundred thousand believers in Novosibirsk. They were already organized and had developed a sound curriculum for leadership training. Yes, the New Siberia was the future of the nation, but it was not the future Stalin had envisioned. From this center of education Christian leadership has come for all of Europe.

Russia was not the only country in those years to be impacted by prayer. In the United States, which bans the public reading of Scripture and the Lord's Prayer as well as Christian symbolism in public schools, a group of young people set themselves to meet at the flag pole of the school at the beginning of each school year and dedi-cate the year to the Lord.

In those school districts where "See You At the Pole" has taken place, teen suicides have decreased, drug sales and usage have decreased, and in many places Bible clubs are being established. Jesus will give the victory to those who pray. We know that if we ask any-thing according to His will He hears us and grants the petition we desire of Him (John 5:15[103]). The truth is, He is more eager to answer your prayers than you are to pray them.

Any school can be a target for prayer walking: public schools at all levels, trade schools, colleges, and even Christian schools.

Some friends of mine pray for a Hebrew Academy in their town every time they pass it. They raise their hands toward the buildings

---

103. [15]The man departed and told the Jews that it was Jesus who had made him well

and speak salvation and a knowledge of their true Messiah to everyone in the school, students, faculty and staff.

CENTERS OF COMMERCE

The fourth pressure point is **Centers of Commerce**.

This is the domain of the *kosmokratos*. Using people to get things is the method of operation for this crippling force. Centers of commerce can include legitimate businesses as well as those not so honest, such as places where drugs are sold. I leave it to you to determine where this force is operating in your town.

On a global scale, I feel that Cali, Colombia, is a center for the *kosmokratos* because of the millions of people who are destroyed by their number one export, cocaine.

Several years ago I was in Cali to visit a fine ministry. One morning I took a walk. Actually I was looking for a place to park the ark and get in touch with Jesus about this force. I walked quietly, focusing on Jesus in praise. I found myself at a small park in the middle of a very well-to-do residential section. Quite accustomed to Latin America, I thought little of the broken glass sills or of the high walls. The barbed wire too was not unusual for those days.

In front of me was a beautiful little lake with beautiful huge willow trees. It was just the sort of morning prayer place I love so much. I sat on one of the cast iron benches and began to commune with the Lord, offering praise. I was soon ushered into worship and was having a really wonderful time as the warmth of a new day complimented the peaceful presence of the Lord.

I was not alone. My right ear filled suddenly with the sound of an automatic weapon being cocked.

"Why are you here?" The question in Spanish was not offered in gentle tones.

I answered quietly and gently in Spanish, "I am here to pray." The responding laughter highlighted the irony of the moment.

"Do you know where you are?" Of course I didn't know in earthly terms, and I really didn't think mentioning heaven was a good idea right then. I shook my head to indicate that I did not.

"Get up...keep your eyes straight ahead...keep walking...do not stop...do not come back here!" The terms of release seemed fine to me, and the ark slowly moved away from the pressure point. Yes, you may meet some resistance from those who occupy for the Enemy.

When I returned to the home of my host I told him what had happened and where I had been. His face went pale as he asked me to not go there again nor even leave the house without escort. I had "stumbled" into the central court of four of the very highest families in the drug cartels.

Within a year the man on whose bench I had sat was in jail. Several of the others have died. Drugs still flow from Cali, but I believe if we intercede (enter into that city to pray) we can see Jesus overcome what man cannot.

Commerce has several types of pressure points because it operates on several levels. They are raw materials, manufacturing, distribution sites and end-users. Let the Holy Spirit direct you to exactly where to apply pressure.

CENTERS OF SPIRITUAL ACTIVITY

We have talked about Centers of Government, Centers of Communication, Centers of Education and Centers of Commerce. What is the fifth center? The most obvious — **Centers of Spiritual Activity**. From the text of 1 Samuel 5:1–5[104] we know that false gods

104. [1]Then the Philistines took the ark of God and brought it from Ebenezer to Ashdod. [2]When the Philistines took the ark of God, they brought it into the house of Dagon and set it by Dagon. [3]And when the people of Ashdod arose early in the morning, there was Dagon, fallen on its face to the earth before the ark of the Lord. So they took Dagon and set it in its place again. [4]And when they arose early the next morning, there was Dagon, fallen on its face to the ground before the ark of the Lord. The head of Dagon and both the palms of its hands were broken off on the threshold; only Dagon's torso was left of it. [5]Therefore neither the priests of Dagon nor any who come into Dagon's house tread on the threshold of Dagon in Ashdod to this day

bow down in the presence of the ark. We know that false gods lose their heads in the presence of the ark. When we park the ark in the temples of the false gods, we cause the Four Forces behind them to bow down.

Twenty-five percent of the world's population is Chinese. These wonderful people can be found on the mainland, but also in every major city on earth. Their language and culture remain a mystery to the remaining seventy-five percent of us. We wonder about the dragons and food tastes and think little about the people. It has been said that even if we win everyone else on earth to Christ and fail to reach the Chinese, the highest grade we can get is seventyfive percent…a "**C**."

I was consecrated to minister among the Chinese through the laying on of the hands of Wang Ming Dao, the father of the house church movement. I had the honor of meeting with him in 1985 in Shanghai. His prayer has seriously altered the course of my life.

In the years of working among the Chinese, my relationship to their centers of spiritual activity has progressed from curiosity through consternation to compassion. They are a people trapped in the past and trying to stretch toward the future. The reforms of communism were designed to move these people from a life of "superstition" to a life of "pragmatic socialism." The new reforms are designed to move them to a sense of "spiritual community." However, the spirit that community is based upon is the human spirit.

CHINESE NAMES…A CLUE

Chinese names are a puzzle to most Westerners. For example, in our home church in Singapore we have Pastors Song, Ong, and Hong. Their full names are Song Mieng Lien, Ong Tian Chuan, and Hong Chi Her. Chances are you just glossed over those names, but if you did, you missed something very important. The point is that a Chinese name will tell you much about the person.

The first word tells you from which part of China their family comes. The second name is a prophetic telling which the monks felt was auspicious for the person. The third name tells you the clan identity and temple to which they pertain. When you know this, you are ready to park the ark.

I was teaching a Prayer Walking Seminar in a church in Singapore. Of the 1,500 participants ninety percent were Englishspeaking Chinese. I suggested that they should identify the spiritual centers — in their case, the temples to which their families related — and should park the ark there while holding some small group outreach for the families of that temple. I suggested they bind the generational curses and the familiar spirits which kept their loved ones from receiving Christ.

Saturday afternoon of the seminar the church's pastoral team took a little walk with me. We went to a principal temple in the heart of Singapore. They realized the Power Presence of the Holy Spirit as we parked the ark in front of the ancestral tablets and prayed for the families represented. They told me later that the joy which filled their hearts there in the midst of so many idols, with our lungs burning from the incense, and the stench of rancid palm oil filling the place, was greater than any they had known before.

Within six months the church added one thousand new members. One thousand! The impact of prayer walking and specifically targeting the centers of spiritual activity, combined with evangelistic outreach, has caused such a migration of former Buddhists to Christ that Buddhist chanters have been sent from Taiwan and China to try to stem the flow. You can see them in Singapore placing their little triangular flags on ground that they feel they must recapture.

The pastor of that church attributes the mobilization of his followers to reach their loved ones to prayer walking. There is power in prayer.

WRESTLING THE ENEMY

Every winning wrestler knows the principle of pressure points. Now you do too. Think with me. Where are the centers of government in your town? Pinpoint them and set out a walking course which will cause you to park the ark on that pressure point. The false gods will bow down in the presence of the ark.

Think further. Where are the centers of communication? Try to take a tour or find a way to spend time there. Many television and radio stations offer tours of their facilities. Pray as you go, and then park the ark and release the Power Presence of God. False gods will bow down in the presence of the ark.

Next, identify the centers of education. Whoever holds the children holds the future. You can be most effective in that place. As you pray, there will be changes. If you need instruction, contact us for the two-part video testimony of opening the public schools in America through prayer.

Next, identify the centers of commerce. Remember, there may be types of commerce which are not listed on the Dow Jones industrial averages. Ask the Lord to show you the place to go and pray. Pray for Christian businessmen that they would have the highest profits with the lowest taxes.

Lastly, find the centers of spiritual activity. Do a church walk in your city and ask God to drive the Four Forces from the church and light the candlesticks again. When you see the temples of the Devil in your town, go there and pray. Park the ark; the false gods will bow down for greater is He that is in you than He that is in the world.

When you have identified these five centers, you have identified the principle infrastructure of your city. Now you must invite a few friends to begin to pray for those who live, work, and study in these centers. Take a prayer walk through them and ask the Lord to direct you with specific prayer strategies to reach those souls. As you park the ark there, you will receive not only fresh vision for the place, but also God's direction for reaching the souls there.

Just as the false god bowed down before the ark, so the Four Forces will be neutralized by the glory that dwells in you. Why can't you just stay at home and pray for the places and see change? Because to intercede is to step into the gap. The Holy Spirit is moving in all the earth looking for those through whom He can be glorified. Go on, call some friends and take a prayer walk around a center in your city. You will be amazed at the clarity with which you will hear from the Lord when you meet Him at His place of work.

You are beginning to define your city according to centers of influence, now let's define your nation according to the keys which God has given for reaching it.

CHAPTER 19

FOUR CULTURE KEYS

Before the days of the 10/40 Window missions emphasis, countries were referred to as Open Access Nations, Limited Access Nations, Restricted Access Nations or Closed Nations. I was always most interested in that last group.

Perhaps it was my parents repeatedly telling me all things were possible to those who believe. It might have been my coach's frequent admonition that attitude, not aptitude, would determine my altitude. It could have been Ann Kiemel's book, *I Love the Word Impossible* (Wolgemuth and Hyatt). Something caused me to believe there is no such thing as a closed country to a praying people. Over twenty years of doing missions has proved it to me.

There is no closed door which cannot be opened. Prayer establishes a beachhead on the Enemy's territory as nothing else can. As George Verwer puts it, "Try the door. If it doesn't open, kick it open. If you can't kick it open, fast till you fit through the key hole. If that doesn't work let the Holy Spirit take you in prayer under the door to the other side."

Now, however, we are able to go to any culture, anywhere. I have always enjoyed my friend Nick Burt's method of reaching unreached peoples. "Get on the plane to the end of the flight. Get a cab to the bus station. Take the bus to the end of the line and walk down the first street. You will be in the midst of unreached people."

PRACTICING AT HOME

Let's say we are at the local high school, and we have parked the ark. In the ten minutes before the basketball game begins, we park on the bleachers. You don't like basketball? Never mind, you are there to pray for the people. You don't like the people? Well, all the more reason to keep your focus on Jesus.

Looking to the Lord, we softly praise Him. Imagine that, praise in the public high school. This is Attack Lamb stuff. We pray for what? Perception. We need to perceive the Four Forces and how they operate in this place. Now remember, you are on the inside of a "pressure point" so you will discern some pressure. It's natural to be somewhat nervous.

The Lord shows us the forces of intimidation. He shows us the "pecking order" or social structure of the faculty, students, and parents. He shows us the worldliness or *kosmokratos* of the location and event. He causes us to feel "at risk" if there is malice present. Jesus will show you these things as you focus on Him.

We pray, binding these forces. Actually, at this point my wife often takes a little walk around the place, especially if she discerns malice. You see, our sons regularly participate in these events so I am sharing a regular practice of our family.

In this perception time, God will bring many ideas to your mind on how to reach the people in that room.

GOD GIVES THE FOUR KEYS

Several years ago I attended a basketball game at our local high school. My older son Sam was playing, and I was very happy to find the son of Pastor Jay Passavant, one of our SEAPC board members, playing for the other school. Jay and I arrived at about the same time and sat together on the top row of the bleachers. High points are often most effective for parking the ark.

My wife and I had spent hours in that gym. We had supported our two sons throughout their high school years. The Lord had given us particular and specific insight into the lives of each person we prayed for. As the different people came in, I shared with Jay the key to reaching each one with the Gospel. In the course of the conversation I realized that the keys to reaching them fell into four categories;

Language Keys

Culture Keys

Humor Keys

Power Keys.

Let's look at how these keys work to unlock various cultures for the Gospel of Jesus Christ.

LANGUAGE KEYS

In every language there is a reference to the Gospel. These are often called **redemptive analogies**. In our work with the Chinese we have been made aware of several of these.

The Chinese have enjoyed a written language for five thousand years. No matter how the characters are pronounced in the various dialects, the meaning is the same to all Chinese in their written form. Imagine, one fourth of the word with the same written language!

The concept of right relationship is basic to everything in Chinese life. The question of right relationship to heaven, to God, is perhaps the most perplexing to the Chinese. They see themselves as very small and creation as very big. You can see in their paintings very small people surrounded by gigantic mountains with waterfalls. Above and larger than the mountains are the clouds of the heavenlies. They often occupy more than a third of the frame.

Three thousand years before Jesus was born, the Chinese created their symbol for right relationship or "righteousness." The root of the symbol, or first part of the character to be drawn, is the symbol for "ego" or "self." The second part of the symbol is a lamb. In Chinese you must "take the lamb for yourself" to be righteous. Three thousand years before the birth of Jesus the Lord gave the prophetic instruction for all Chinese that "righteousness" can be obtained only by taking the lamb to cover the self.

This is a **language key**. When you are sharing with a Chinese you know they are already thinking of the lamb as long as you use the word "righteousness." Often I say to a Chinese person, "You already believe in the Lamb." Then I explain to them how this is so. Or I ask them, "Do you know who the Lamb is?" When they tell me they do not, I ask, "Would you like to know?" When they say yes, I have the perfect opening to share Jesus, the Lamb of God that takes away the sin of the world, and makes us righteous before God.

BACK TO THE GYM

You're not planning on going to China? Well, at least we got you to the gym. What was the language key there? One of the coaches kept yelling the name of Jesus in his frustration. Have you ever heard it? While the practice is very offensive to me personally, it tells me he does not know the Precious Person behind that name.

After the fifth or sixth time of hearing the name of Jesus mistreated, the thought occurred to me, *"This is a language key. This is something I can capitalize on for souls."*

The next time he shouted, I asked those sitting around me, "Why Jesus, why not Mohammed or Buddha or Shiva? Why does he shout the name of Jesus?" They were dumbfounded. No one had asked the question although they were also uncomfortable with the abuse of the Lord's name.

Into their silence I inserted the answer for them, "Because Jesus is the only One who has true power. He has to use that name because the others have no power. The demons in the Bible called out the name of Jesus in much the same tone." I quietly asked the Lord to deliver that coach from the oppressive spirit which controlled him.

About a year later I saw the man outside the school. He told me he had seen me preaching on a TV show and liked what I had to say.

I asked if he had prayed the prayer with me at the end and he said he had.

In the four years since then we have had many close basketball games. He has yelled at players. But not once in all those years have I heard him abuse the name of Jesus. Chinese or American, the principle works. God will give you the language key, and when you slip it into the door of their hearts, you will set the prisoners free.

THE CULTURE KEY

High in the mountains of Guatemala is a small Indian village called Zaqualpa. Several years ago my wife and I were working with a group of missionaries attempting to reach the Quiche people of the region. We flew up to the village in a single-engine plane to spend time at a very small mission station there.

My wife and I are both of German extraction so our oldest son's hair was that white silky blonde which adorns the heads of European children. He was just learning to walk at the time. On the mission field we carried him in a back pack frame rather than letting him crawl about in the dust because of the risk of parasites.

The day was fraught with a string of interruptions and much last-minute packing. Finally, we took off and arrived at the village; it was nearly dusk. The pilot buzzed the dirt strip to chase off grazing cows and playing kids. Then, with a tight "hammerhead" type turn we reversed direction and landed out of a huge red sun. Heads spinning, but laughing with relief and joy, we tumbled from the plane and quickly unloaded our gear so the pilot could get back to the city before dark.

I hoisted Sam into his carrier on my back and walked the thirty meters or so to the three by four meter wooden shed that would be our home for the next few days. Ellie brought armloads of "stuff" for the mission station there, and we were pleasantly greeted by Audrey who lived there.

Getting settled was fun. We had things for Audrey and shared the news from the city and around the globe. She was a wonderful grandmother who was ministering the love of Jesus in those remote mountain villages.

Our socializing was interrupted by the sound of many people outside the building. It sounded as if the place was surrounded and a guerilla war was going on in the region. We became quite concerned.

I was chosen to answer the knock at the door.

As it swung open we could see hundreds of Quiche people. They were dressed up in their beautifully colored earth tones of woven wool. Their jet black hair was braided with beautiful streaming ribbons.

The men were quite small, but appeared very strong. The leader addressed me in a dialect which I did not understand and then in Spanish.

"We have come for you to tell us," he said in a clear dignified voice.

"To tell you what?" I asked, without the faintest idea what he meant.

"The way to God. Our legend tells us that at the time of the red sun a man will come from the sky carrying a child with golden hair, and he will tell us the way to God. You have come from the red sun, and there is the child of golden hair, and we have all come to hear of the way to God."

I looked at Sam now toddling his way to the door. God had given him to us for a purpose, and a nation would be released because he was the fulfillment of a **culture key**.

We had great success in that place. Doors opened to the people which had been closed for over one hundred years of missions. Audrey went out to the villages and many children were raised from the dead as she prayed. Jesus was lifted up among the Quiche. They still think God lives in the sun, but they know to get to Him you must serve His Son Jesus. Culture keys are some of the most powerful keys to reaching a people for Jesus.

BACK TO THE GYM...AGAIN

As I watched Sam play in that basketball game so many years later, I asked the Lord for the culture key to this society. America is too young to have identified its culture. Many of the keys are going to have originated in other cultures from which this melting pot of a nation has been derived. African-American, Italian-American, Irish-American, European and other cultures have all brought their culture keys to this country.

For the people in that gym the common culture key was a **priority for their family.** I started talking with one of the men sitting near me. We had known each other since childhood. As kids we each had a reputation for violent strength. While he spoke I realized he had been through enough life experience to have been broken. The gentleness which came from his heart was so genuine. We began talking about Jesus, and he quoted his favorite TV preacher. He didn't attend a church, but there was a culture key that could unlock him to serve the Lord. He loves his family. The culture keys to your circle of friends and acquaintances are probably things you value highly as well.

THE HUMOR KEY

When I teach the Prayer Walking Seminar in person, one of my favorite sections is the typology of the ark. You read it in Chapter 7. When I stand in front of the people to teach I do hand motions which describe each part of the ark, but without saying anything. When I come to the part about the "pot of manna," I reach with both hands and bounce my stomach. My ample flesh makes for a humorous illustration. The people laugh and laugh, but they do not forget the point. This is a **humor key.**

Much of humor is at the expense of another. It can be very hurtful especially when you are the brunt of the joke. In the gym crowd, everyone loves humor. We take pleasure in being together. A merry heart does good like a medicine (Proverbs 17:22[105]). The happy person brings joy to the place. But, I realize when I'm parked in a pressure point like the gym, I'm in the midst of broken marriages. There can be great pressure as the two new couples come to watch a child play who is in the middle of the families. The Four Forces work extra hard to defeat them.

The Lord has given me a key in this area to defeat the Four Forces. Instead of being critical, I try to be gently kind to those who are hurting. Sharing humor with them often opens the door and communicates your acceptance of them. As a result of the open door created by my attitude, the opportunity to lead several to Christ has softly come. Pray that the Lord will give you a special love and understanding for these folk.

THE POWER KEY

All you need to plant a church is a good miracle.

We were prayer walking on Bintan Island in the Riau Province of Indonesia. (Just follow the equator around and you will find it). A family from the team was invited to a local home for lunch and of course went. Home-cooked Indonesian food is incredibly wonderful.

While they were there they met a lady whose face was being eaten away by leprosy. With no medical facility available for her, she was kept at home. The female team member asked if she could pray for the lady. She was permitted and did so. Then she also gave her a verse about new skin. Nothing appeared to happen so they encouraged the family, thanked them for lunch and went on their way. She shared the experience with us over dinner.

That evening we were in a church and the Holy Spirit was moving. The female team member was standing next to me on the platform as we were all caught up in worship. Focused on Jesus, I was interrupted by her incessant tugging on my shirt.

---

105. [22]A merry heart does good, like medicine, But a broken spirit dries the bones

"Look, Pastor Mark," she said, "there is the lady."

"What lady?" I asked, having only half-listened to her lunch testimony.

"The leper lady," she said.

As we watched, a breeze blew across the woman, and the light pastel veil covering her face was gently whisked aside. Her face shone as tears of love washed across brand new skin. Her nose had been restored as well as her cheeks and ear lobes. Jesus was making her over as we worshiped. We could not speak. We could barely breathe as the anointing of God was so intense. No one called her forward or dared to interrupt Jesus as He touched her with healing.

The news spread quickly and the church has been packed every night since. Four years later, they are opening a training center to send people throughout all of Indonesia. Muslims in that part of the world are coming to Christ because they have seen the manifestation of a **power key**.

BACK TO THE GYM...ONE MORE TIME

Across the gym is a big man. His powerful three hundred and fifty pounds glide through the place on a 6' 6" frame. He loves every kid on that floor and watches over them like his own. In a wheel chair next to him is his oldest son. He loves Jesus.

Late last October the weather had been bitter cold. I found out the young man was about to have his twenty-something operation. He had been born with tremendous difficulties and had been con-fined to the wheel chair. His three younger brothers, by contrast, had each been star athletes on a national scale. He has not missed a single game of theirs.

I went to visit him before his operation at the request of his par-ents. The doctor had not given them a good prognosis. In fact, the feel of death was very much in the air. He and I spent a half hour together and I gave him my pocket cross which I had carried for years. He received Jesus and declared he had experienced a change in his heart. I went on home and continued to pray for him.

His dad told me the rest of the story. They had prepared him for surgery and told both he and the family things did not look good. As they were taking him to the operating room he became very distressed, calling out to his father. Dad leaned in close to him and asked what he wanted. He wanted the cross. He said he wanted to know Jesus was with him as He knew He had been with me so many times. They went back and found the cross and gave it to him.

Now, several months later, there he sits alive and well, next to his father. His recovery is a **power key** which has allowed me an open door to share Christ with student athletes throughout the school. Jesus touched him. His family testifies he is a new person. His language has changed. His attitude has changed. His life has changed.

YOUR TURN AGAIN

As the game ended we rejoiced in the testimonies of the Lord. Jesus loves every one of these people. We must go to where they are and park the ark. We do not wrestle with flesh and blood. We wrestle with four forces that want to keep them from being saved. You have the in-dwelling ability as a child of God to go and neutralize the power of the Enemy in your school. You can get in the gap and begin to pray. You can become involved in the life of the place.

How are you going to access your local school? Develop an action plan. Ask your prayer partners to pray for you as you go. Become involved as a volunteer at some level. If this generation is lost to hell it will be because the adults let them go.

How are you going to access your local government? Develop an action plan. Ask your prayer partners to pray for you as you go. Find a place to park the ark. Pray for the people who work there. Make yourself aware of their world. Let the glory of God flow through you to the community.

How are you going to access your local communication center? Develop an action plan. Write letters to the editor, small papers love them. Take out an ad for a place of prayer. Infiltrate through activity. Find a place to park the ark.

How are you going to access the center of commerce? Develop an action plan. Get churches and individuals to rent a store front for prayer. Open a coffee shop. Start a lunch-time prayer walk around the complex. Get a few associates to join you in fasting one lunch a week, pray for the business and the souls in it. Find a place to park the ark and let the glory of God flow through you in it.

How are you going to access that center of spiritual activity? Develop an action plan. Ask your prayer partners to pray for you as you go, and take someone with you. Enter in for the souls of the people. Find a place to park the ark and let the glory of God flow through you and release the people.

The Lord will show you the way for it is His great pleasure to give you the Kingdom (Luke 12:32[106]). He has, after all, given you the keys. To use these keys, you must "enter in" to the gap-like doorways of the world. You can do this because Jesus is the Way. As you pray to be used of Him, remember your feet. Let them be swift to walk in His way.

....

In this chapter, we are going to consolidate many of the points made in chapters 17 through 19 of the first edition. Living the principles of this book for the 20 years since its publication, and seeing it become an embraced teaching around the world , we will look at the five pressure points and releasing the anointing from Luke 4 and Isaiah 61.

God's purpose is that every man, woman, and child on the face of the earth have the opportunity to know Jesus Christ as their personal Lord and Savior.

---

106. [32]"Do not fear, little flock, for it is your Father's good pleasure to give you the kingdom

His plan is to use you and me to accomplish His purpose.

He promises to be with us in every place as we walk in His plan and purpose.

He promises to provide the power to accomplish the purpose.

He is looking for the person who will prioritize for His purpose, participate in His plan, practice His presence, produce in His power, and be His person. For more on this, I refer you to our upcoming book, *Five Things You Need to Know.*

Being a person of structure, I have adopted a weekly hour of prayer strategy for Attack Lambs. Let me warn you, late-night TV is out. Like many who serve in professions, I am an early morning person. The highlight of my day is an hour of personal prayer. "Early will I rise to greet thee," is my motto and hours before sunrise you will find me with my bible, journal, and coffee seeking the Lord. If you read the chapter on giving, you will know that I firmly believe in the principle of the tithe. And if time is money, then why not tithe the day in prayer, one hour for ten hours productivity?

You probably work in one of the five centers we taught in the first edition: Government, Commerce, Communication, Education, or Spiritual Activity. God has you there to stand in the gap for others. This is a place in which your prayers will affect the culture and productivity of the team He has assembled. Because you take the time to put Him first, He will honor you by answering your prayers. You do not have to draw attention to yourself, in fact, it would be good not to. Just be the lamb of lambs while the King of kings works through you.

For people like me who have retired from the everyday "go to the office" world, we can be very mobile in support of the working Attack Lambs.

Prayer is good for us. Walking is good for us. Prayer walking is a double blessing for us.

CENTERS OF GOVERNMENT

On Mondays, we can go for one hour to the centers of Government. This would be wherever your city or county council meets. You arrive early, if weather permits take a walk around the building praying for the members by name. If it is also a police station, pray for your local police.

As you walk—or, if the weather is bad, sit in your car— you can begin by praising the Lord for these civil servants. They are often volunteers or part-time people. They carry the representation of your community including services and public safety. If you have made your community your prayer parish, then they are those who the Lord has given to serve in your parish. Think about it, they are the people who dress and keep your garden.

As the Lord manifests His presence, listen to Him about how to pray. For me, a scripture will often come to mind and I just speak that over the government and the community. "Thy Kingdom come thy will be done" is a great prayer at your Government Center. The Ten Commandments or The Lord's Prayer, while perhaps not allowed to be published, can certainly be prayed.

What you are doing is releasing the anointing or the presence of God to dispel the forces of Archas, Exousias, Kosmokratos, and Poneerias. You are invoking righteousness, peace, and joy in the Holy Spirit which is the Kingdom of God (Romans 14:17[107]). You are speaking the name of Jesus and announcing the manifold wisdom of God. Go often enough and maintain the presence and you will see the promises of God fulfilled in your community. Crime will go down as praise goes up. The key in community is not the actions of the evil, but the prayer power of the righteous.

We are not political activists, but we do influence elections through prayer for God knows the thoughts and intents of the heart of each candidate and what they will or will not do once in office.

---

107. [17]for the kingdom of God is not eating and drinking, but righteousness and peace and joy in the Holy Spirit.

He sees and knows it all. Pray as though the life of your community depended on your prayer. Think about and learn about your neighborhood or highrise. Speak well of those in authority and if they are horrible, simply say, "I am praying for them." Remember Lot, for that righteous man was deeply disturbed by the culture around him, and God heard his prayer and answered it (2 Peter 2:7[108]).

If you are invited into the building, ask for the opportunity to meet the highest available official and offer to pray with or for them. If you have your best "lamb of lambs" behavior going, they will not be put off by your offer. In this way I have been able to lay hands on and pray for the Lord's blessing to and through many civic leaders.

One hour on Mondays for the government. We get the community we pray for.

Taking this a little further, we have developed Pray Americas in which we encourage and lead prayer teams to go to their state capitol and pray at the government headquarters. This has resulted in wonderful breakthroughs which we measure in a decrease in crime, a decrease in drug overdoses, and an increase in the economy. You might really enjoy getting a van full of like-minded folks and heading over to the capitol to pray. Make an appointment with your representative and offer yourselves to be a prayer support for them. I have seen a real turn around in legislation and a decrease in crime in the states where we have done this.

When this door opens, remember to be on time, dress with respect, pray what the Lord gives you, and leave without asking any type of favor. You are an Ambassador from the King of Kings. Behave like it.

CENTERS OF COMMERCE

Tuesdays are commerce days for me. I love Tuesdays. Centers of commerce are the Chamber of Commerce location and major

---

108. [7]and delivered righteous Lot, who was oppressed by the filthy conduct of the wicked

employers in your community. Health care is one of the big industries as well as information technology. Both are under terrific pressure these days. One of the communities I have adopted for prayer is Mahoning County, Ohio. Located in the Rust Belt, this once-thriving coal, steel, and car manufacturing center is now abandoned and the target of the gang and drug outlets of the spirit of malice, Pneumatika tae Poneerias. This fourth, of the four forces in Ephesians 6:12[109], features gang battles, killings, drug addiction, and other forms of brutality. Eastern Ohio and particularly Youngstown were brought to my attention by a Pastors Coalition. We studied Attack Lambs together, reading and implementing chapters. We walked the streets together. We located where the drug trade was happening as it was rapidly becoming the leading industry in town.

Pastors, black and white, walked together and prayed for this city. They ministered to each incoming mayor and school director. Funding and favor were found to bring businesses into the area. The greatest commercial challenge we faced was the opioid epidemic. This has to be seen from a greed driven business plan that includes pharmaceutical companies, doctors, and dealers who prey upon the public for personal gain.

Our first step was "Unity in the Community" and we worked through many racial issues. We, as leaders, had to get real with God about our prejudices. He worked in wonderful ways to show black and white community members alike the inherent value of the other. As unity began to happen, so did breakthrough.

The University received grants and new leadership to move it in a Godward way. Housing grants were obtained so that people could live in decent housing. A former hospital was obtained and converted to a high-security drug rehab and family development center, so hope came alive.

---

109. [12]For we do not wrestle against flesh and blood, but against principalities, against powers, against the rulers of the darkness of this age, against spiritual hosts of wickedness in the heavenly places.

With peace, local manufacturing companies took advantage of lower business taxes and began to develop their industries. With the declaration of vision for the government, the place began to change.

And with the church, police, federal agents, and federal courts working together, drug deaths decreased 48% in one year of focused intercession. To intercede means to intervene between two with a view of reconciling their difference. Tuesday is the day to enter into the commercial centers of your community.

In a less dramatic setting, I like to walk. Malls are great for walking and speaking life into the businesses there. Walmart's are great for walking as are Target stores. Walk and pray and pray and walk and especially visit the checkout counters for I feel these are the most stressful commercial locations in America.

Those of us who are retirement age should own the malls if the word is true, "**Every place that the sole of your foot will tread upon I have given you**" (Joshua 1:3).

CENTERS OF COMMUNICATION

Wednesdays are communication days.

You are going to enter a space between where communication is and where it can be. Communication is, by definition, the imparting or exchanging of information or news. In the Garden of Eden, at the beginning of the human experience, flawed communication brought the fall of man. The devil miscommunicated (by intention) the directive God had given. Eve, not knowing the nature of God, though created in His image, repeated the miscommunication and her innocence was lost.

Ephesians 2:2[110] reminds us that we once walked in the cloud of miscommunication created by the enemy but now have been raised with Christ high above all powers and principalities. You are now

---

110. [2]in which you once walked according to the course of this world, according to the prince of the power of the air, the spirit who now works in the sons of disobedience

going to enter a gap and pray for those whose lives are controlled by the devil's miscommunication and the resultant loss of innocence.

You enter with the mind of Christ and though you discern all things, you are discerned of none (1 Corinthians 2:13-16[111]). You are an instrument of the restoration of innocence as the cloud is disbursed and the light shines in the hearts and minds of the people. The anointing you carry as the ark in the flesh dispels the cloud that has been foisted on the minds of those who do not hold the truth of scripture in their hearts and minds. The gospel is foolishness to the carnal mind. It is not a marketable commodity because it is the only Word of the only true God who sent His only Son as the only way to the Father. It cannot be put in a competitive setting because it has no equal. The competition was won when Jesus rose from the dead according to the prophecies that came hundreds of years before His death.

Wednesdays we go to radio and television stations, IT centers, companies that produce and publish information or news. We focus on the throne and release the anointing. Our desire is to bring clarity to what is being produced.

News is a big business today and each broadcast, podcast, or tweet is a classroom for the tactics of the prince and power of the air. Who is number one? It is the most often asked question in media. Who has the primetime news show? Which newscast is watched by the most people? Which program has the highest rating because I want my advertising dollar to be spent reaching the largest market for my product. As long as there are sponsors promoting products, this is not a news show. News has become the tool of the devil to again feed the flesh of humanity with the lust of the flesh, eyes, and pride. He

---

111. [13]These things we also speak, not in words which man's wisdom teaches but which the Holy Spirit teaches, comparing spiritual things with spiritual. [14]But the natural man does not receive the things of the Spirit of God, for they are foolishness to him; nor can he know them, because they are spiritually discerned. [15]But he who is spiritual judges all things, yet he himself is rightly judged by no one. [16]For "who has known the mind of the Lord that he may instruct Him?" But we have the mind of Christ.

gives who he is through the message he sends. This product will cause you to know more, look better, and feel really good about yourself.

And yet, you have the best news. Your news has not been corrupted by the prince. Your news is about the innocent being slain to restore innocence to man. Your news is redemptive and can be received by everyone. People with whom you come in contact in centers of communication are deeply under the influence of the four forces. Who is number one? Why should I talk to you? Who are you? Are you important?

Movies, games, and print materials have become more violent since the Bible was replaced as the moral code of ethics. The spirit of malice is manifested on these platforms with ever-increasing reality as the virtual world of the game becomes a reality in the minds of youth. It is no longer morally questionable for a young person playing a game to obtain a gun and take the life of another. In fact, the anarchy of the generation is all about the Archas manifesting with the power of the Poneerias.

As an anointed Attack Lamb, you can enter into the space between the student and that spirit. Because the One living in you is greater than the one trying to dominate that person, you can, by declaration of the presence, power, or person of Jesus, dispel the work of the enemy. May I suggest that you visit the gaming center or the producers of the games, park the ark, let the anointing flow forth and see the changes in the young people.

At all times remember, God is love. Approach this gap in the spirit of love. Do not condemn but rather embrace this generation. When your child or grandchild wants the latest game, research just how violent it is and do not ever be afraid to stand in the gap and refuse to purchase it. They may pout a bit, but they will not learn mass murder.

This spirit of malice and Archas combination is the root of bullying and intimidation, the physical brutality is fueled by the spirit of malice (malice is the desire or action to cause harm to another human being) and the fear and intimidation by the Archas. This tag team of terror can be evicted by the demonstration of God's love. **"There is no fear in love; but perfect love casts out fear, because fear involves torment"** (1 John 4:18a). The prophet, Isaiah spoke of this in Isaiah 26:12-13,14b, **"Lord, You will establish peace for us, for You have also done all our works in us. O Lord our God, masters besides You have had dominion over us; But by You only we make mention of Your name... You have punished and destroyed them, and made all their memory to perish."** Night sweats, cold fears, anxiety attacks, and hyperventilation are all measures of the impact of the tag team of terror, but the declaration and the demonstration of God's love will break their power.

Bullying has become lethal in this generation. Multiplying fear cripples the lives of those under the influence of a bully and its charges. When the victim reports to those who love him, he is often told to just stay away from the offender. Few people understand that the tag team of terror, very real spiritual forces, are driving the often bruised individual to bully those perceived to be weaker just to feed a need for worth. "Just stay away" does not help when the spirits are driving the bully to feed the frenzy. Someone needs to be in that gap releasing the power that is greater than any other power. Action must be taken. Intervention must occur.

The end game for the tag team of terror is teen suicide.

Authorities may reprimand the bully, but they can not block the spirits and he will be a repeat offender, actually beginning to sound and look like the force that is driving him. This bullying needs the Attack Lambs' attention in our government, businesses, schools, and churches. Fed by the communication industry of violence and outrage, the bully seeks out lives to destroy.

For Attack Lamb power to be released in this gap, an Attack Lamb must park that ark at this pressure point and release the Holy Spirit through declaration and demonstration, declaring the person and victory of Jesus Christ.

CENTERS OF EDUCATION

Nowhere is this warfare more evident than in places of education. Often a good student is compromised because they are being bullied by a jealous peer. Students and faculty suffer as the control of the tag team flaunt its power in the halls, restrooms, and classrooms. What is a teacher to do? They are not there to be the police. They just want to impart value to the students in their charge.

Thursdays are school days for the Attack Lamb.

Ron Luce initiated See You at the Pole almost 30 years ago and it is still going strong today. Fellowship of Christian Athletes has Huddles in thousands of high schools and most universities. I have personally visited 42 NCAA Division One Campuses and found faith alive on each. Yet, there is a crying need for people to pray. Many programs, though good, often do not release the anointing that will break the yokes of bondage that seek to control campus life.

There are social gaps, academic gaps, political gaps, and a gaping hole when it comes to Jesus and personal faith. I once interviewed a grad student at the University of Minnesota. As a gay man of color, I asked him about human rights and whether there is a hierarchy within human rights. What takes priority? Perhaps assuming I'd never understand as a straight white man, he brushed me aside and transitioned into a speech on the topic.

Glad to hear him give me the mantra, and listening very closely to every word, I tried to release the Holy Spirit. Jesus loves the man, though his words were hate-filled. After about five minutes of non-stop profanity in describing me to myself, I asked him who had hurt him so badly that he had to vent with such venom to a person about whom he knew nothing except the color of his skin.

At these words, he switched courses to explain that he knew everything he needed to know about me, because "we" are all the same. Of course, the four forces were feeding his head with the language of intimidation and division that is their nature.

I interrupted to say, "How old were you when you first understood that Jesus is the Son of God?"

Increasing his volume and becoming quite impassioned, he shared that "Jesus is the white man's God." In doing so, he became quite physical, stepping closer to me. The others in the team stepped up and for a moment it looked like a campus truth-finding conversation was going to end badly.

I waited for the Holy Spirit to touch him and slowly he lost some steam. He cocked his head and looked at me with a strange look, "Who are you, anyway?"

"I am Mark Geppert," I said extending my hand.

When he took the hand, I felt the power flow. He held my hand for a moment and, disarmed, sheepishly said, "I have to go."

My last words to him were, "Jesus loves you. When you need Him, call on His Name."

Consider Christ who endured such contradiction of sinners before you lose heart in praying for people.

After that encounter, we went to the office of the President of the University. Unavailable at the moment, we were ushered into the office of the Dean of Academic affairs. At the mention of the purpose of our visit, she shut down. Cold does not describe the atmosphere she emanated. She told us that her job was to prepare young people for adulthood by selecting courses and instructors that would teach them today's ethics.

I love that phrase, "today's ethics." You have to contact SEAPC and ask for the book *Where Have the Children Gone?* They will give it to you as a gift so that you can benefit from their in-depth exploration of the term, "today's ethics." Simply put, "today's ethics" deny the existence of God, His Son, and Salvation. The young man we had just met was a perfect example of this mindset.

"So, where do God and prayer fit in?" One of our team members, a mother of a college-age boy, couldn't take too much more of this conversation.

"Each student is free to choose how they want to answer that." A well-seasoned answer if there ever was one.

"So, self-determined ethics?" Asked another team member. He is a local businessman, well known in the community and also a parent of a college student. "Is there a code of conduct or ethical stance for the university or do the students just do what they think is right? Is there a standard at this university?"

These lambs were getting a bit rowdy.

"I am sure the Provost can explain that to you." The Dean retorted, showing us to the office of the Provost and suggesting to the secretary that we might do better there.

The secretary assured us that the Provost was not in, but if we would like to pray there in the office it would be fine with her and with him. We formed a circle and gently prayed for the university and its leadership and asked the Lord to put angels in the doorways to prevent the agents of the enemy from coming to the campus. The dean did not stay.

Leaving the administration building we took a loop past the student union. There we encountered a young man who was nearly seven feet tall. A basketball recruit no doubt, I stopped him to ask a few questions about spiritual life on the campus and whether he had connected with Intervarsity or Fellowship of Christian Athletes. Towering of us, his response touched me deeply.

"You are Christians? He asked.

"Yes, we are here praying for the school," the mom answered.

"Please, pray for me. This place is crazy. I think I made the wrong choice to come here. I had other offers but chose here and it is not at all what I expected. I feel so isolated as a believer. The social scene is not at all what I expected and the teams are racially divided. I am afraid every day. As soon as I am labeled as a Christian, I become a target for rants. Please keep me in your prayers."

And off he went to class. He is the reason. He and thousands like him who are leaving secure homes and entering into a world that has lost its moral code. We pray for him and millions like him on our college campuses.

CENTERS OF SPIRITUAL ACTIVITY

Friday, we go to centers of spiritual activity.

Pastor Isaac Lim was the TRAC Chairman for Methodist Churches in Singapore. He attended an Attack Lambs Seminar in that city and invited us to come with him on a hired bus and visit each Methodist church on the island republic. With joy, we joined his vision to pray for each Methodist church staff. He set the schedule and hired the bus and we spent a few wonderful days going to these centers of spiritual activity with the purpose of relighting the lamp-stand. Isaac saw us laying hands on the pastors and asking the Lord to refill them with the Holy Spirit.

Pastor Nathaniel Chow, a leading pastor in Taiwan also decided to hire a bus. This time our team of Attack Lambs went to Buddhist centers and prayed for the people who were part of those temples. The centers are family and clan-based. We prayed that the Lord would break through in the family line and start bringing those families into Christian faith. Within six months the churches in each city reported significant growth.

Pastor Joshua Cheung hired a helicopter and many double-decker busses and we traveled to each district of Hong Kong and flew through the Central Business district, among the tall towers, and cried out to the Lord for souls to be saved. The church in Hong Kong has realized unprecedented growth especially among those mainland Chinese who have come down for work.

Pastor Bulmaro Valle Martinez gathered his group of pastors in Oaxaca, Mexico and we walked from church to church and through very violent sections of the city. We hired a bus and took the team to the outskirts of Oaxaca where witches and spiritists operated in caves. With loud praise and worship at the roadside, a team of us actually walked into the caves. Passing instruments of witchcraft, we confronted the spirits. They manifested in cloud-like forms rising from the depths of the cave. Several were photographed, the sense of fear was crippling, but as we proclaimed the name of Jesus, they fled the region. New churches are coming up where love has displaced fear in the hearts of the people.

These are just four examples of the pastoral leadership we have enjoyed. Pastor Rusty Wills has led a prayer walk every Wednesday to centers of spiritual activity in his adopted Youngstown, Ohio region. Joined by a few regular walkers, and through the direction of the Holy Spirit, they have dispelled forces of evil throughout the city. Perhaps the most wonderful manifestation of the success of their prayers is the unity they now enjoy across racial and denominational lines.

Our team of four was in the Shiva-Vishnu temple in a Pittsburgh suburb. No stranger to this atmosphere of bondage, I took a bit of time to interview the head priest of the temple. A bit of a seer, he had been giving "blessing" sayings to a family worshipping the idols. I respectfully put on my "lamb of lambs" demeanor and patiently waited until he indicated we could talk.

He had come from Varanasi, India which is one of the holiest places in Shiva-Vishnu worship. Sponsored by the temple and given an employment visa from the government, he was there to minister to the needs of the Indian community.

I shared that we, too, were there to minister to their need to know Jesus as their Lord and Savior. He was happy to chat about this as he had seen our respect for the people.

I suggested we move away from the altar toward an open window, more to get out of the incense than any other reason, and as we looked out the window he gave a surprised jump and said to me, "Sir, you have a very important message for me, what is it?"

I asked how he knew.

"Look in the sky" he said excitedly. "There are two eagles. They carry the presence of God. They have never been here before. It is a sign from heaven for me. You must share with me."

So, I did. I shared that the true and living God loves him and brought him to America for this moment so that he could hear about the love of God in Jesus Christ, receive Jesus as His Lord, and be free from the fear he had every time he came near lord Shiva.

"How do you know about the fear?" He asked.

"God has shown me your heart," I responded. "You must open your heart to Jesus. You cannot add Him to your six million other gods. You must serve Him alone."

Amazed, we walked out of the temple together and watched the two eagles as they soared above the temple.

"I shall do it," the former priest declared. "Never have I seen such a thing. I shall do it today."

He is no longer employed by the temple. Jesus has taken him a new way.

When we enter a center of spiritual activity, we must be mindful that this confrontation is not with us. It is the Holy Spirit within us that is confronting every anti-Christ force in the place. Manifestations are between the two of them. Just as Jesus encouraged the 70 in Luke 10, He encourages us to keep our focus on the throne and not get distracted by those things that go on around us.

People come to temples in an attempt to find a solution to a problem they are facing. The tag team of terror will try to grip them with terror, but you are there to block it, to neutralize the power of the enemy so that you can clearly speak the love of God to them. The true victory in spiritual warfare is souls saved, healthy growing churches, and communities changed.

Centers of government, commerce, communication, education, and spiritual activity are five pressure points in which you can park your ark, focus on the throne, release the anointing and set the captive free. Make a schedule, build a team of like-minded people, ask the Lord for direction and follow through. I pray that your testimonies will reach my ears that I might be blessed that you took this book and went out and did it.

CHAPTER 20

OPENING THE DOOR TO A NATION

I was sitting on a housetop in Kathmandu, Nepal, talking with our team of eight prayer walkers who had gone trekking to take literature to the western region of the mountain country. After sharing our experiences, it became obvious that, in order to reach our goal, we would have to split up. We had already mapped out the area we were going to, and now we assigned territories. Rick Mains, a man of God from Kansas, and I went with one porter to the snowline while the rest of our group went through a more densely populated area in the direction of India.

Rick and I had climbed to twelve thousand feet and made the mistake of not descending to sleep. As a result, we had difficulty with altitude sickness and circulatory problems. The Lord intervened and we did not fall off the mountain; as a result, the next day we were able to get along at a reasonable pace.

That evening we stayed at the home of a Buddhist trader in the town of Dohrpatan. It is at this town that the mule teams from Tibet and India meet and the cultures transact business. Salt for silk, spices for saddles and so forth. Our host was the middleman for these trades and quite wealthy.

I DIDN'T SMELL SO GOOD

When I awoke in his house I became aware of a very pungent odor. Of course, given where I was at the time it could have been anything. As I sniffed about, I realized it was my own body. I stank. Body odor is not news for anyone who has trekked in Nepal, but this smell was way beyond that. Removing my shoes and socks I was startled to find pus running from several open sores. During the course of our trek I had contracted a local disease called *pani*. This Hindi word for "water" lets us know the bacteria involved are water borne. Actually, they enter through any sore in the feet causing a very serious infection, which spreads rapidly. I tore away dead skin and administered a salve and then wrapped my feet with adhesive tape. With clean socks and new shoes, I felt it would be alright to do our prayer walk that day.

We began to walk that morning and after about an hour had to ford a clear stream. Like true Nepali we just walked into it. The stream was run off water from ice and snow less than a mile away. Its numbing cold gave me some relief to what was already becoming a difficult situation with my feet.

By noon we crested a ridge we would now descend for several days, working our way along granite paths to a roadhead we would take just over a week to reach. Since there are no roads in these mountains, you become accustomed to walks measured in weeks as opposed to hours. In Nepal there is no direct route from anywhere or to anywhere. You just keep climbing either up or down. There is no level ground to be found. After a while, the heart pounding, lung burning "ups" become more pleasant than the knee twisting, toe crunching, gut wrenching "downs." In Nepal everything that goes down must again come up.

THE THIRD DAY

By the third day I knew I was in real trouble. The infection was spreading rapidly. The swelling had gone beyond the limits of the tape, which I determined I would not remove until I couldn't walk any more. My overall health was deteriorating as the infection raced through my blood. Each heart pound sent tiny bacteria to homes where they would build colonies and start pumping waste into my system. Prayer was a groan.

I used a walking stick and, shuffling my feet, I slid along as best I could. My ego was destroyed when I had to give the porter my pack so I could keep up with Rick. My partner had been assaulted with Spina Bifida as a child but was really getting along well, and his great victory left little room for my complaint. We must have been a sight.

After two more days we reached a village along the bank of a good-sized little river. We would stay here and, I was told, it was just one full day's walk to reach a place where we could get a bus back to Kathmandu. Relieved, I lay down on a bed made from a wooden door in the back room of a shack, and dropped into the deep sleep of the exhausted. I awoke a short time later with the strange feeling something was eating me, and when I inspected myself I found hoards of bed bugs feasting on me.

When morning mercifully came upon us I was the picture of misery and disgust: filthy, unshaven and bug infested, inside and out. I was determined, however, and we began our last day's walk. I crossed the river without feeling the coolness of the water at all. In fact, my reddened upper legs told me something disastrous was about to happen to my already sorry state.

TIRE TRACKS

As we emerged from the river, there in the silt at the river's edge was a most wonderful sight. A tire track. Never before or since have I so enjoyed the appearance of a tire track. And this one was not alone! There were more. It was a group of tire tracks. Saved!

"Where there are tires, there are wheels," I explained to the guide. "Where there are wheels there are vehicles." My excitement built as he stared at me. "Where there are vehicles one does not walk, one rides!" My joy was lost on him. He had been paid to guide us on a walking trek, and didn't understand why we wanted to ride now.

"We walk just half day and be there," he insisted.

"No, man, we sit and vehicle come and carry us." Was there pleading in my voice?

"Just six hours, very close." He turned and started on the trek.

I sat down. Sitting down is the "full stop" of many cross-cultural communications. Just sit down. He got the message and came and sat beside me. His concern was he had been hired to travel the distance on foot and to bring us safely through. I was ill, we were going to ride instead of walk. He was afraid of losing face as a guide. I assured him I would put plenty of face back on him by telling the world he was a wonderful guide, and that none of my plight was his fault, and I thought he was a great guy, and now couldn't we please ride?

We worked it out.

OUR TAXI COMES

The vehicle that came was a Chinese tractor pulling a wagon. It was our taxi to the next town. We took it. Three hours later we all arrived.

By now it was late afternoon and Rick and the guide went to buy our bus tickets. I sat down on a bench under a rough lean-to and, knowing I wouldn't have to walk anymore, gave my feet some welldeserved attention. I was joined by three street beggars. My appearance must have put them off for they did not even ask me for alms.

The two men wore filthy cotton shirts and rag skirts. With them was a young woman. She was filthy. Her hair was matted with livein dirt and bugs. Her filth-encrusted face rested atop shoulders covered only by the ragged remnant of a man's undershirt. On her hip was a naked baby who was equally filthy. This sight will never leave me. They just stared at my feet. They knew what was wrong with my feet, and they also knew I probably wouldn't have them long. I could see the pity in their eyes.

GOD'S OPEN DOOR

When I removed my first shoe, I was nauseated by the stench. They stood back a bit, this odor overcoming their own, while I removed the now shredded sock and took hold of the tape.

Have you ever pulled adhesive tape from skin? Can you imagine the dead skin and tissue coming with it? As I pulled the final layer, pus flew in every direction. My feet burst into the air. I think all the flies of India converged on that rotten flesh.

The young girl reached out to touch my feet. Tears washed rivulets down her dirty, crestfallen cheeks. Her tears fell to the dust before me, and her hand of compassion reached across culture and time to comfort me. I was ministered to by the lowest of the low caste of Asia. God had brought me lower than the lowest that I might have ministry among them.

I would never forget them, nor they me.

God had opened the door.

JOURNEY OF FAITH

I did what I could to bind up my feet again and, tickets in hand, we boarded the bus. As we pulled out of the village I waved good-bye to my three friends. I didn't know it then, but I had just started on what would be the longest journey of faith I have ever taken, even to this day.

They delivered me to the Mendies Haven children's home in Kathmandu. At first the doctors thought they would have to remove both of my legs above the knees. Not a good prognosis for a prayer walker. Much prayer was offered by the whole team. The doctors examined me again and reconsidered. Now they were going to remove them just below the knee. More prayer was offered. My legs and feet began to heal. The infection retreated and began to leave.

I took antibiotics regularly and Indira, a wonderful worker at the Haven, ministered to my feet. She pulled away the dead and decaying tissue and applied topical antibiotics regularly. The Lord intervened to do what the doctors were sure was beyond their power to do, and I was healed.

My journey of faith was complete, and behind me was an open door to India. I would return soon to walk through it again.

CHAPTER 21

THE VISION AND THE STRATEGY

Back on the roof in Kathmandu, near the close of my time in that city, the Lord had allowed me to see a vision.

I saw the beautiful Kathmandu valley filled with a dark cloud. Above the cloud was brilliant sunshine. Beneath the cloud was total darkness.

"What is this?" I asked the Lord in prayer.

"This is the way the world is," He said clearly. "Above the cloud is the way I want it to be; I want to bless all people everywhere. Below is the way they live, in darkness."

"What is the cloud?" I asked.

"The cloud is what separates them from my blessing," He said. "It is sin and religious systems."

"What shall I do?" I asked.

"Be a mobile earth station," He said.

I'm not sure what I expected His response to be, but that was surely not it.

A mobile earth station is a television transmitter which sends the signal to the satellite. The signal is then beamed down to an area where it can be received by a dish or another earth station. The area in which the beamed signal can be picked up is called the satellite's "footprint." Earth stations are very big, pulled by trucks and very heavy.

"Lord, I cannot carry a TV station around the world," I said.

"Not TV," He replied, "prayer! You go where I show you and pray. As you pray I will respond from heaven. When we effect an uplink I will send government-changing revival."

"Where do I go first?" I asked.

"Go to Beijing and take the train across Siberia to Moscow," was the reply.

I agreed to do it, and began planning for the trip. The Scripture the Lord brought to mind was Psalm 119:105[112], **"Thy word is a lamp unto my feet...,"** which were now totally healed.

It was the fall of 1985 and for the next three and a half years, my family and I went to Asia ourselves, or sent trained teams of intercessors to Moscow and the Trans-Siberian region. As we all know, the Lord did, in fact, send government-changing revival to the USSR. It didn't happen overnight, but it did happen!

THE DIVINE MANDATE

At the time I received the earth station vision, it was against the law to become a Christian in Nepal. The penalty was one year in prison for converting, three years for leading someone to Christ, and six years per person for water baptism. Yet, in the face of these restrictions, the Lord is faithful concerning His promise. We have a divine mandate to walk the earth. With that mandate we have the promise that He will give us the land.

The Lord moved on the Prime Minister of Nepal, and then the King and now you can become a Christian, plant a church, or even preach in the street. We have freedom.

When we go forth with faith in the One who has called us, all things are possible. There is no such thing any more as a "Closed Country." There is no "Closed City." You can get a visa to visit Mecca,

---

112. [105]Your word is a lamp to my feet And a light to my path

put on the right clothes and walk that place for Jesus. You can believe God and take New York City.

God is going to add to your account in heaven every soul which is won as you walk your neighborhood. Each place you go He will breakthrough for you.

Even your city can be taken for Christ. Yes, even yours. To win a city you must have a strategy. Let's learn a little about how it's done.

THE STRATEGY

There is a very simple strategy which will guide us in taking the promised nations.

First, we have to **map it out**. I thank God for AD 2000 and Global Harvest ministries. These people, and the Joshua Project, have teams over all the earth cataloging people groups and finding the four keys to release them. Just a few years ago we had prayer walking teams throughout the 10/40 Window. The year before YWAM celebrated the completion of a phase of their commission with the Cardinal Points Prayer Day.

Next, we must **determine the gateway cities and centers** in the earth. This is being done, but more workers are needed. Get a couple of partners, trust God for the tickets, get a visa and get out there. Walk that land; God is going to give it to you.

After we discern the gateways, we have to **do research**. I was recently in Ankor Wat in Cambodia and discovered there are lines of control which extend from that city to Bali, Indonesia, and then to Dashankali, Nepal. Many are researching the influence of the four forces which have prevented the Gospel from reaching the people within this triangle. Recently, we brought teams to the prayer summits of China and coordinated prayer throughout that vast land. We had to leave one peak of the five untouched because we did not have the manpower to get there. We must see God's plan and get in it.

Then, we need to **apply the knowledge** the Lord is giving. I thank God for the networks that are being established. The Body of Christ is coming together through the Internet and we are able to rally multinational teams to meet at specific prayer points and create those uplinks all over the world. You must become involved in the flow of what the Lord is doing. Ignorance is not bliss when the voice of the trumpet calls you to come up to a new level and see the purpose of God.

The Body of Christ has, finally, come to the point where we can **evaluate one another's work with a heart to help.** Selfprotective territorialism and self-exaltation are passing from the scene as we see the One who sits on the throne, and get free from self. Finally, the Body is working in unity, bringing racial reconciliation around the world.

Each of us must walk in the synergism of spiritual unity. You have a part to play. You are important in all that God is doing. You are the fulfillment of His power picture.

You are an Attack Lamb for Jesus.

Move with the flock!

WHAT GOD IS DOING

For a moment let's follow Joshua into the promised land. In spite of God's promise to give Joshua every place where his foot shall tread (Joshua 1:3[113]), living that promise was a difficult task. Remember, Israel had been a nation of slaves not conquerors.

To make matters worse, one of the Israelites kept some of the spoil for himself from the first city they attacked. One man's greed broke the ranks of the entire nation, bringing not only defeat in the next battle but disgrace for his tribe and his family. Instead of everyone receiving the fullness of the promise, one man stole a few treasures for himself, only to lose them, and his life and family later.

Today the Lord has brought together many of the mainstreams of Christianity into a unified network of prayer. This has not been accomplished through the work of one or more key men. Instead,

---

113. ³Every place that the sole of your foot will tread upon I have given you, as I said to Moses

God has spoken very gently and providentially to individuals worldwide and caused them to walk to the same goal. The sense of unity is pure not contrived. The openness to work together comes from a common focus on the throne of God.

Within the fibers of this network we find similar patterns. They are the genetic strands of global harvest. Guess what? You are a part of that. Your interest in this book, and the topics it touches, indicates a God-given desire to be part of His plan for these days. I welcome you to the fellowship of mobile intercessors who are taking the land for the resurrected Jesus.

FIVE PRACTICAL POINTS AS YOU GO

We must move in order and at the pace of the whole net. Here are five practical points I have learned in over twenty years which help keep me in the timing and flow of the whole. I share them with you, not to give you a strict method or put you under any bondage, but as principles which help keep me focused on the throne and safe from counterattack.

1. The Lord sent them out in pairs. Let's be smart and do the same. The Christian marriage is God's number one weapon in spiritual warfare. My wife and I have celebrated twenty-six wonderful years of marriage. We are in agreement on God's plan for our lives. We are focused on the throne and desire His will beyond all else. Our home is dedicated to serving Jesus.

Because of my mission's travels we are apart much of the time. Yet, as parents of teenage children, we feel one parent should be at home. Yes, I trust my sons. Yes, I trust the Lord. But, I also trust the Enemy to be the Enemy. As a result, many of my prayer journeys are made with people other than my wife.

The Lord has knit me to several men who also have a heart to see the nations reached. When it is not possible for my wife to travel, one or more of these men join me in targeting a nation. Once a year I lead a large group which includes men and women. I try to arrange it so that my wife and sons are with that team. The principle of family unity is vital to our success.

As a mobile ministry team, we realize each of us has a part to play. I have learned the Lord can, and generally will, speak through any team member at any time. Remember, it was a young musician who had the word for Jehoshaphat and the children of Israel (2 Chronicles 20). So, let's glean a little from this. Your spouse is God's first choice for a prayer partner. If you don't have a spouse then a same-gender partner should be your choice. Before you go on specific prayer walks into the pressure points to wrestle the four forces, you should have gone through the process of developing a prayer partnership with someone you trust completely, both personally and spiritually.

Of course you can pray by yourself. Of course you have a daily prayer life, and your own time of intimacy with Jesus. I am talking about when you target a perceived pressure point, and you are going into it for the purpose of releasing the people under its influence, then you need a partner.

2. You must be specific in your mapping. The initial prayer walk should be one of exploration and identification, a leisurely walk through town with your spiritual antenna up. On our central Singapore route, I walked it first and then invited intercessors from different churches to walk on different days. I did not share the findings of one group or my personal impressions with another group. The groups were diverse; Methodists, Anglicans, Pentecostals, charismatics, and Lutherans.

They each perceived exactly the same pressure points and gateways. It was amazing!

From that mapping we were able to send two-person teams to the pressure points while the others prayed for them. In Singapore you cannot have a group of more than five without a permit. We found teams of two and four worked well for us.

But they were disciplined enough to go to the specific points mapped and confirmed by those who had gone before.

In this way the Lord allowed several streams to "own" the prayer vision. Working together, they cast the net in the heart of the city. The Christian population of Singapore has increased so much in five years the Parliament had to publish a "White Paper" concerning the revival's impact on the balance of ideologies on the island!

Asia Week published an article on the revival's impact on business in the region. Centers of government and commerce have been impacted by two people standing on a corner in a completely irrelevant fashion with an uplink to the throne of God!

3. Discipline yourself to a specific report format. There are many available through Global Harvest Ministries, P.O. Box 63060, Colorado Springs, CO, 80962-3060. It is most important that we avoid time-wasters and nit-pickers in a report form. Essentially, what needs to be in a report is where you went, what you perceived, how you prayed, advice for those who will follow and any specific prayer direction you took. When you compile the findings of all the teams you see the multitude of counsel with which there is safety, and the assurance of victory.

4. Volunteer the information of your plans to your pastor to maximize your effectiveness in prayer walking. He will appreciate the information. As a pastor, I always appreciated knowing where the active ministries of our church would be. It gave me the opportunity to pray for them, to watch for books and tapes that would encourage them in their ministry, to drive by that location and encourage them in the course of my duties, and to be ready to answer the phone should the police call wondering why several of our members were walking around their building.

As a result of this pastoral involvement, I have seen the Lord do wonderful things in foreign nations and in the US. We have stressed that we are one Body, and if you, as a member of that Body, are involved in expanding the Kingdom, then we are all involved. Please take the time and make the effort to inform your pastor of the places in which you are praying. You never know, he might just show up one time to encourage you.

5. Develop prayer partner support. There are those who are not going to go out on the streets of your city to pray.

You have to be willing to accept that and love them anyway.

They might be confined to their homes by illness or responsibility. They might work incredible hours to make ends meet. You must not make them feel like lesser citizens in the Kingdom because they cannot get out and walk with you.

I spend much of my time walking among totally Christless people in nations which try to prevent the preaching of the Gospel. If there is anyone on earth who has cried to the Lord for workers in the face of such harvest it is me. But I tell you, you cannot become estranged from the Body of Christ as an intercessor or you will end up with a small group of pseudo-spiritual people casting the demons out of each other, and totally distracted from the throne of God. If you love Him, you must love His Church.

Therefore, find a way to recruit members of your church or cell group to become a part of your prayer team. Inform them of the goals of your team, such as, "We are praying together for the principal of our local school to receive Jesus. Please, while you are microwaving your popcorn at the office, take the four minutes of wait time and join us in this prayer time." Or, "As you drive to work you will pass through the very congested intersection at the bridge. Your delay will be about five minutes. Please use these five minutes to pray for a visitation of the Spirit of God on our community." Or, "As you take your child to daycare, please pause to pray for their safety and for the evangelization of all the children in daycare centers in our community. Please pray for centers of education; whoever holds the children holds the future." Use a few examples that embrace rather than divide. Not everyone has the freedom and ability you have to serve the Lord, so please allow Jesus to give you more great ways to embrace them into prayer ministry.

THE GREATEST NEED

Often I am asked, "Mark, what is missing in the Church today?" More than anointing, more than finances, more than vision, more than leadership, I feel our greatest need is **perseverance**. Hebrews 6:12 gives us the key to receiving the promise of the nations. **"Be not slothful, but followers of them who through faith and patience inherit the promises [of God]."**

As we walked and prayed for Nepal, the forces of resistance were great. The power of government and malice were set against us. In 1983 the Lord declared that He would break through. In 1985 He showed the power of the "uplink," and in 1990 He changed the government. Today you can preach Christ openly in Nepal.

In 1985 God promised change in Russia. In 1988 He confirmed the "uplink," in 1991 the government changed and today you can preach Christ openly in Moscow.

Through those years many thousands — that's right, thousands — of intercessors have been led to travel in those lands and pray. Many have been burdened, have made the choices and gone. Perhaps you have been, or have supported, one or more of them. In these cases the results did not come quickly. If we think of the grandma in Novosibirsk, it has been a prayer time since the fifties. But God is faithful concerning His promises. He does watch over His Word to perform it. What He says will come to pass.

Pastor Wang Ming Dao spent over twenty years in prison believing that one day he would see China free from the atheistic rider of the communist horse. He died never having seen the fulfillment. He imparted a calling to many and they continue on. China is now 10 percent Christian and some reports say that 35,000 people a day are coming to Christ. Pastor Wang is part of that great cloud of witnesses who watch us walk and pray. His tears and prayers for China are before the throne, mingled with yours and mine. We shall see the day he envisioned!

Persevere for your city. Persevere for your loved ones. Steve Lightle, a wonderful intercessor for the Soviet Jews, once said to me, "Mark, you will succeed in prayer ministry only if you don't have to have something happen every day to keep your faith up. If you can just see Jesus and His promises, you will persevere until you receive your answer."

Faith is the key to all the strategies of God. Prayer walking, interceding in the gap and being an Attack Lamb is no exception.

Dear Friend,

This Updated and Revised Edition of Attack Lambs commemorates the twentieth anniversary of the release of the first edition. In it, I have shared with you some of the things I have learned by doing. And that is the key to it all.

When Jesus called the disciples he simply said, "Follow me." They did, and the good news has circled the globe so many times. Carried in the bags of businesspeople, government leaders, teachers, field workers, oil drillers, taxi drivers, doctors, nurses, administrators, camel drivers, and some actual clergy, this gospel of the Kingdom is soon to cover the whole earth.

We have a very important role to play in the completion of the great commission, for we just might be around when the last person receives the last gospel message and gives their heart to the Lord. It could happen any day. So, what are we to do?

Watch therefore and pray for no man knows the hour of His coming (Matthew 24:42[114]).

Please take what you have learned here and apply it. Information without application is just information.

Thank you for reading the book or utilizing the accompanying resources. Please remember SEAPC in your prayers and please do make a gift to Every Home for Christ. By bringing prayer and mission together and getting a gospel message to every home, we are living our lives in the plan and purpose of God. You make the crucifixion worth the suffering as you multiply the kingdom.

God Bless You,
Mark

---

114. [42]Watch therefore, for you do not know what hour your Lord is coming.

END NOTES

Chapter 8 — "Know Your Enemy"

1. Discussion of the *archas, exousias, kosmokratos* and *pneuma tae ponerias* is based on insights gained from the Theological Dictionary of the New Testament by Gerhard Kittel and Frederich Gerhard, William B. Eerdmans Publisher, © October 1994.

2. Strong, James. *Strong's Exhaustive Concordance of the Bible.*

"Hebrew and Chaldee Dictionary," "Greek Dictionary of the New Testament." Nashville: Abingdon, 1890. "Greek,"

entry #746, p.16.

3. Strong, "Greek," entry #1849, p.30.

4. Strong, "Greek," entry #2888, p.43; and entry #2902, p.43.

5. Strong, "Greek," entry #4189, p.59.

Chapter 13 — "And Again I Say Rejoice"

1. John Lennon, *Imagine*, Apple Records, Copyright 1971,

Maclen Music, Inc., BMI, SW-3421 Chapter 14 — "A Fresh Word"

1. W.E. Vine, *Vine's Expository Dictionary of Old and New Testament Words*, Thomas Nelson Publishers, © 1984, 1996 Chapter 15 — "Dawn of A New Day"

1. *What A Friend We Have In Jesus*, lyrics by Joseph M.

Scriven, music by Charles C. Converse, public domain.

ABOUT THE AUTHOR

Mark Geppert was selling insurance to a Baptist pastor in 1970 when the Holy Spirit touched his life in an irrevocable way. Under careful training, he began walking out the call of God in his life. Leaving business in 1973 he received Bible and ministry training in the Assemblies of God at Western Pennsylvania Bible Institute.

From there Mark and his wife Ellie went to Guatemala where for three years he directed the Guatemala Assistance Project. Their first son, Samuel, was born in Guatemala.

In 1979 God spoke to Mark to return to Pittsburgh, Pennsylvania, and serve the Church in the establishment of the Dayspring Bible Training Center which opened its doors in 1980. A second son, Matthew, was born in Pittsburgh.

Mark served as Co-Pastor, Missions Director, and Bible Training Center Director until 1988 when he accepted a call to serve as Vice-President and Director of Operation Unreached with the Association of International Missions Services in Virginia Beach, Virginia.

In 1991 Mark and Ellie established the South East Asia Prayer Center. Committed to "Creating New and Networking Existing Prayer Cells in South East Asia," this foundation has brought forth fruit in many nations. Much of their success has been accomplished through Mark's Prayer Walking Seminar which has been taught to more than 50,000 in Asia, both through live conferences as well as audio and video cassettes.

Now with over 40 years of international experience, Mark has lived the principles of prayer. His life is a testimony to the faithfulness of Jesus to those who walk with Him. The focus on Asia continues with works in many nations.

WHAT LEADERS ARE SAYING...

"As early as 1992, a man by the name of Mark Geppert was already blazing through the land in prayer. For weeks on end, Mark would walk and pray through the thoroughfares and back alleys of Singapore visiting strategic sites and sowing prayer seeds every step of the way."
— **Lai-Kheng Pousson**, Director Prayer Wave Asia

"My prayer life was dramatically changed after Mark Geppert introduced me to prayer walking...this book will open your understanding to how you can maximize your prayer time to benefit the kingdom of God."
— **Oleen Eagle**, President Cornerstone Television

"EVERY PLACE YOUR FOOT SHALL TREAD is birthed in the heart of a frontline missionary and bathed in sound scriptural interpretation.
Mark Geppert doesn't speak from an ivory tower about abstract theory and cold theology. He talks of principles which have been proven in Asia and America, in mosques and temples, in metropolitan cities and mud huts."
— **Rev. William Ellis**,
Sr. Pastor Riverside Comm. Church, Oakmont, PA

"The principles and practices you'll read in this book are transformational! I've prayer walked in China with Mark Geppert, and seen God's hand open doors to ministry and miracles through such targeted intercessory prayer. Every follower of Jesus Christ, and particularly church leaders, needs to read this book!"

— **Dr. Chris E. Marshall**
Glade Run United Presbyterian Church, PCUSA

OTHER WORKS BY MARK GEPPERT

Bridges Getting From A to Z

Stepping Stones Sure Footing for Troubled Times

A Faith to Die For Your Roadmap to Hope

TO CONTACT MARK GEPPERT

write to:

South East Asia Prayer Center
Post Office Box 127
Oakmont, Pennsylvania 15139

or email:

seapc@hotmail.com

Please include your prayer requests and comments when you write.